GW00537283

Walk!

the
Axarquía

with

Charles Davis

DISCOVERY WALKING GUIDES LTD

Walk! Axarquía
First Edition - May 2005

Copyright © 2005

Published by
Discovery Walking Guides Ltd
10 Tennyson Close, Northampton NN5 7HJ,
England

Maps
Original mapping reproduced under licence from:
The Instituto Geográfico Nacional - Centro
Nacional de Información Geográfica

Cartografía original:
INSTITUTO GEOGRÁFICO NACIONAL -
CENTRO NACIONAL DE INFORMACIÓN
GEOGRÁFICA

Photographs
All photographs in this book were taken by Charles
Davis and Jeanette Tallegas.

Front Cover Photographs

Los Cahorros on the
Río Chillar Route   Walk 8 The Path to Los
(Walk 15)   Pradillos

Admiring the view on   Walk 10 La
Walk 24   Maroma
              from Malas Camas

ISBN 1-904946-08-9

Text and photographs* © Charles Davis 2005

All rights reserved. No part of this publication may
be reproduced, stored in a retrieval system or
transmitted in any form or by any means,
electronic, mechanical, photocopying, recording
or otherwise, without the prior written permission
of the publishers.

The author and
publishers have tried to
ensure that the
information and maps
in this publication are
as accurate as possible.
However, we accept no
responsibility for any
loss, injury or
inconvenience
sustained by anyone
using this book.

Walk! Axarquía

CONTENTS

Contents 3

The Author 8

Introduction
Holy Stone of the South 9
The Mountains: oreography and man's impact 12
Scope & Aim: what we cover and who it's for 15
When to Go: climate and state of the walks 16
Getting there, getting about, getting a bed 17
The Walks 18
Equipment 19
Problems 20
Flora & Fauna 20
Eating & Drinking 23
Tourist Stuff: what to do on a day off 25
Language 26
Acknowledgements 27

Map Information
Map Notes 27
Location Maps 28

Walking Information
Symbols Rating Guide & Notes 30
Using GPS in Axarquía 31
Walking Equipment 33

THE WALKS: SIERRAS TEJEDA & ALMIJARA

SIERRA TEJEDA 35

1   Cueva de la Fajara from Alcaucín 38
3 walker, 3 hours 10 mins, 10 kilometres, ascents &
descents 450 metres, 4 refreshments (circular)
A bucolic tour of classic Axarquía countryside

2   Los Castillones from Cortijo de la Alcauca 42
4 walker, 2¼ hours, 8½ kilometres, ascents & descents
300 metres, 0 refreshments (circular)
Big mountain, small walk: suitable for an energetic
family outing

3   La Maroma: El Alcazar 44
5 walker, 6-7 hours, 16 kilometres, ascents & descents
1200 metres, 0 refreshments (linear two-way)
The Iberian peninsula's westernmost 2000 metre summit

4   La Maroma: Sendero El Robledal   **48**
5 walker, 5-7 hours, 13 kilometres, ascents & descents
975 metres, vertigo risk, 0 refreshments (linear two-way)
Possibly the prettiest approach to La Maroma

5   El Robledal   **51**
1 walker, 1½ hours, 6 kilometres, ascents & descents
215 metres, 0 refreshments (circular)
A way into the great oak woods of the north without
busting a gut on a big climb

6   Loma de la Fuente   **53**
3 walker, 3½ hours, 10 kilometres, ascents & descents
550 metres, 3 refreshments (circular)
Grand tour of the grandiose landscape behind Sedella

7   Two Short Walks from La Fábrica de la Luz
    (a) Arroyo Turbilla   **57**
3 walker, 2 hours 20 mins, 7.6 kilometres, ascents &
descents 400 metres, 0 refreshments (circular)
    (b) Cerro de la Cueva del Agua   **59**
2 walker, 1¾ hours, 6 kilometres, ascents & descents
250 metres, 0 refreshments (circular)
Excursions off the walker's beaten track

8   Puerto Blanquillo from La Fábrica de la Luz via   **60**
    Los Pradillos and Arroyo del Cueva Melero
4 walker, 4 hours, 12.3 kilometres, ascents & descents
700 metres, 0 refreshments (circular)
An unconventional version of a classic ascent

9   Camino del Río   **63**
2 walker, 1 hour 50 mins, 5¾ kilometres, ascents &
descents 300 metres, 3 refreshments (circular)
Delightful, easy riverside walking leading to lovely farmland

10 Malas Camas via Haza del Aguadero   **65**
4 walker, 4 hours 40 mins - 5 hours, 18 kilometres, ascents
& descents 800 metres, 0 refreshments (pan-handle circular)
Little visited summit with very spectacular views

SIERRA ALMIJARA   **69**

11 Paraje Natural de los Acantilados de Mar
    y Cerro Gordo
    (a) 2 walker, 1 hour 20 mins, 4½ kilometres, ascents &   **73**
descents 180 metres, 4 refreshments (circular)
    (b) 1 walker, 1½ hours, 5 kilometres, ascents & descents   **75**
200 metres, vertigo risk, 4 refreshments (circular)
    (c) 1 walker, 2 hours, 5 kilometres, ascents & descents 250   **77**
metres, vertigo risk, 5 refreshments (circular)
One well-known short walk (Torre de Maro) & two
alternative adventure-strolls exploring the best of the
Costa del Sol

12 **Puerto de Frigiliana**   **79**
     5 walker, 5-5½ hours, 20-22 kilometres, ascents & descents
     750 metres, 0 refreshments (circular)
     A step back in time, following one of the great mule trails

13 **Río Higuerón**   **83**
     2 walker, 6-7 hours, 15 kilometres, ascents & decscents
     350 metres, vertigo risk, 4 refreshments (linear two-way)
     The greatest river walk of them all

14 **Cuesta del Sordo from Frigiliana**   **86**
     3 walker, 2 hours, 6½ kilometres, ascents & descents
     350 metres, 4 refreshments (circular)
     Short tour of the Sierra de Enmedio

15 **Río Chillar**   **88**
     4 walker, 6-9 hours, 13 kilometres, ascents & descents
     200 metres, vertigo risk, 0 refreshments (circular)
     Wading in the water: the Axarquía's most famous stream

16 **The Limán Trail**   **92**
     5 walker, 6 hours, 19 kilometres, ascents & descents
     800 metres, 0 refreshments (circular)
     A classic linear walk turned into a major loop

17 **Cortijo Imán from Pinarillo**   **96**
     4 walker. 5 hours, 14 kilometres, ascents & descents
     750 metres, 0 refreshments (linear two-way)
     Perhaps the most spectacularly located ruin in the
     parque natural

18 **Venta Los Pradillos and Cerro Gavilán from**   **100**
     Casa de la Mina
     3 walker, 3-3½ hours, 12½ kilpmetres, ascents & descents
     400 metres, 5 refreshments (circular)
     A walk on the wildside for those who'd rather not stray too far
     from domesticity

19 **Lucero from Rambla de la Mota**   **103**
     3 walker, 2 hours, 14 kilometres, ascents & descents 450
     metres, vertigo risk, 0 refreshments (linear two-way)
     The region's most spectacular peak

20 **Navachica via Barranco de los Cazadores**   **106**
     5 walker, 6½ hours, 16 kilometres, ascents & descents
     1300 metres, vertigo risk, 0 refreshments (linear two-way)
     Culminating point of the Sierra Almijara

21 **Tajo Almendrón and La Puerta**   **110**
     5 walker, 4 hours 20 mins, 11 kilometres, ascents &
     descents 900 metres, vertigo risk, 0 refreshments (circular)
     Dramatic rocks and dizzying panoramas

22   Tour of Tajo de los Bueyes   **113**
     3 walker, 3 hours 20 mins, 14 kilometres, ascents &
     descents 500 metres, 3 refreshments (circular)
     Two lovely ravines and some great views

23   Alto de Cielo from Barranco de la Higuera   **116**
     descending via Cortijos de la Civila
     5 walker, 5 hours, 11 kilometres, ascents & descents
     1300 metres, 0 refreshments (circular)
     Knocking on heaven's gate - the hard way

24   Two Short Walks off Loma de las Cuadrillas
     (a) Peñon de los Castillejos   **120**
     2 walker, 1 hour 5 mins, 3.2 kilometres, ascents & descents
     200 metres, 5 refreshments (off route) (linear two-way)
     (b) Barranco de los Gigantes   **122**
     2 walker, 1 hour 40 mins, 5 kilometres, ascents & descents
     100 metres, 5 refreshments (off route) (linear two-way)
     Easy access to wild places: turning the perfidious works
     of the tarmacadam cowboys to our advantage.

25   Pico de Lopera via the 'back door'   **123**
     1 walker, 2-2¼ hours, 9 kilometres, ascents & descents
     200 metres, 5 refreshments (circular)
     Small summit, short on effort, long on spectacle

26   Barranco Bacal & Cuerda de los Morros   **125**
     2/4 walker, 3/6 hours, 6.4/16 kilometres, ascents & descents
     175/350 metres, 0 refreshments (linear/circular options)
     Wet-footed fun for children of all ages

27   Río Cebollon   **128**
     2 walker, 2¾-3 hours, 10 kilometres, ascents & descents
     100 metres, vertigo risk, 0 refreshments (linear two-way)
     More messing about in rivers

28   The Waterfall of Petrified Wood   **131**
     3 walker, 3 hours, 9.3 kilometres, ascents & descents 350
     metres, vertigo risk, 0 refreshments (circular)
     Exactly what it says: one of nature's marvels

29   Río Verde   **134**
     3 walker, 2¾-3 hours, 14 kilometres, ascents 350 metres,
     descents 1000 metres, vertigo risk 0/5 refreshments
     (linear/circular options)
     The grandest gorge of them all and the best river-bathing
     in the region

30   Alternative Walks, Sierras Tejeda & Almijara
     (a) Traverse of the Sierra Tejeda: El Alcázar to Canillas de   **138**
     Aceituno descending from La Maroma (Walk 3) via Camino de
     la Casa de la Nieve
     5 walker, 2½/9 hours, 16½ kilometres, descents 1400 metres,
     4 refreshments (linear one-way)

Making a big walk bigger: the most spectacular of the three La Maroma paths

(b) Traverse of the Sierra Tejeda: El Robledal (Walk 4) to **141** Sedella via Tacita de Plata and Llanadas de Sedella
5 walker, 5-6+ hours, 16 kilometres, ascents 850 metres, descents 1200 metres. 3 refreshments (linear one-way)
The Ballet of Natty Bumppo: spectacular traverse for the more inspired pathfinder

(c) Sierra de Almijara: The Apretaderos Ridge path (Walk **144** 16) and Chillar acequia (Walk 15) from Pinarillo (Walk 17).
3 walker, 2½-3 hours, 12 kilometres, ascents & descents 400 metres, vertigo risk, 0 refreshments (circular)
Easy way onto wild ways

GPS Waypoints Lists   **146**

Glossary   **150**

Appendices
    A Useful Information   **152**
    B Cycle Routes   **154**
    C Bibliography   **154**

Place Names Index   **156**

Charles Davis was born in London, and has lived and worked in the United States, Sudan, Turkey, Ivory Coast, Spain and France. With the onset of middle age, he realised that the urge to roam was better satisfied by walking than bouncing about on the back of a lorry in the middle of the desert, and now divides his time between mountain tops, desk-tops and laptops. He is the author of numerous highly praised and wholly unpublished novels.

Jeanette Tallegas has spent thirty odd years labouring for the French education system, from which she has finally, gleefully, taken early retirement. Asked what she intends doing now, she resolutely replies, "Nothing". Nonetheless, she does follow the author up various gruelling mountains, frequently alarming younger ramblers who seem to assume that remote and inaccessible places are the preserve of youth.

Charles Davis is also the author of:-

34 Alpujarras Walks
ISBN 1-899554-83-1

Walk! La Gomera
(2nd Edition)
ISBN 1-899554-90-4

Walk! Mallorca (North & Mountains)
ISBN 1-899554-92-0

Walk! Mallorca West
ISBN 1-899554-98-X

Walk! La Palma
ISBN 1-904946-06-2

Walk! Andorraa
ISBN 1-904946-04-6

- published by **Discovery Walking Guides Ltd.**

The Axarquía is one of the world's great places, and among the greatest places within it are the **Sierras Tejeda** and **Almijara**, which form the backbone both of the region and the present publication. Blessed with high summits, dizzying pinnacles, dramatic crags, deep ravines, dozens of springs, delightful rivers and the best coves on the **Costa del Sol**, this is an area that has something for everyone. And the only prerequisites for benefitting from all this are a desire to get off the beaten track and a set of relatively, sometimes very, sturdy legs.

The appellation of the mother chain, the **Baetic Cordillera**, comes from the Latin name for Andalucía, Baetica, which in turn was taken from the River Baetis, now the Guadalquivir. By a happy coincidence this neatly echoes the word '*baetyl*', a magical or holy stone like the *ka'bah* in Mecca, which probably stems from the Arabic *be'tel*, House or Seat of the Gods. One glance at the Sierras Tejeda and Almijara will tell you why I regard this as a matter of serendipity*. This really is a place fit for the gods, hence the conceit of dubbing it The Holy Stone of the South.

If you've not seen them already, you can get an idea of how dramatic these mountains are from one simple fact, that the high peaks, including **Lucero** (1779 metres), **Navachica** (1828 metres) and **La Maroma** (2065 metres), are all within ten kilometres of the coast, rising out of the sea like a succession of immense

Lucero (as seen from the north)

Peña del Sol on Walk 4, 'La Maroma: Sendero El Robledal

pedestals, just waiting for humankind to enthrone whoever or whatever we find most sacred or simply most lacking in our quotidian lives.

And that is precisely how they've been used, much as other wild and spectacular places have been in Spain, as a kind of *tabula rasa* on which

---

* Sadly, the connection is no closer than that. Though the Spanish *Cordillera Penibético* and the alternative spelling of Baetica, *Bética*, sound tantalizingly close to *be'tel* they don't appear to have any etymological link. Baetis seems to have its origins in an Etruscan word that later became the root for various river names.

people can project, even inscribe, their frustrated yearnings, ranging from a mundane desire for material wealth to more inchoate cravings for an uncluttered arcadia.

In former times when there was no National Lottery to feed dreams of freedom from daily drudgery, the departed Moors were drafted in to inspire the fantasies of impoverished Spanish peasants and hungry day-labourers dependent on the whims of feudal landlords. Regarded as quasi-mythical creatures from the past, the Moors were endowed by fanciful memory with fabulous fortunes which, given their peremptory dispossession and expulsion, must indubitably be buried in Spain! With the insuperable optimism of the truly desperate, Spaniards decided their newly reconquered land was riddled with hidden riches, as a result of which it sometimes seems as if there's scarcely a vale, cave, or crevice in the country that doesn't have its resident Moor and, more importantly, Moor's treasure. Walkers will still occasionally stumble upon a cavern excavated with less than archaeological delicacy and I can almost guarantee that, if **you ask about local legends in any** village in Southern Spain, you will eventually hear something along the lines of, "Well, there was this rich Moor, you see …".

The Axarquía is no exception to this long and honourable tradition. The Costa del Sol's most famous marine grotto, the **Cueva del Tesoro** behind **La Cala del Moral**, has been explored by treasure hunters since the 17th century, some dedicating their lives to the search and, in one instance, the afterlife too, the cave allegedly being haunted by the ghost of a 19th century Swiss adventurer who contrived to blow himself up while trying to breach a new chamber. **La Rábita**, meanwhile, on the southern approach to **La Maroma**, is cited as the burial site of four Moorish *santons* (Muslim saints, transformed for the purposes of treasure hunting into princes), who doubtless had their fair share of lucre wrapped around them when they were interred.

Nowadays, living as we do in a culture premised on the assumption that most treasure is to be found in other people's pockets, we look to the land for relief from more nebulous pressures than mere poverty. Harried by crowded lives, a surfeit of things, and a want of time and space in which to enjoy them, we hanker after tranquillity and ease, dream of 'getting away from it all' and living 'the good life', exalting an idealized notion of nature and its apparent simplicities when contrasted with our own increasingly complex lives. It's not the Moor's treasure we crave, but something more than treasure and, inevitably, in Southern Spain the enduring grandeur of the mountains stands in marked contrast to the frenetic scramble for a quick profit down on the coast.

While large tracts of Andalucía are being submerged in a superfluity of golf courses ribboned with bloated villas, incongruous 'chalets', and terraces of rabbit-hutch *adosadas* (almost literally, 'lean-tos'), the Sierras Tejeda and Almijara have remained aloof and largely intact, evolving from a working and heavily-worked landscape into a numinous playing field for local ecologists, entomologists, birdwatchers, botanists, amateur naturalists, ramblers and outward bound enthusiasts, who would otherwise spend their days sat at home wringing their hands and bewailing the massacre of the Costa del Sol by King Concrete.

The mountains were certainly the saving of us when we moved to the coast and, though we no longer live in the area, it's always a pleasure to return to our former playground, which isn't always the case with favourite spots from the past.

Haza del Aguadero

The joys of these mountains are manifold, comprising bulky expanses of rock sculpted by karstic erosion (like the massive dome of **La Maroma**), vertiginous pinnacles flanked by sheer cliffs (such as the **Tajos de Almendrón** and **Sol**), spectacular peaks draped with ragged crags that seem newly emerged from the earth's core and look like they may very well continue surging upward at any moment (**Lucero**), steep slopes cloaked with cork oak groves (**El Robledal**), ancient alpine pastures (**Llanadas de Sedella**), abandoned terraces swaddled in a buttery blanket

View from Alto de Cielo

of yellow-flowering shrubs (**Cuesta de los Galgos**), picturesque ruins of deserted *cortijos* (**Haza del Aguadero**), obscure *fuentes* tucked away in unlikely austere corners (**Tacita de la Plata**), immense ridges dominating the deep blue Mediterranean (**Alto de Cielo**), broad spurs spreading from the higher slopes like the splayed toes of a giant's foot (the great flat *lomos* to the north of the **Sierra Almijara**), fabulous riverbeds winding between tight towering chicanes known as *cahorros* (**Ríos Higuerón** and **Chillar**)

Río Chillar

… and all of it accessible within fifteen minutes of the coast, which means we have the inestimable privilege of climbing a high peak in the morning and having a bathe in the Mediterranean in the afternoon.

Seat of the gods? It's enough to make any self-respecting deity weep with envy.

Though the two *sierras* are superficially coherent - their morphology is comparable, both are part of the Baetic Cordillera, and both have been lumped together as a single *Parque Natural* - the ranges are distinct, the **Sierra Tejeda** being a discrete massif defined by cliffs, gullies and gorges, and culminating in the Iberian Peninsula's westernmost 2000 metre summit (**La Maroma**, 2065 metres), while the **Sierra Almijara** comprises numerous mini-ranges aligned on a very approximate north-south axis and separated by a series of ravines draining into the sea.

Cueva Melero (Walk 8)

The **composition of the mountains** consists of a Palaeozoic metamorphic plinth mantled with dolomitic marble from the later Triassic period. The mix of gneiss, quartzite, and schist with compact marble and more friable limestones created the conditions for the karstic erosion that has wrought the shallow *grykes* (furrows caused by solution), blade-like *clints* (puckered rock between the grykes), deep ravines, sharp ridges, and *terra rossa* (ferruginous sedimentary deposits that accumulate in erosion cavities giving vegetation a purchase on the inhospitable rock face) so characteristic of this terrain.

Rock formations (Walk 3)

Of particular interest in this respect are the *simas*, sinkholes up to forty-five metres deep (**Sima de las Nieves** near the summit of **La Maroma**), hollowed out by the solution of bedrock and consequent subsidence.

Sinkhole encountered on Walk 4

The **historical record** of man's presence dates back some 200,000 years to the Acheulean Period, while Neanderthal bones have been found in the vicinity of the **Boquete de Zafarraya**, and the **Cueva de Nerja** was apparently in use from the Solutrean Period (circa 20,000BC) to the Bronze Age.

Andalucía as a whole was a significant trading outpost during Phoenician and Roman times (there are still Phoenician ruins in the hills behind the Costa del Sol, though I know of at least two bulldozed into the ground by recent developments, while the Romans relied on Baetica for their supplies of *garum*, a fermented fish sauce comparable to nuoc-nam in contemporary Vietnamese cooking), but inevitably it is the Moorish dominion that has most profoundly shaped the region and, some would say, the entire mentality of southern Spain.

Most place names in the Axarquía (Arabic *sarq*, or *sharquiyya* meaning east, or the way in from/place to the east) are of Arabic origin: **Canillas de Albaida** prefigures the modern denomination of The White Villages by taking its epithet from the Arabic word for white, **Nerja** was named for its abundant springs (Arabic *narixa*), and **Alcaucín** stems from *Al-cautin*, the arches.

In more concrete terms, the Moors built the villages that are such a distinctive feature of the Andalusian landscape, they introduced the ceramics that would become a Spanish tradition adorning every gatepost and souvenir shop in the country, and most importantly they developed the patterns of farming that would shape the Andalusian countryside for centuries to come: the cane sugar industry, which presaged modern plantations of tropical fruits and culminated in the building of fine 19th century sugar-mills (**Máro**, **Nerja**, **Frigiliana**); the viniculture that called for the terracing of low-lying foothills; the sericulture that lead to the planting of mulberry trees in medium range mountains; olives, almonds, figs, honey all emerged as major local products during the emirate of Al-Andalus.

And even the expulsion of the Moslems and the resettlement of the villages by Christian settlers from as far north as Galicia could not exorcise the customs and lifestyle cultivated over seven centuries by the Moors. It is largely thanks to the inhabitants of these villages, regardless of professions of faith, that the **Sierras Tejeda** and **Almijara** enjoy such a fine network of paths, tracks and trodden ways today.

The **origin of the paths into the mountains** can be ascribed to various activities, notably mining, snow-gathering, and grazing, but the most important points of access are the old trading routes linking the coast and villages of the *solana* (sunny side of the mountain*) with **Granada** and **Alhama de Granada**, trails taken by countless mule trains exporting the local products listed above, especially silk, and importing wheat, salt, cotton, copper and other precious metals.

It's thanks to this traffic that the **Puertos de Competa** and **Frigiliana** became such major thoroughfares, as evidenced by the existence of what today seem like improbably remote *ventas* (a kind of inn minus the fancy bits plus some unfancy bits like groceries, gossip, barter etc.) and of a long, legend-rich history of banditry, the latter an integral part of Andalusian culture that persisted until comparatively recently in some areas - I've even seen an interview on local TV with a man from Cordoba who was an active *bandolero*

---

* Though never invested with a comparable philosophical connotation, *umbría* and *solana* are the Spanish equivalents of *yin* and *yang*, which originally referred to the dark and sunny sides of a mountain.

(all the traditional stuff, swish of the cape, gold teeth, daring hold-ups, blood-curdling deeds, hiding out among the peasants, giving to the poor and so forth) thirty odd years ago!

Cortijo Imán (Walk 17)

Apart from the concentrated settlements on their fringes, the mountains have also been shaped by farmers taking advantage of the *terra rossa* in larger valleys, most obviously on the northern side in the still productive **Zafarraya** basin, but on a smaller scale on the southern face, too.

Each farm was linked to its neighbour by a well trodden way and at one stage it must have been possible to traverse the component ranges from east to west simply following the paths between *cortijos*. Nowadays, the southern farms like the **Cortijos de Almáchar**, **Conca**, and **Imán** are largely abandoned, and many of them are likely to become inaccessible if paths aren't consciously maintained, but there are still some working farms, while others are partially maintained as goat pens or *huertas* (vegetable gardens), are used as arboretums by the park authorities, or have been restored as hotels or *casas rurales*.

La Herrerizas (Walk 8)

The **forests** meanwhile have also been heavily managed and frequently damaged, either by over-exploitation or wildfire. Much of the woodland has been replanted with Scots and Austrian pine, impacting both the topography and access to the mountains, one of the main dirt tracks into the *sierras* being via **La Resinera**, a resin processing plant that was still operational in the 1970s.

Finally, man's influence can be seen in **marble quarries**, like the one below **Puerto de Competa**. Though still active, these are nothing like the calamitous excavations seen further west, where they seem to be making a determined effort to dismantle entire mountain ranges, but are on a much smaller scale, and in some instances even complement rather than mutilate the landscape. From a distance, the **Puerto de Competa** quarry stands out like a shining white temple. Quite what they're worshipping, apart from bathroom fixtures and bank counters, I wouldn't like to say, but it remains a striking spectacle, and is a boon for the walker, since it means the dirt track used for approaching **Lucero** is well maintained.

Strictly speaking, we have strayed beyond the commonly accepted **geopolitical boundaries of the Axarquía**, but I'm not terribly interested in strict speaking, still less in a merely bureaucratic definition of borders, being rather more inclined to go where the good rambling is; hence the incursion into the administrative district of Granada (the provinces of Granada and **Málaga** are officially divided by the summits of the **Sierras Tejeda** and **Almijara**) so we could squeeze in walks around **Río Verde**, an otherwise arbitrary annexation happily justified by the borders of the *Parque Natural*.

Río Verde

This also brings in the attractive rural landscape on the northern flank of the **Sierra Almijara**, which rarely features in guidebooks and then only for one or two better known walks.

View north from Almáchar
(Walk 22)

The true Axarquía is defined by the **Montes de Málaga** in the west, the provincial border to the north, and **Cantarriján** in the east. There are plenty of short walks in **western Axarquía**, the town of **Almáchar** in particular having made an effort to signpost local paths, but redevelopment and the rapid transformation of paths into tracks and tracks into roads mean that, for the present, any attempt to produce an up-to-date comprehensive map for this area is a hopeless task, as you can guarantee something vital would go missing, mugged by a golf course or bundled up a dark alley by a new urbanization, well before any map emerged from the printers.

Fortunately, our chosen catchment area contains the finest, wildest and most extensive walks in the region, and is on the whole sufficiently well protected to ensure there will be little radical change in the lifetime of a given print run.

The traditional dividing point between the two *sierras* is **Puerto de Competa**, which doesn't mean a huge amount on the ground, but provides a rough **organizing framework for the book**, which is divided between the two principal *sierras* and their subsidiary ranges; essentially west = **Tejeda**, east = **Almijara**.

The book is intended for a **wide range of walking capacities**, encompassing both holiday-makers who just want to potter about within easy reach of the car and the hard-boiled walker determined to scale the most obdurate summits. However, by far the greatest number of walks are aimed at the adventurous leisure rambler, people who will on the whole have some experience of hiking in mountains, are happy to invest a little and sometimes a lot of effort for a corresponding reward, but who do not necessarily measure pleasure by pain and potential danger.

Of course, all this is very subjective, and you may find yourself dismissing me as a decrepit old fool who should be padlocked to his Zimmer-frame, or lamenting the trust you invested in a whirly-eyed lunatic who ought to be removed from the day-release scheme without delay. Both scenarios seem unlikely to me, but then they would, wouldn't they? Consequently I suggest you first do a relatively short walk (e.g. 2/5/7/9/11/14/24/25), one that can be easily and satisfactorily cut short (e.g. 13/15/17/27), or one calculated to give you an idea of the terrain (e.g. 1/14/22), before tackling more ambitious itineraries.

If at a glance there seem too many walks at the higher end of the range, bear in mind that the strolls would only merit an exertion rating of 1 or 2, while most short versions are within the capacities of nearly all walkers.

WHEN TO GO: CLIMATE AND STATE OF THE WALKS

There's a faintly irritating sign at the entrance to **Torrox** claiming it has **the 'best' climate in Europe**. They don't actually specify what for and I rather doubt downhill skiers, reindeers, tobogganing enthusiasts and The Snowman would go a bundle on it, but taking the boast at face value and stripping it of its municipal boundaries, it has to be said, they do have a point.

Boquete de Zafarraya

The summits of the **Sierras Tejeda** and **Almijara** are a climatic as well as administrative frontier, as you will find if you drive through the **Boquete de Zafarraya** between November and March, when one seems to change season within half a mile, passing from an eternal spring to something recognisably wintry.

But on that southern, sunny side, the *solana*, the weather really is superb. It's no accident that entire tribes of Brits, Germans, Swiss, French, Belgians, Scandinavians and lately Russians have come to the conclusion that, with modern communications, what can be done in the damp cities of the north can as well be done on the warm shores of the Mediterranean, and are consequently upping sticks by the suburb-load and moving south to establish parallel communities on the Costa del Sol. Setting aside questions of cultural affinity, kinship and friendship, only the most lugubrious spirit would prefer daylight-saving time, wet tarmac and grey skies to the golden light, tawny hillsides and bright blue sea of Andalucía. And with rare exceptions, it really is as good as the picture postcard clichés claim. The Axarquía enjoys three thousand hours of sun a year - yes, that's it, an average of eight hours a day, which makes even the busiest sunbed look a little silly.

That said, it does **rain** sometimes and though annual precipitation is so very nominal (400-800 millimetres) it sounds like a dosage of cough medicine, when it does fall it tends to do so all at once, turning otherwise dry gullies into raging torrents, sweeping away negligently parked cars, and generally making you wonder whether you shouldn't start brushing up your carpentry skills with a view to cobbling together an ark. On the whole though, there's good walking here throughout the year.

La Maroma under snow

La Maroma can be crowned with snow for weeks at a time in **winter** and I've even seen it sporting a thin white tonsure as late as April, but providing visibility is good, it's still an easy walk-up, one which many local people only do when it's under snow.

Come **spring** the river walks can be either impassable or severely curtailed, but the fabulous flowering elsewhere amply compensates for that. Meanwhile, **autumn** is best for the light. The only months I would recommend you **avoid** are late June, all July and August, and early September, since it will be too hot to do most of the walks in comfort. Even in June and September though, some walking is possible. We once did a traverse of the entire range via the high summits from **Alcaucín** to **Prados de Lopera** in June.

GETTING THERE, GETTING ABOUT, GETTING A BED

Getting there couldn't be simpler given that **Málaga** is THE premier destination for winter charters. You could probably turn-up at your local airport and take the first flight out with a reasonable chance of reaching the Costa del Sol. Given the volume of traffic, fares are correspondingly low and, so long as you're flexible, can be found at give-away prices.

Getting about is also simple as the mass-tourism of the last twenty years has lead to the development of a full range of tourist services. Many people rely on buses, however, if your trip is premised on getting into the mountains and walking, I recommend hiring a car (or possibly mountain bikes), as this allows greater flexibility and a broader range of walks.

Getting a bed … yes, you've guessed it, easy! Looking around the Axarquía, one sometimes gets the impression there are so many hotels, rooms to rent, studio-apartments, and *casas rurales* that the indigenous population must be hard pressed to find a place to let by the year. Naturally, the largest selection of accommodation is in the touristy triangle of **Nerja - Frigiliana - Torrox**, however, there are plenty of small hotels and rentals further afield. For the experience of being off the standard tourist trail without being totally lost, I would recommend looking for something in the **Canilla - Competa** area. To be totally lost, head for the northern side of the mountains. If you want to be on the coast, **Máro** is best. For competitive prices and a selection of services, go for **Nerja**, **Torrox**, **La Herradura** or **Almuñécar**. If you're camping (see Appendix A), bear in mind that the northern flanks of the mountain can get very cold in winter. We've experienced daytime temperatures in the mid-twenties dropping to minus 8C at night! See Appendix A for recommendations and a few slightly eccentric options.

We've aimed to provide a good **range of walks** covering the classic itineraries and several little known or even entirely 'new' routes, including short strolls suitable for walkers of all ages and aptitudes, and tough high-mountain itineraries only recommended for experienced hikers. At the request of the park authorities, a number of itineraries were dropped from the projected outline, either to avoid disturbing nesting grounds, or to avoid opening up more remote corners of the park to too many visitors. Please bear this in mind if improvising your own itineraries.

The **paths** are often rough and frequently little more than natural ways, however, in virtually every instance, the ways *are* natural and, once on the ground, only require rudimentary path-finding skills.

There are few official routes in the area (though the authorities have recently sign and wayposted ten classic itineraries) and, apart from the **GR7** which traverses the north of our area (generally on tedious dirt tracks), even fewer consistently waymarked paths. However, local hiking groups have marked many routes with cairns, often indicating itineraries that appear on no maps, and these cairns can generally be trusted - off hand I can think of no occasion in these mountains when I've taken a chance on a cairn-marked route and found myself in difficulty as a consequence, which is by no means always the case in Spain.

Río Chillar

Despite the commonplace depredations, the **condition of the land** itself is generally good, however, there are signs that the increasing popularity of the area is bringing some unwelcome visitors with it. Motorbikes have been seen going up the **Río Chillar** and even the *cahorros* in the **Río Higuerón** (and it doesn't get much more inaccessible than that) are marred by graffiti.

Other walks, like the classic ascent of **Peñon de los Castillejos** via **Rio de Miel** have been reduced to scramble-strolls by the asphalting of dirt tracks, while the superb descent of the **Río Verde** now involves a fee-paying parking area (for a non-paying version, see Walk 29).

Happily though, the *parque natural* should protect the heart of our region and, so long as there are no major forest fires, all the walks described here ought to remain a delight for generations to come.

Spectacular falls, Río Higuerón (Walk 13)

The **descriptions** are relatively straightforward since in most itineraries the route is reasonably obvious. I've tried to give enough detail for those wanting reassurance they're not about to topple off a cliff, but not so much as to irritate more confidant pathfinders with superfluity. A 'track' is something that might, sometimes in extremis and with extraordinary delicacy, be driven; a 'trail' is narrower than a track and wider than a path, and was probably made for mules and donkeys; a 'path' is a path, a 'way' an aspirant path; anything premised with the word 'goat' should be viewed with suspicion - goats go into some godawful places by ridiculous means, but occasionally they are worth following (see individual itinerary descriptions to decide if you agree). For ease of reference, 'place names written on signposts' are in inverted commas, while **bold text** indicates where we are on the ground. Italics are used for discrete Spanish words. Consistency rather than deficient vocabulary accounts for all **climbs** being 'gentle', 'steady', or 'steep'.

All **timings** are 'pure' excluding snacking, snapping and simply standing still staring. It is highly unlikely you will complete any of these walks in exactly the time specified. Before you tackle the longer routes, time yourself against one of our shorter itineraries, then curse me for a slowcoach or a racing maniac as seems appropriate. All global timings include the return unless otherwise specified. **Exertion ratings** are also subjective. Do an 'easy' walk first then judge more ambitious routes accordingly.

EQUIPMENT

On the whole, these are very forgiving mountains and most of the walks can be done with minimal equipment. I'd recommend wearing good walking boots, but trainers or walking sandals are adequate on most routes and, indeed, an advantage when splashing knee deep up a river. Obviously, anyone who climbs **La Maroma** when its under snow (highly recommended, though not for a first ascent) or sets off without adequate sun protection or a supply of water on a hot day, is asking for trouble, but on the whole, if you don't ask for it, you won't get it, a quality of forbearing that is not always forthcoming in other ranges. For an outline of Discovery Walking Guides' general recommendations concerning equipment, see page 33.

Man-made problems are infrequent, always excepting the risk of forest-fire toward the end of the summer. If, in autumn, you see a sign on a country road for a '*matanza*' (sometimes bizarrely spelt '*batanza*'), it's probably best to steer clear as the chances are it refers not to the communal killing, cutting and curing of a pig (the traditional meaning) but an organized boar hunt conducted, judging by the disparaging comments of non-hunting farmers, by gun-toting tyros with only a very approximate, fairground facility for pointing their weapons in the right direction.

Despite the concentration of tourism along the coast and the journalistic habit of calling the Costa del Sol the *Costa del Crimen*, petty crime is rare in the vicinity of the mountains.

The major risks one runs are the obvious ones of negligence or lack of foresight: **dehydration** when it's hot or **disorientation** on the high plateaus when visibility is poor. Always take plenty of water, even when there's a *fuente* en route, and if you're not navigating by GPS, don't venture onto high ground in cloud or mist.

The only two **natural hazards** you are likely to encounter are processionary caterpillars (either nose-to-tailing their way across a path or clustered in cottony nests in the trees), to which many people are allergic (take some antihistamine if you're susceptible to allergies), and brucellosis, a very aggressive bacterial infection endemic among the goats on the Costa del Sol; if you have to cross a herd of goats, hold your breath.

Nests of processionary caterpillars

There are 1300 plant species within the *Parque Natural*, including fifteen **endemics**, among them a couple of species of flax (*linaria amoi* and *linaria salzmanni flava*), a type of vetch (*anthyllis plumosa*), a cognate of sea holly (*eringium grossi*), a subspecies of gorse (*ulex parviflorus rivasgodayanus*), and a member of the mignonette family (*reseda paui almijariensis*).

Allowing for variations according to altitude, orientation, humidity, soil and the impact of fires, you can expect to see the following **flora**. Two of the hardiest and traditionally most useful plants to be found in our area are esparto grass and dwarf palm, the former being plaited into matting and shoe soles, the latter used for fans. The most common herbs are rosemary and thyme, though you will also see various types of sage, including Jerusalem sage, a woody shrub formerly used as a diuretic and called *matagallo* in Spanish - basically 'kill the chicken'!

It's worth noting here that the Spanish don't beat about the bush when naming plants, wolfsbane becoming the considerably more candid *matalobo* (kill the wolf), while *morcilla* (black pudding) is sometimes flavoured with a type of aniseed called *matalauva* - kill the grape! If you're short of something to eat with your herbs, keep an eye open for wild asparagus, which is particularly good incorporated in a *tortilla* or *revuelto* (the Spanish version of scrambled eggs), while digestion can be aided by *manzanilla*, a type of wild camomile frequently found beside dirt tracks.

Typical landscape, wild olives in the foreground

Apart from the flowering shrubs (see below), **wildflowers** are not quite so fine here as further west on lower, grassier ground, though it is worth keeping an eye open for orchids, wild iris and paeonies, while in winter the northern slopes are carpeted with crocus.

Shrubs abound, including box, cistus, furze/gorse, honeysuckle, juniper, at least two types of lavender, lentisc/mastic, mediterranean daphne (poisonous and formerly used as a purgative), meadow rue (*thalictrum speciosissimum*, sometimes dubbed 'poor man's rhubarb'), oleander, retama, rockrose, whin, and more varieties of broom than I'd care to identify, though one can generally distinguish adenocarpus (Spanish *rascavieja*, which sounds suspiciously like 'scratch the old lady'; in keeping with the customary linguistic candor noted above there is another untranslatable plant, *rascaculo*, that involves scratching of a considerably more intimate, non-gender specific nature), blue hedgehog, spiny (very spiny) and slender broom.

Collecting chestnuts (Walk 8)

Trees are inevitably restricted due to the increasing dryness and centuries of forest fires, however, you will see wild olive, more often a shrub than a tree, but if left to its own devices said to live for over a thousand years.

Cork oak (*alcornoque*)

There's yew (*taxus baccata*, likewise more a shrub than a tree), maple, the resilient Carob tree, Maritime, Aleppo, Scots and Austrian pine, and - on the more humid northern face - cork, holm, gall, Pyrenean and stone oak.

There's an official arboretum at **Cortijo del Nevazo**, which includes amongst its saplings some *pinsapo* (Spanish fir), the prototype fir only found wild in the *sierras* of western Andalucía (**Bermeja, Blanca, Grazalema** and **de la Nieves**).

The last wolf in these mountain -always presuming none of the local property developers have strayed up here more recently- was killed in 1900. Nowadays you may spot a dark-furred fox sloping through the twilight and will certainly see some sign, if only the soil churned up by their foraging, of wild boar.

Despite spending several years ranging these mountains and occasionally bivouacking outdoors, I have only once glimpsed a mountain cat (about twice the size of the domestic variety and considerably more galumphing, distinguished by a dark ringed tail and muddy, mottled back).

The smaller **mammals** meanwhile are represented by equally elusive marten, genet, weasel, dormice and bats.

But the king of the **Sierras Tejeda** and **Almijara**, indeed one of the principal reasons why the area was declared a *parque natural*, is the *cabra montés* or Spanish Ibex (*Capra pyrenaica hispanica*), and you will be very unlucky indeed if you don't see a few of these. Now that their principal predator has been obliged to take his twelve-bore elsewhere, these fine animals are losing their timidity and you can often come within thirty metres of a herd before they scatter. Even if they don't let you get close, the spectacle of a disdainful buck nonchalantly strolling up a near vertical cliff to distance himself from the impertinent biped staggering about on the path, is quite as rewarding despite being mildly galling - the casual over-the-shoulder glance has been studied to such perfection, you get the keenest impression it's been cultivated solely to put you in your place, as if to say, "And you call yourself a walker!". This regal demeanour is acknowledged by the name older people use for *cabra montés*, La Montesa (you can hear the capitals), as if they were members of a lesser but still admirable nobility.

Birds of prey are regularly seen, including golden, booted and short-toed eagles, peregrine falcon, buzzards and goshawk. There are said to be tawny and eagle owls, too, and you may occasionally catch a nightjar blinking in the car headlights on a country road.

Other birds include bunting, chaffinch, cuckoo, doves, stonechat, robin, tits, warblers, wheatear, woodpecker and, among the most characteristic, partridge, which are particularly appealing when seen scurrying across a track, Indian file, their babes in line behind them.

Axarquían Robin

However, my own favourite is the hoopoe, by nature if not appearance the robin of the south, settling on a particular territory, generally close to humankind, and returning year after year. With their distinctive crest, fine plumage, chaotic take off - as if launched by a cackhanded blow from a tennis racket-, and swooping gravity - challenged flight, they're unmistakable and unforgettable.

Reptiles are represented by toads, frogs, salamanders, triton, chameleons and numerous types of lizard including the vivid green Ocellated Lizard (*Lacerta lapida*) and the smaller greeny-brown yellow-striped Spiny Footed Lizard (*Acanthodadactylus erythrurus*). Snakes are rarely seen, though vipers are said to be common in some places, and in low-lying scrub you may come across the odd 'harmless' grass snake - 'harmless' in inverted commas because they can grow as thick as your arm and as long as your leg and my heart has hopped out my mouth every time I've seen them.

As elsewhere in the south, grasshoppers are the most omnipresent **insects,** but there are also many varieties of butterflies and moths, notably Swallowtails (*Papilion machaon*) (rare in Britain) and the fabulously patterned Monarch (*Danaus plexippus*), which isn't found anywhere else in mainland Europe.

EATING & DRINKING

English travellers are increasingly familiar with classic Spanish cooking and **Spanish menus** are increasingly familiar with travellers who aren't, almost always featuring a translation, sometimes a slightly surreal translation, but generally adequate for avoiding anything you desperately dislike. Nonetheless, a few key words may be helpful.

A great institution in bars, hotels and restaurants is the *menu del día*, offering a three-course meal with wine for between seven and twelve euros. *Sopa de picadillo*, a hambone broth laced with bits of meat and hard-boiled egg, is a standard starter. Other regulars are omelettes (*tortilla española* and *francésa*, the latter comparable to what we're used to in Britain), potatoes fried with garlic and green peppers (*papas* or *patatas a lo pobre*), meatballs (*albondigas*), black-pudding (*morcilla*), classic *chorizo* sausage, often served with *migas* (literally crumbs, actually the Spanish take on *couscous*), chicken (*pollo* - get the gender right, the feminine *polla* no longer means 'hen'but is a euphemism for the male reproductive organs, a double-entendre giving rise to a famously filthy shaggy-dog story about a man being followed about by a hungry hen having prayed God give him a *polla insatiable*), pork chops (*chuletas de cerdo*) and possibly a fish (*pescado*) option.

Dessert is generally a bit dreary, often as not taking the form of something lamentable perpetrated in a distant factory. The key phrase for avoiding this is *¿Hay algo de la casa?* If there is "Anything homemade?", it will probably be flan (*crème caramel*) or *pudin* (a sort of semolina concoction), though personally I think you're better off ending with a *carajillo* (coffee with a tot of brandy).

If you're taking the *a la carta* option, go for a *solomillo* (loin) of pork or *chuletas de cordero* (lamb chops) rather than *ternera* (beef), which is generally elderly veal. Otherwise, local specialities include *chivo en salsa de almendras* (goat in an almond sauce) and *choto al horno* (roast kid).

Vegetarians will soon find eating in restaurants a little monotonous, while vegans must self-cater or die. Your best hope of something substantial are *garbanzos* (chick peas), *judias* (beans), *lentejas* (lentils), or *habas* (broad beans) though these are nearly always laced with chunks of ham (*tacos de jamón*) or boiled in meat stock (*caldo de carne*). You'll just have to emphasize *sin carne* (without meat) and watch the waiter weep. Eggs (*huevos*) most commonly appear in *tortillas* (see above) or *revueltos* (scrambled with vegetables). If you don't eat fish and order an *ensalada mixta*, ask for it *sin atún*, since a mixed salad is usually topped with tinned tuna.

No trip to the coast would be complete without a visit to a *chiringuito*, a beachside eatery that can range from a weather beaten shack to a full scale restaurant. They are far and away the best place to eat fresh fish, often delivered on the day direct from the boat by local fishermen. Specialities include *pescaíto frito* (lit. fried fish), seasonally available grilled sardines (*sardinas*), *boquerones* (fresh unsalted anchovies resembling overgrown whitebait), *almejas* (small clams griddled *a la plancha*), *chipirones* (baby squid), *dorada* (bream), and numerous locally caught fish that lack even a name in English let alone any familiarity with the English palate. *Rosada* is a particularly good example of these mystery fish. Not only does it lack a name in English or French, it doesn't even appear in Spanish dictionaries! It's very good, though.

The great days of **wine** making died with phylloxera at the end of the nineteenth century, but there are still enough *bodegas* and *ventas* selling local wine (generally tapped from a barrel into your own bottle) to keep all but the most exigent toper happy. The wine is not fine and is generally sweet, drier versions tending to be a tad too rough, but it's definitely worth trying. The nearest area producing quality red wine is Jumilla, a scandalously neglected denomination that is, for my money, preferable to most of the well known, tannin-laced Riojas. If you happen to be staying in **Nerja** and see a bottle of 'Vino Tinto de Nerja', don't be deceived. It probably comes from Valldepeñas and is available in dozens of resorts along the coast with an appropriately local label slapped on the bottle.

The famous **White Villages** of the Andalusian mountains are perhaps a little too famous for their own good nowadays. Many have lost their local flavour under one layer of whitewash too many, surrendering themselves to a simulacrum of their past and filling their high streets with the sort of shops that can only be called, with no great merit implicit in the term, 'boutiques'.

That said, even the least vital of these museum pieces will still probably have the odd ground floor stable with a mule hanging his head from the window, watching the world go by; a tour of the backstreets will generally reveal a few elderly men and women clad in black clothes and crumpled faces and an air of having missed the twentieth century altogether (they haven't, indeed they've probably experienced the sharp end of the twentieth century more intimately than their contemporaries in Britain, but at a glance they definitely give the impression they're more familiar with feudalism than capitalism); and the winding alleys, flower-decked dead-ends, and higgledy-piggledy houses help explain just why these places became so popular in the first place.

Among the most famous villages are **Frigiliana**, **Cómpeta**, and **Comares**. Others are becoming increasingly well known as the property developers encroach on parishes like **Alcaucín**, **Moclinejo**, **Iznate** and even hamlets such as **Periana**, the sort of place that was once so out of the way you half wondered whether they'd got the glad tidings about Franco's death.

Frigiliana

My own favourites are **Totalán**, **Macharaviaya**, **Almáchar**, **Canillas de Aceituno**, **Salares** and **Sedella**. Many of these villages are connected with the coast by a bus service, generally only twice daily, but a day can be amply filled exploring the village, strolling round the surrounding countryside, and having a leisurely meal in the local *venta*.

Otherwise, take to the car for a **driving tour** of the hinterland, either following one of the signposted routes (e.g. *Ruta de las Pasas* climbing from **Rincón de la Victoria** and exploring the Western Axarquía and **Montés de Málaga**, or *Ruta del Mudejar* through the southern villages of the **Sierra Tejeda**) or just nosing around as the urge takes you. To circumnavigate the area covered in the present publication, take the SO2 or *Carretera de la Cabra Montés* north from **Almuñécar** (signposted 'Jete'), then turn left after forty kilometres (28km after **Otivar**) to follow the backroads through **Jayena** and **Fornes** to **Alhama de Granada** before returning to the coast via **Ventas de Zafarraya**. It's a drive I can pretty well guarantee you will not forget in a hurry.

If you're looking for **gifts or souvenirs**, I'd strongly recommend opting for something to put in your mouth rather than on your shelf. It maybe marginally more ephemeral, but the pleasure is all the more intense. Mountain *ventas* (the **Venta de Cardenas** on the MA169 between **Málaga** and **Comares** is particularly recommended) will generally sell sweet Málaga wine, homemade cheeses and home-cured charcuterie (in particular *morcilla* and *chorizo*), and superb honey (full of flavour and free of the crystal-forming, taste-spoiling sugar more northerly apiarists are often obliged to use to maintain production), any one of which will be more striking back in Britain than a T-shirt splashed with a 'humorous' slogan. And if you're feeling strong, you might go the whole hog (ouch!) and buy a ham (they travel well so long as you let them 'settle' for two or three days after the trip before taking the first slice) or five litres of olive oil from one of the innumerable local co-operatives (the **Puente Don Manuel** press enjoys a particularly good reputation, but buy the oil made from the ripe olives harvested after the New Year rather than the pre-Christmas batch made from unripe fruit for seasonally visiting city-slickers).

Standard **tourist attractions** like the **Cuevas de Nerja**, **Torcal de Antequera**, **El Chorro**, and the range of facilities and amusement parks along the coast, are well covered by promotional leaflets available in local Tourist Information Offices, but there are less well known sites that would be suitable for a day-off walking, like the **spa** at **Alhama de Granada** and the **dolmens** at **Antequera**.

In terms of **major cities**, **Cordoba**, **Ronda** and **Seville** are within striking distance though a little far for a comfortable day-trip. **Málaga** has more to see than reputation suggests, boasting a fine unfinished cathedral (I believe the prelate overseeing construction was in need of a country retreat), an attractive old quarter, a theatre with an eclectic programme of performance arts, a Picasso museum, an absolutely wild *fería* (the English translation, 'fair' or 'festival', is a bit wan for the sort of round-the-clock bacchanalia this denotes in Spain), and some of the most celebrated Easter parades in the country.

The real star of the region though is **Granada**, a city that is essential visiting for anyone wanting to claim even a cursory familiarity with Spain. It's easily done as a day-trip from anywhere on the coast between **Málaga** and **Almuñécar**, but don't just turn up expecting to get into the **Alhambra** (www.alhambra-patronato.es) on spec. The daily number of visitors has been restricted for several years (greatly improving the quality of the experience) and you need to book in advance, either at a branch of the Banco Bilbao Vizcaya or by phone (958 227525).

If you're venturing further afield, other less well known areas worth exploring include **Aracena** and the **Alpujarras** (see Discovery Walking Guides' respective publications), the mountains behind **Marbell**a and **Estepona**, the Spaghetti-western land round **Tabernas**, and - my own favourite - the fabulous unspoiled coast of **Cabo de Gata**.

LANGUAGE

There are large areas of Andalucía where Spotting The Spanish Speaker is like an elaborate, animated version of a Where's Wally puzzle. Many will sigh with relief at not having to plough through their phrase book, but I strongly recommend taking it nonetheless and making the effort to learn a few key words for greeting, guiding and eating. Even a passing familiarity with the language will help reveal the landscape behind the toponym, the meal behind the menu and, most importantly, the man behind the chance meeting. Of course, elderly mountain folk will be so glad to hear you speaking Spanish, there's every chance they'll launch into an enthusiastic stream of impenetrable dialect in which the last letter of every word, sometimes other key consonants, too, the odd vital syllable, and occasionally entire phrases are elided, but that's another matter altogether.

ACKNOWLEDGEMENTS

Mike Casdi for an insider's knowledge of the bits I hadn't previously been inside.

Antonio Pulido Pastor for doing his level best to keep the mountains intact.

Jeannette for La Loma de las Rosas and everything that entailed.

Ros and **David** for going places other publishers don't reach.

Antoine for hot water, clean clothes and Almódovar.

MAP NOTES

The map sections used to illustrate our walking routes in **Walk! Axarquía** are licenced from the 1:25,000 scale maps published by Centro Nacional de Información Geográfica (CIGN) of Madrid, Spain. Each section is then re-scaled to our traditional 1:40,000 scale and the walking routes and waypoints added.

Eight CIGN 1:25,000 scale map sheets cover the Axarquía; 1054-II, 1040-I, 1040-II, 1040-III, 1040-IV, 1041-I, 1041-III and 1051-I. CIGN maps can be ordered direct from:-

Centro Nacional de Información Geográfica
General Ibañez de Ibero, 3
28003 Madrid   Spain/España
http://www.cnig.es website and email at consulta@cnig.es

Discovery Walking Guides Ltd expect to have copies of CIGN maps used in our Walk! books available for direct purchase in UK, but at our publication date for **Walk! Axarquía** we are still negotiating our Distribution Agreement with CIGN.

Ventas de
Zafarraya

Alcaucín

Canillas
de
Aceituno

Canillas
de Albaida

Archez Competa

Arenas

Corumbela

Velez-
Malaga

Algarrobo

Torre
del
Mar

Torrox Costa

SPAIN

enas de

Jatar

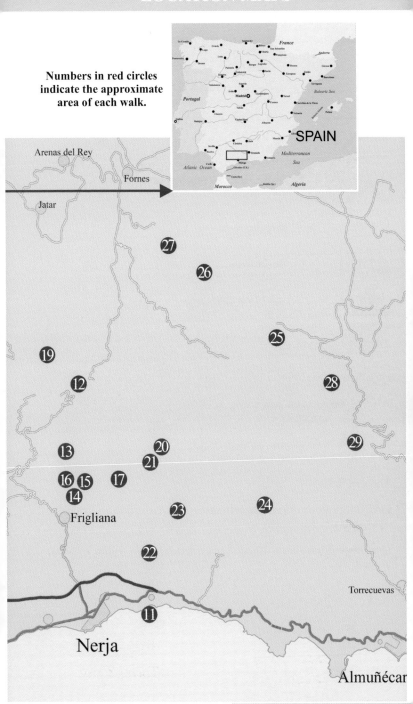

Numbers in red circles indicate the approximate area of each walk.

SPAIN

our rating for effort/exertion:-
1 very easy   **2** easy   **3** average
4 energetic   **5** strenuous

approximate **time** to complete a walk (compare your times against ours early in a walk) - does not include stopping time

approximate walking **distance** in kilometres

approximate **ascents/descents** in metres (N = negligible)

circular route

linear route

risk of **vertigo**

refreshments (may be at start or end of a route only)

Walk descriptions include:

- timing in minutes, shown as (40M)
- compass directions, shown as (NW)
- heights in metres, shown as (1355m)
- GPS waypoints, shown as (Wp.3)

Notes on the text

Place names are shown in **bold text**, except where we refer to a written sign, when any place names are enclosed in single quotation marks.

Spanish words are shown in *italics*, and if also in *purple*, will be included in the glossary (P.150).

The GPS Waypoint lists provided in this **Walk! Axarquia** guide book by Charles Davis, are as recorded during the research of the walk descriptions contained in the book. In the interests of clarity, not all waypoints included in these lists are shown on the maps which accompany each detailed walk description. Where a waypoint symbol is shown on a map it is numbered so that it can be directly identified against the walk description and waypoint list.

All the GPS Waypoints quoted in **Walk! Axarquia** were recorded during the research of the walking routes, and are subject to the general considerations as to the accuracy of GPS units in the location concerned. The **Axarquia** is a rugged region, as you would expect for a *Parque Natural*, and this ruggedness can make for potentially poor GPS reception in the more extreme areas of the region. In the deep ravines/*barrancos*, GPS reception is poor, very poor or non-existent; though in these situations there is usually only one logical route to follow. When we do encounter poor GPS reception you should stay with the detailed walk description.

GPS reception is surprisingly good for the majority of our walking routes. Routes where poor GPS reception was experienced are; Walk 3 between Wps.3 to 6; Walk 4 poor reception until Wp.2; Walk 8 between Wps.1 & 2, 7 & 8, 9 & 10; Walk 12 between Wps.16 & 17 at end of route; Walk 14 poor/nil reception along floor of the *barranco* until Wp.3; Walk 15 poor/nil reception in *barranco* and between Wps.6, 7 & 8; Walk 16 *barranco* floor again; Walk 17 between Wps.8 & 9 and 11 & 12; Walks 20 & 21 *barranco* floor with poor/nil reception; Walk 22 poor between Wps.4 & 5 and Wps.14 & 15; Walk 24 accuracy reduced in the *barranco*; Walk 25 between Wps.9 & 10; Walk 26 between Wps.3 & 4; Walk 27 between Wps.3 & 4; Walk 28 areas of poor reception but all wps are secure readings; Walk 29 poor between Wps.10 & 11; Walk 30A between Wps.3 & 4; Walk 30B poor reception until Wp.4; Walk 30C poor reception between Wps.11 to 16.

It is virtually impossible to reproduce the exact GPS Waypoint co-ordinates in practice when walking a route. While GPS Waypoints are quoted to 00.0001 minutes of arc, in practice you should expect 10 metres as an acceptable standard of accuracy when you have '3D navigation' (four or more satellites in view).

Signal Strength
Signal strength from sufficient satellites is crucial to obtaining an accurate location fix with your GPS unit. In open sky, ridge top, conditions you may have up to 11 satellites in view to give you a GPS location accuracy of 5 metres. Providing you have good batteries, and that you wait until your GPS has full 'satellite acquisition' before starting out, your GPS will perform well in the Axarquia for the majority of our walking routes.

To Input the Waypoints
GPS Waypoint co-ordinates are quoted for the WGS84 datum in degrees and minutes of Latitude and Longitude. To input the Waypoints into your GPS we suggest that you:

- switch on your GPS and select 'simulator' mode.
- check that your GPS is set to the WGS84 datum (its default datum) and the 'location format' 'hddd°.mm.mmm'.
- input the GPS Waypoints into a 'route' file with the same number as the walking route number; then when you call up the 'route' while in the Axarquía, there will be no confusion as to which walking route it refers. If your GPS will accept only three places of decimals, then 'round off' the waypoints; e.g. waypoint 7 in Walk 30 42 31.1994 N 1 35.7558 E would 'round off' to 42 31.199 N 1 35.756 E.
- repeat the inputting of routes until you have covered all the routes you plan to walk, or until you have used up the memory capacity of your GPS; even the most basic of GPS units will store up to 20 routes of up to 50 Waypoints for each route, and you can always re-programme your GPS while in Axarquía.
- turn off your GPS. When you turn the GPS back on it should return to its normal navigation mode.

Note that GPS Waypoints complement the detailed walking route descriptions in **Walk Axarquía** and are not intended as an alternative to the detailed walking route description.

Personal Navigator Files (PNFs) CD version 2.01
Edited versions of the original GPS research tracks and waypoints are available as downloadable files on our PNFs CD. In addition to **Axarquia** the CD contains **Tenerife**, **La Gomera**, **Lanzarote**, **La Palma**, **Mallorca**, **Menorca**, **Madeira**, **Andorra**, **Aracena** and **Alpujarras**; plus **GPS Utility Special Edition** software and examples from our **Walk! UK** series of guidebooks. See DWG websites for more information:

www.walking.demon.co.uk   www.dwgwalking.co.uk

Confused by GPS?
If you are confused by talk of GPS, but are interested in how this modern navigational aid could enhance your walking enjoyment, then simply seek out a copy of **GPS The Easy Way**, the UK's best selling GPS manual. Written in an easy to read, lively, style and lavishly illustrated, GPS The Easy Way takes you through all aspects of GPS usage from absolute basics up to GPS Expert and debunking the myths about GPS along the way; an essential purchase for anyone thinking of buying a GPS.

"A compass points north"

but

"A GPS tells you where you are, where you have been, and can show you where you want to go."

"Ask not 'What is GPS?' - ask 'What can GPS do for me?' "

GPS The Easy Way is available from bookshops, outdoor shops, over the internet, and post free from:
Discovery Walking Guides Ltd.
10 Tennyson Close
Northampton NN5 7HJ
www.walking.demon.co.uk & www.dwgwalking.co.uk

WALKING EQUIPMENT

From reading the postings on uk.rec.walking internet news group, it is obvious that walkers are very interested in the clothing and equipment used by other walkers. For some this interest borders on obsession, with heated debates over walking poles, boots versus sandals, GPS versus 'map and compass' navigation etc. Walking magazines are packed with clothing and equipment reviews, opinions and adverts, but few walking guide books give more than a cursory mention to recommended clothing and equipment.

The Axarquia is only a few minutes drive from the Costa del Sol but presents a rugged contrast to the 'easy strolling' promenades of the resorts, and you should come prepared. In spring and autumn, you can expect some wet weather and if it does rain, or is forecast to rain, stay out of the *barranco* routes. Summer are hot in this region and dehydration is a serious risk unless you carry enough water. Protection against sunburn, sunstroke and dehydration should not be relaxed for even the easiest of routes.

At the risk of upsetting some walking fundamentalists, here's a brief rundown on what we've used.

BACKPACK

A 25-30 litre day pack should easily cope with all the equipment you think you will need for a day's walking. A design with plenty of outside pockets to give easy access to frequently used items, such as ½ litre water bottles, is a good starting point. Well padded straps will spread the load and a waist strap will stop the pack moving about on the more adventurous routes. A ventilated back panel will help clear sweat on hot days and tough routes; a design with a stand-off frame is best for ventilation and worth the small increase in weight. Do spend time adjusting the straps so that you get the most comfortable fit. As an alternative to traditional backpack designs, you might find the cyclist's packs produced by **Nikko** (which we use), and similar companies, a good compromise of stand-off frame, capacity, pockets and weight.

FOOTWEAR

Rugged landscapes call for good footwear. Whether you choose boots, shoes or sandals they must be up to the task. Take note of the advice in each walk introduction, particularly for the 'wet' river routes. You will need a hard sole with plenty of grip and a well padded foot-bed. Our boot choice is **Bestard** boots or shoes, worn with thick walking socks. Bestard boots and shoes are not widely available in UK but if you are ever on Mallorca call in at their factory shop in Lloseta. Good rugged walking sandals we've used include those made by **Merrell**, **Cat** and **Teva**, amongst others. Whichever footwear you choose, do make sure that you've covered plenty of kilometres in them before coming to the Axarquia.

Sunburn and sunstroke are a real danger, particularly in the Summer months. Wear comfortable loose clothing and always carry a comfortable sun hat. Choose a design that gives you plenty of shade, is comfortable to wear, and stays on your head in windy conditions; our choice are the **Rohan** 'Legionnaire' style which protects neck and ears, while the **Tilley** is Charles Davis' choice You'll be spending several hours a day outdoors and sunburnt ears (and neck) are both painful and embarrassing. Use a high-factor sun cream on all exposed skin. We favour wrap-round sunglasses which, as well as reducing UV radiation, protect from getting grit in our eyes on windy days. When you do take a break always sit in the shade; if there is any, and leave the sunburning to the Costa's 'booze and snooze' visitors.

Dehydration, like sunburn, is a real danger in the hotter months and particularly on the longer, more energetic routes. Always carry as much water as you think you might drink. A couple of ½ litre bottles, a few pence each from local shops, is the minimum, and add extra for the longer and more energetic routes. Even on shorter routes, we would advise that you carry some survival rations. Chocolate bars and the like can provide welcome comfort when out in the wild.

Antiseptic wipes, antiseptic cream, plasters and bandage are supplemented by lip salve. Also include tweezers, which you will soon appreciate if you catch a splinter or spine, and a whistle to attract attention if you get into difficulties.

Do not compromise - buy the best guide book and carry it with you. A compass is useful to orientate yourself at the start of a route and for general directions, but a GPS unit is far more useful - see 'Using GPS in the Axarquía' on page 31.

Choose loose comfortable clothing and add a lightweight jacket to your back pack.

You won't want to be carrying excess weight during your walking, especially on the longer routes with major ascents/descents. Digital cameras generally weigh far less than their film equivalents, and a monocular is half the weight of a pair of binoculars. A mobile phone, and money (refreshments, taxis, public telephones, drinks machines etc.) are also recommended.

David & Ros Brawn

Named for the abundant *tejos*, a shrubby type of yew (*taxus baccata*), the Sierra Tejeda is the best known of the various *sierras* covered in this book, largely becomes its culminating point is the westernmost 2000 metre summit on the Iberian Peninsula.

Given its altitude, **La Maroma** has become the emblematic mountain for the people of **Málaga**, its only serious rivals for the affections of local walkers being **La Concha** (1215m) behind **Marbella** and **Torrecillas** (1918m) in the **Sierra de las Nieves**. Given this pre-eminence, the walk to the top is considered something of a pilgrimage, literally so during the full moon in Summer, when the mountain is climbed at night in order see the sunrise. It's also very popular after snowfall, when local lads enjoying the immortality of youth launch themselves head-first from the top of a slope and slide down the mountain on their unprotected bellies, hoping they won't fetch up against a sharp rock poking out of the snow - in a country that already has one of the lowest birth rates in Europe, it's a terrifying sight.

La Maroma under snow

Among the conventional usages of the word *maroma* in Spanish is a cable or rope, which in Latin America has been extended to a tightrope act. I don't know why the mountain is called **La Maroma** (hazarding a guess, it may have something to do with the fact that ropes used to be made from the esparto grass that's such a feature of these *sierras*), but the literal meanings are deceptive when applied to this particular summit.

Despite the fact that all ways to the top (save one requiring a 4x4 to reach the start) involve climbs of 1000 metres or more, there's nothing very acrobatic about the ascent and the walking is relatively easy, certainly within the capacities of anyone who is reasonably fit, even if they have little experience. However, there are very few landmarks and the top is dotted with sinkholes, so you shouldn't attempt it in poor conditions. The summit itself is not that spectacular, but the views are extraordinary, including a large tranche of **Málaga** province, the silvery peaks of **Sierra Nevada**, the fabulous azure blue sweep of the Mediterranean, and on a clear day the African coast.

However, those people - and they are many - who walk up **La Maroma** once and think they've 'done' the **Sierra Tejeda**, are making a serious mistake. For one thing, the three classic ascents (there are others, but three should be enough for most people), are sufficiently different from one another for it to be worth doing all of them. More importantly though, there are many other walks in the **Sierra Tejeda** and, as any experienced walker will tell you, getting to the top is often the least engaging part of exploring a mountain. The **Fábrica de la Luz** above **Canillas de Albaida** is a well known starting point for other **Sierra Tejeda** walks, but many of our itineraries are either little known or have been more or less invented by myself, so I strongly recommend taking the time to explore some of the less celebrated facets of this fine mountain.

I don't intend describing all the villages and towns flanking the mountains, but it's worth mentioning a few details about those from which we start our walks.

For many years, **Alcaucín** was a back-of-beyond place, rarely visited by tourists and only used by non-local Spaniards as a point of access to the mountains. It's now been 'discovered'and the customary colonization is underway, which is no great surprise, as it enjoys a privileged position, overlooking the Western Axarquía, the **Embalse de la Viñuela**, and the inevitable golf course that's being laid near the dam. For our purposes though, the most important piece of information is that **Alcaucín** is the start of one of the best dirt tracks around the **Sierra Tejeda**, leading to the **Llanos de Zafarraya**, and passing en route the **Alcázar** and **Alcauca** picnic/camping zones. Even if you don't do any walks here, I strongly recommend a car tour along this track. See Walk 2 for details of access.

Canillas de Aceituno, **Alcaucín**'s southern neighbour, has long been known as one of the region's prettiest villages, which makes it doubly remarkable that the place remains distinctively Spanish and, despite some new building on the outskirts, well-preserved without becoming a museum piece. Apparently the name refers not to the cultivation of olives (Sp. *aceitunas*) but to the olive (Ar. *azzeitun*) drab silk produced here in Moorish times. Its Moorish origins are also evident on the ground in fine *mudéjar* architecture (**Casa de los Diezmos** and **Casa de la Reina Mora**) and the Arabic cistern at **Casa Esgrafiada**. Not that every trace of the past has proved so resilient: the sixteenth century church is built on top of an old mosque while the only memory of the old Moorish fortress is in the name of **Plaza de Castillo**, which is where it was located.

Until comparatively recently, **Sedella** was a bit too inaccessible for most holidaymakers, second-homeowners and the plague of estate-agents currently breaking out all over the Axarquía. A classic Andalusian *pueblo* tucked away in the mountains, it seemed its inhabitants could only look on in envy as more conveniently located villages filled themselves with what seemed like fabulously wealthy foreigners willing to pay what seemed like fabulously absurd sums for ancient, drafty houses. **Sedella** was beyond the pale, stuck in time and unlikely to change until new roads were built. But such an estimate misjudged the determination of later expats and one now gets the impression that nine out of ten children in the street are blue-eyed, blond, English-speakers. Always presuming some fruitful and enterprising immigrant with a winning way hasn't set himself the task of saving the village school, this suggests the place is rapidly being bought up by English families, and yet it remains hard of access and classically Andalusian. A healthy sign for the future: the English-run hotel is the watering hole for local farmers as well as foreigners, suggesting this is one invasion intent on preserving rather than denaturing the locale.

A similar observation could be made of **Canillas de Albaida**. This *pueblo* has always been comparatively easy to reach, being just down the road from **Cómpeta**, and yet it's only in the last year that it's got its first hotel. It's another great village that seems to have got the balance between insiders and outsiders right. The local shop sells wine, olives, honey, ham, cheese, fruit and veg', dry goods … all the basic foodstuffs, plus buckets, hats, boots, working clothes … and Marmite and Lea & Perrins! This suggests a sane balance of tastes that puts to shame the dismal chauvinism of an advert I once saw for a Costa del Sol Safeways: "Labels you can read / Food you can eat". Confronted with an attitude like that, all I can say is, "¡Viva España!" - which it is in **Sedella** and **Canillas**.

Competa

Apart from the towns, I should also mention **Sierra de Alhama**, the range of mountains lying behind the western Axarquía and the poor relation of the *Parque Natural*, apparently tacked on to complete the trinity, like a chaperone shoe-horned into the party, grudgingly acknowledged in the invitations, but otherwise ignored. Apart from the title page, it doesn't even appear on the official *Parque Natural* map, and consequently falls outside our own catchment area. But like many a neglected relative, it's not without its merits, despite its inevitable diffidence in the face of its big, burly, better-known, larger-than-life cousins to the south-east. So once you've exhausted this book, check out the rocky ridges either side of the **Boquete de Zafarraya**.

Cueva de la Fajara, a kilometre-deep cave at the source of the **Río Bermuza** below **Canillas de Aceituno**, maybe of more profound interest to spelunkers, but for our purposes it merely serves as a pretext for exploring the classic domestic landscape of the Axarquía. Indeed, though we glimpse it, we don't actually go all the way to the cave itself, but instead spend our time meandering along the tracks and mule trails linking the cabins and *cortijos* scattered across the *lomas* between the two *pueblos*.

A *cortijo* on the route

The landscape is a joy, a matrix of valleys and hills cloaked with prickly pear, agave, vines, retama, and cane, and spattered with pomegranate, olive, orange, almond and carob trees, with hundreds of tiny cabins, *cortijos* and grape-drying beds perched on every available ridge.

Alcaucín itself is so busy building, you half suspect the village is staging a bid to host the next Olympic Games, but it retains its charm and would be a good base for a walking holiday, boasting several restaurants and a variety of accommodation options.

3 | 3H 10M | 10 km | 450m / 450m | ↻ | 4*

Access: on foot from **Alcaucín**   * in **Alcaucín**

As is frequently the case on land that's been mucked about by man, description makes the route sound more complicated than it really is. However, some care is required to follow the described itinerary at Wp.6 and between Wps.13 & 20 and Wps.24 & 28. There's a risk of vertigo at Wp.14, which can be avoided by turning left at Wp.10.

The walk starts at the southern end of **Alcaucín**, in front of the **Casa de Cultura** (Wp.1 0M) between the two signposted entrances to the central car-park. Walking uphill, we take the stairs to the left of the long row of low houses directly behind the **Casa de Cultura**. Turning left on the dirt track behind the houses (Wp.2) then right on the concrete track it joins (Wp.3), we pass the town cemetery, where the concrete gives way to dirt. Ignoring a major, concreted branch climbing to the left (Wp.4), we follow the main dirt track, bearing left at the next junction 200 metres later (Wp.5 11M).

The track passes the **Las Nogueras** quarry and, immediately afterwards, our return path (Wp.28). A long gentle climb with fine views over lowland

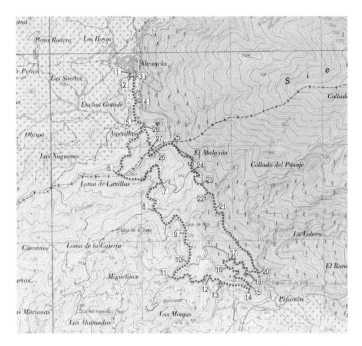

Axarquía brings us to a T-junction below two telecommunications masts on the **Loma de Canillas** (Wp.6 25M), within sight of the sea. Turning left and immediately forking right at a Y-junction below a cottage called 'La Loma', we follow the main track as it descends into the vine-clad valley of **Barranco Cárcomo**, passing a branch on the left to the optimistically named 'Casa Bedrock' (Wp.7 34M) (optimistic because Spanish builders are none too picky about the stability of foundations). Following a brief climb, we maintain our southerly direction at a staggered crossroads (Wp.8 42M), sticking with the main track.

After passing a cabin topped with a solar panel, we ignore a branch forking left (Wp.9) and descend steadily along the western flank of a long spur capped with a succession of cottages and cabins. 100 metres before a large modern bungalow, we pass a track branching left behind a building platform (possibly built upon by the time we go to press) (Wp.10 57M). This is the track to take if you don't like the sound of the little scramble at Wp.14, rejoining the described route at Wp.17. Otherwise, stick to the main track, which curls round to the east below the large modern bungalow (distinguished by eagle-topped gateposts) (Wp.11).

After passing a second bungalow with similar gateposts (they evidently had a bit of a run on the raptorial statuary down at the builders' merchants) and a minor track doubling back to the right, we cross the **Río Bermuza** (Wp.12 73M) and start climbing on a concrete lane leading to **Canillas de Aceituno**.

Climbing steadily, we pass a fenced cottage, immediately after which the concrete gives way to tarmac (Wp.13 78M) and we fork left on a narrow path that soon dips down to run between an *acequia* and olive terrace. 250-metres from the tarmac lane, erosion has washed away both path and *acequia* (Wp.14

82M). The *acequia* has been replaced by a metal pipe. The path hasn't! For five metres we're obliged to pick our way over the rocks above the erosion cavity, which isn't life-threateningly dangerous, but is precarious and won't be to everybody's taste.

The stream at Wp.15

Afterwards, we drop down a couple of metres to recover the path, crossing a second erosion gully before descending to a delightful pedestrian bridge over the stream (Wp.15) 50 metres from Wp.14. On a hot day, there's a lovely little waterfall and plunge pool to the right, just after the bridge.

On the far side of the stream, a cobbled way climbs under overhanging brambles to a small ruin, from where a dirt path skirts to the west of a well-maintained cottage, then follows a partially interred pipe along a contour line, eventually joining the end of a dirt track below a roofless ruin (Wp.16 95M). We follow the track as it climbs behind a cottage, where we take the first branch to the right (Wp.17 102M), passing below a large, abandoned corral 100 metres later. 125 metres after the corral, we fork left on a rough branch (Wp.18) climbing to an oblong reservoir, the interior of which has been painted swimming-pool blue (Wp.19 113M) (N.B. at Wp.18 the main track descends to the cottage above the bridge, a more direct and obviously unpublishable route).

The track ends here, but from the far end of the reservoir, we cross a pathless olive grove (ENE) and, 50-metres from the reservoir, emerge on a rough path along the fence defining the *parque natural* (Wp.20). For a glimpse of **Cueva de la Fajara**, descend to the right, otherwise, we bear left and follow the rough but clear way along the fence. After a long, level stretch, this path, which is obviously popular with your more circumspect fence-sitting poacher (it's littered with shotgun cartridges), climbs across a patch of cobbles, betraying its origins as the old mule trail linking **Canillas** and **Alcaucín**.

After a steady climb, the path levels out again (Wp.21 130M) within sight of two large electricity pylons. We then descend very slightly to cross **Barranco de la Hoya**, after which we come to a Y-junction (Wp.22), the branch on the left dropping into a gully between a house and a goatpen/dovecot. We fork right, passing a gate in the fence and joining a dirt track (Wp.23). Bearing right, we curve behind **Casa Concha**, the house just above the track, and climb steeply to a line of three bungalows (among them, presumably, Casa Bedrock) on a ridge below the twin electricity pylons seen earlier (Wp.24 146M).

Leaving the track, we turn right and approach the electricity pylons. Immediately next to the first pylon, which is set in a 2 metre tall concrete base, we bear left on a very narrow path defined by an almond grove on the left and invasive clumps of retama on the right. Within 50 metres, this path becomes clearer, bringing us back alongside the fence toward the head of **Barranco Cárcomo**. We then climb past a lime kiln, 150 metres after which, we descend onto the eastern end of the telecommunications masts track passed at Wp.6 (Wp.25 162M).

We follow this track (WSW) for 150-metres, then fork right behind a large bunker-like structure (Wp.26) onto a minor track winding down across terraces of olives to the south of the quarry (N.B. This is private property. If anyone's working among the vines or olives, a polite request would be in order. A simple '¿Podremos pasar?' is sufficient. In the unlikely event of the response being negative, return to the track and follow it past the telecommunications masts to Wp.6.). When the terrace track divides at a T-junction (Wp.27 170M), we bear right to join a narrow dirt path faintly beaten in the bare soil between the olive trees. Descending directly to the north-west, the path briefly approaches the quarry fence, then winds between vines, olives and almonds, passing a grape drying bed before rejoining our outward route (Wp.28 176M).

2 LOS CASTILLONES FROM CORTIJO DE LA ALCAULA

A pleasant woodland walk amid pine and mixed oak, culminating with some spectacular rocks and enjoying excellent views over the eastern Axarquía, **Sierra Alhama**, the **Zafarraya** plain, and the **Alcauca/Puente de Piedra** ravine. Very easy walking on clear paths and good tracks (easy enough to be done in poor conditions), but just scraping a high exertion rating for the stiff climb across the lower slopes of **Loma de las Víboras**. Of the two approaches to the *área recreativa/zona de acampada*, the northern one is perhaps preferable since, despite beginning with scruffy, litter-strewn, working countryside, it soon sheds the debris and traverses some of the finest oak forest in the park.

Access: by car

Alternative access to Walk 3: turn left at Wp.5 to join Walk 3 at Wp.12, cutting 200 metres off the full climb to **La Maroma**.

To reach the start from the south, immediately after the green ceramic welcome sign at the entrance to **Alcaucín** ('Alcaucín / Paraiso Natural / Bienvenidos'), turn left on a concrete lane signposted 'Cortijo El Alcázar Área Recreativa', setting the odometer at 0. After 600 metres the concrete gives way to dirt (though the rash of new building above **Alcaucín** suggests this section will soon be surfaced). We follow this track all the way to the **Cortijo de la Alcauca** *área recreativa/zona de acampada*, ignoring all branch tracks. The only slightly confusing junction comes at km1.5, where we fork right, ignoring the branch on the left, which is signposted 'Casa Rural Las Alberquillas'. We pass **Cortijo del Alcázar** at km5.5 and reach **Cortijo de la Alcauca** at km11. There's ample parking just past the *cortijo* ruins.

To reach the start from the north, take the tarmac track south between kms88 & 89 of the A335, signposted with a large Parque Natural sign and a smaller sign for 'Mercaventas Corrida de Frutos', setting the odometer at 0. After 600 metres, we pass the **Mercaventas** fruit & veg packaging plant and the tarmac gives way to dirt. Thereafter, we follow the signs for the **Cortijo de la Alcauca** *zona de acampada*, which we reach at km4.7. There's ample parking just before the *cortijo* ruins.

From the main, stepped entrance to the **Cortijo de la Alcauca** *zona de acampada* (Wp.1 0M), we follow the **Alcazar** dirt track (S) for 250 metres, ignoring a first path climbing left directly behind the área recreativa (an alternative start soon joining the described route), and taking a second path (Wp.2 4M) climbing alongside the dry, densely wooded gully of **Arroyo de la Alcauca**.

Crossing the *arroyo* 50 metres later below a tiny, trickling waterfall, we climb past densely mossed rocks before bearing away (W) from the stream 100 metres later, following a pleasant path carpeted with pine needles. After crossing a second broader gully (Wp.3 15M), we climb steadily to steeply between pine and several varieties of oak onto the back of a spur distinguished by decorticated cork oaks (Wp.4 26M).

We now simply climb straight up the spur (S), part of the **Loma de las Viboras**, ballooning calves rapidly coming to resemble Popeye's (this is the short stretch that squeezed in the high exertion rating), until the path emerges above the pine and veers left (SE) to join the **Castillones** dirt track climbing from **Cortijo de Alcázar** (Wp.5 42M).

Turning right, we descend past the superb little pinnacles of **Los Castillones**, below which there are some pleasant picnic spots amid the rocks. The track then curves through a U-bend into a long northwesterly descent flanked by partially cleared woodland. After a little over a kilometre, the track veers left through a second U-bend (SSE) and, 200 metres later, we turn right (NW) on a minor logging track (Wp.6 66M).

La Alcauca

Ignoring the spurs at each bend, we stay with this track as it zigzags down through the pine, eventually rejoining the main **Alcázar-Alcauca** track (Wp.7 97M). Turning right and ignoring all branches, we follow the main track for just under three kilometres to return to our starting point.

The westernmost 2000 metre summit on the Iberian peninsula and the highest point of the **Parque Natural**, **La Maroma** is in a certain sense the definitive Axarquía walking experience and one which many otherwise sedentary Malagueños regard in much the same light as practising Moslems consider the *hadj*: a not necessarily agreeable experience, but a pilgrimage that one is duty bound to undertake at least once in a worthy lifetime. And much as devout and wealthy Moslems will go to Mecca time and again, so dedicated and healthy ramblers will be up and down **La Maroma** at every available opportunity. The summit itself is not the most spectacular in the chain, but it is The Big One, the views are fabulous, and the sense of achievement is comparable to that felt at any culminating point: Ouf, done it!

The route from the **Alcázar** *área recreativa* above **Alcaucín** is not the easiest climb in normal conditions (that honour goes to the Robledal route), but it is the most direct and is the recommended route when the summit is under snow. That said, it does involve a long off-path section at the end when a certain confidence (and accuracy!) is required for orienting oneself. Finally, remember there's no shame in turning back. In our early explorations of these mountains, wind, mist and snow prevented us getting to the top of **La Maroma** on several occasions, a history of failure since confirmed by the experience of other ramblers. Definitely a place to be safe rather than sorry. The itinerary can be extended into a traverse descending to **Canillas de Aceituno** (Walk 30) while the climb can be reduced by starting from the **Alcauca** *área recreativa* (Walk 2).

(All values are for the full return route.)

Stroll/Short Version
Fuente del Tío Pelegran (*see text)

Access on foot:
From **Alcaucín**, probably including a night camping at the **Alcázar** *zona de acampada*, and adding 11 kilometres (return), and a 350 metre climb.

Access: by car
To reach the start, immediately after the green ceramic welcome sign at the entrance to **Alcaucín** ('Alcaucín / Paraiso Natural / Bienvenidos'), turn left on a concrete lane signposted 'Cortijo El Alcázar Área Recreativa', setting the odometer at 0. After 600 metres the concrete gives way to dirt (though the rash of new building above **Alcaucín** suggests this section will soon be surfaced). We follow this track all the way to the **Alcázar** *área recreativa/zona de acampada*, ignoring all branch tracks. The only slightly confusing junction comes at km1.5, where we fork right, ignoring the branch on the left, which is signposted 'Casa Rural Las Alberquillas'. We pass the first riverside camping area and the new *chiringuito* at km4.1 and park at km5.5 in the railed parking area to the right of the dirt track, beside the main **Cortijo del Alcázar** building, now part of the *área recreativa* to which it lends its name.

N.B. A *chiringuito* has recently opened at the lower of the two *zonas de acampada* though it's never actually been operational when I've passed, so I can make no judgement on what is obviously a worthy initiative.

Our path starts at the southern end of the car-park between the 'Sendero de la Maroma' and 'Cortijo del Alcázar' signboards (Wp.1 0M) crossing a pine shaded picnic area to join the **Castillones** dirt track (see Walk 2) where a chain blocks motorized access (Wp.2). We follow the track (NE) for 100 metres till it curves round a bend to a junction with a narrower track on the right (Wp.3 9M), at which point we have a choice of routes. The wayposted itinerary follows the **Castillones** track for a long but relatively sedate climb till it ends at **Loma de las Viboras** (Wp.12). Being both obvious and wayposted, this alternative requires no description, so we've opted for the steeper but more attractive **Barranco de la Higuera**/firebreak climb to **Loma de las Viboras**.

Turning right, we follow the branch track, which dwindles to a broad trail a little over 200 metres later (Wp.4). The trail crosses a stream then climbs steadily before fording the main **Barranco de la Higuera** watercourse between abandoned corrals (Wp.5 25M). Climbing slightly more steeply, we cross the end of a rough logging track (Wp.6 30M). After climbing east for 75 metres, the path curves round to the north, rejoining the logging track 300 metres later (Wp.7 42M). Ignoring a clear gully on the right, we briefly follow the track as it climbs (NE) to a bend, where cairns mark an initially narrow path climbing to the right (Wp.8).

* For a short walk, continue along the logging track past **Fuente del Tío Pelegran**, then turn left at the junction with the **Castillones** track to return to the *área recreativa*. Otherwise, turn right to climb steeply along a spur that gradually reveals itself to be a firebreak.

The path up the firebreak has recently been cleaned and is reasonably clear, though there are one or two points where it divides, generally thanks to the head-banging brigade that just climb straight up regardless of gradient. Unless you're a dedicated headbanger, I recommend taking advantage of every tiny zigzag the pathmakers see fit to offer, favouring the northern flank of the spur whenever possible. It's already quite steep enough.

After a little over ten minutes of steady climbing, we pass a lopsided pine (Wp.9), all its branches reaching south (you'll appreciate the sentiment if it's a windy day), after which we come to an apparent Y-junction (Wp.10 62M), both forks leading back onto the firebreak. Nearly 300 metres later, all of them climbing, we come to another Y-junction (Wp.11 76M), just below what appears to be the top (it ain't). Again, either branch can be taken, each leading through slightly obscure stretches before recovering a clear path for the final slog up to the end of the **Castillones** track beside a snow-metre (Wp.12 85M), from where we already enjoy fine views to the north-east.

From here we follow the broad, beautifully and incomprehensibly (it doesn't really go anywhere) well-made path zigzagging up **Loma de las Viboras** (Vipers' Hill), passing a waypost as the path levels out below a shallow watershed (Wp.13 112M), after which we curve round to a wayposted confluence of *barrancos* (Wp.14 122M).

The faint path bearing right leads into **Barranco del Mojón**, the most direct route, recommended when its windy, as its sheltered by the small summits of

Cerro Mojón and **Cerro del Águila.** Otherwise though, the longer, wayposted route is preferable, as it's marginally easier and a much more attractive climb.

Bearing left, we climb along the southern flank of **Barranco del Espino**, passing after 50 metres the tiny, likely dry **Fuente Espino** spring. The way is much fainter here, but poses no pathfinding problems thanks to the cairns and new wayposts. After a steady climb, we reach **Collado del Espino** (Wp.15 140M) a long, shallow col at the head of the *barranco*, from where we enjoy fine views across the province of **Granada** to **Sierra Nevada**.

The gateway at Wp.16

The path becomes even more obscure, but sticking to the upper traces as indicated by a waypost, we bear right (SE), crossing two thin lines of pine to the east of **Cerro Mojón** and following a cairn-marked way across an otherwise virtually pathless karstic landscape, leading to a small, natural 'gateway' of rock (Wp.16 152M), where the path becomes clear again. After a denser, more sombre line of pine, a natural pathway weaves through the rock to another 'gateway' (Wp.17 163M), this one with a waypost. Shortly after this second 'gateway' we see to our right a tall cairn and another snow-metre silhouetted against the sky.

Climbing towards Wp.18

Our path passes the **Fuensanta** spring (also probably dry), from where a clear, wayposted climb weaving between fabulous little rock formations, leads to the snow-metre (Wp.18 178M), now no more than a bullet-riddled snow-catching ring. This is where the **Barranco del Mojón** alternative rejoins the described route, though if you're climbing the **Mojón** under snow, the tendency is to continue in the swale of the *barranco* till Wp.19. The rest of the climb is off-path, though there are plenty of cairns and the new wayposts are a boon for first-time visitors.

Bearing left, we climb to the south-east, winding between clumps of stunted broom and esparto grass, following the heights between the **Barranco del Mojón** swale and **Arroyo de los Tejos**. Toward the head of the **Barranco del Mojón**, we briefly lose sight of cairns and wayposts, but climbing directly over the ridge above the swale, we find another waypost (Wp.19 193M) and can see the final climb ahead of us, though the trig-point is still invisible. After the next mini-ridge, we cross a shallow depression then climb straight up the remaining rise. Don't worry too much about following the 'right' way. There's no 'right' way, just several more or less cairn-marked routes.

The trig point

After passing a final waypost (Wp.20 204M) 175 metres from the still invisible trig point, we cross a cluster of cairns (Wp.21) and curve round (ESE) to the trig point and the summit of **La Maroma** (Wp.22 210M).

If it's your first visit to the summit, return the same way. If you intend continuing to **Canillas**, see Walk 30.

This is the 'easy' way up **La Maroma**, a mere 1000 metre climb, and perhaps the prettiest of the three standard routes, including the **Loma Contadero** spur, fine views to the north, healthy woodland, and the chance to see some of the yew (*tejos*), formerly so abundant they gave their name to the entire *sierra*. It can be done throughout the year providing the summit's not under snow, when the **Alcázar** ascent (Walk 3) is recommended. It's particularly lovely in autumn when the leaves are turning and the golden light is at its finest. However, 'easy' is a very relative term for a gruelling ascent of this nature and of the three main **Maroma** routes this includes the longest stretch on the exposed, virtually pathless heights of the dome. It should not be undertaken lightly, especially when conditions are poor. Once again, 'safe rather than sorry' is the rule. If in doubt, turn back and try again another day. Schedule at least one long stop en route to the top.

> **Short Version:**
> **Loma Contadero**

Access: by car:
To reach the start, take the track beside **Hotel Los Caños de la Alcaiceria** between kms85 & 84 of the A335, setting the odometer at 0. We turn right at km2.5, km4.8 (both signposted 'Zona de Acampada'), and km4.9, then fork left at km5.1 and park at km5.4.

The km2.5 turning can also be reached via a 'La Maroma' signposted track off the **Alhama-Jatar** road (km1.2 of the old L12).

(The bus between **Torre del Mar** & **Granada** via **Alhama** stops at **La Alcaiceria** twice daily.)

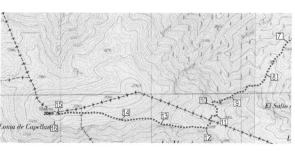

From the chain cutting access to motorized traffic (Wp.1 0M), we follow the pine lined track, passing after 400 metres a lefthand branch cut by a deep trench (Wp.2).

We then climb through more mixed woodland to a signposted junction, where we turn left for 'La Maroma' (Wp.3 10M). This track doubles back to the south-east for a little over 500 metres before veering south-west and meandering through mixed woodland, where it levels off briefly then dwindles to a path (Wp.4 31M) picked out with red and green waymarks.

After a further 250 metres, the path takes a more southerly direction and starts climbing the **Contadero** spur. After climbing onto a rocky promontory, we skirt to the right of a higher spine of rock (ignoring a curiously orientated green arrow) and climb steeply - so steeply my GPS, which claimed full satellite coverage at the time, was kind enough to suggest I was progressing at 0kph!

The Loma de Contadero

Emerging behind the spine of rock (Wp.5 47M) fine views open out to the north-east. If you just want to do a short walk, it's worth following the path for another 100 metres onto the next crag, from where we have even more splendid views (Wp.6).

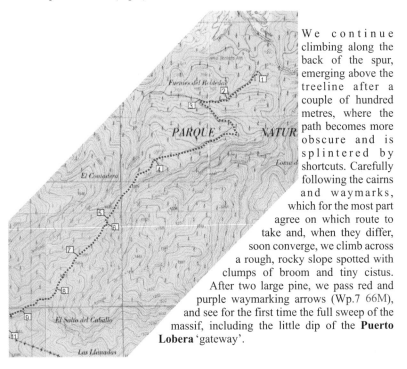

We continue climbing along the back of the spur, emerging above the treeline after a couple of hundred metres, where the path becomes more obscure and is splintered by shortcuts. Carefully following the cairns and waymarks, which for the most part agree on which route to take and, when they differ, soon converge, we climb across a rough, rocky slope spotted with clumps of broom and tiny cistus. After two large pine, we pass red and purple waymarking arrows (Wp.7 66M), and see for the first time the full sweep of the massif, including the little dip of the **Puerto Lobera** 'gateway'.

N.B. The large round summit to the south-west is the **Tajo** or **Peña del Sol** - not the summit of **La Maroma**.

We then stroll along a naturally paved way, meandering between the remaining scattered pine before climbing gently on a faint way, again picked out with waymarks - pathfinding isn't difficult, but you do need to keep an eye out for the waymarks. Midway through the last stand of pine, we pass a line of stones blocking a faint path branching off to the right (Wp.8 77M). Sticking with the broader waymarked route, we climb alongside a 'wall' of eroded rock, onto a broad ledge path below the **Salto de Caballo** (Horse's Leap!) cliffs.

WARNING: though never alarmingly vertiginous, this path does traverse some steep slopes. Moreover, it gets very little sun and, toward the end of winter, can be rendered treacherous with hard compacted ice, even when the summit is clear of snow. Do not venture onto this path if it's icy.

Climbing gently, the path passes the first of two very slightly vertiginous stretches where you wouldn't want to be slipping and sliding on ice (Wp.9 85M). After each slightly vertiginous stretch, it traces a chicane onto higher ground before finally winding past a curiously placed purple waymark cross and going through the gateway of **Puerto Lobera** (Wp.10 103M).

A cairn to the right indicates a pathless route to the top across the heights behind the **Tajo del Sol**, but the final ascent is already arduous enough without forsaking the minimal path that does exist, so we bear left, following the waymarked route into a shallow depression, where the path has been cut by a fence (Wp.11). Skirting to the right of the fenced area, we wind between clumps of hedgehog broom, crossing a rocky rise and bearing right along a shallow trench of exposed soil to a cairn-marked junction with a very faint path to the east (Wp.12 116M), which is where the present itinerary and the Alternative Walk (Walk 30(b)) diverge.

For **La Maroma**, we take the clearer path to the right (W), climbing steadily past new red waymarks - a godsend for a first time ascent; previously it was all too easy to stray dangerously close to the cliffs. Following the waymarks, we skirt the cliffs, fabulous views opening out over the broad sweep of the Axarquía and across the Mediterranean as far as North Africa on a clear day. After 275 metres, the clear path disappears in the bare rock of the **Tajo Volaero**.

Remaining a prudent two to five metres behind the cliffs, we pick our way across the rocks to a large red arrow (Wp.13 125M) with a metal pole set in the stone a few metres behind it. Recovering a faint path, we climb across bare rock toward a long, drab green shoulder, where the path again disappears amid a sea of loose debris (Wp.14 146M), debris that serves for the innumerable cairns that define the remaining climb to the trig point on the main summit of **La Maroma** (Wp.15 166M). Remember, these are 'pure' timings. Allow at least three hours for the climb, but expect it to take four the first time.

Eighty metres south-west of the trig point is a **Mirador de La Maroma** panel (as if you might have missed the views!) and the deepest of the summit's sinkholes (Wp.16) - to be approached with the utmost caution. We return via the same route, taking particular care to follow the cairns (GPS users should leave their receivers on), as the summit can be disorientating the first time. Also take care on the steep slopes descending toward **Tajo Volaero**. For future reference or if you're intending to do Walk 30(b) straight away (not recommended on a first ascent) the **Llanadas de Sedella** are the distinctive green belt separating the two major ranges of rocky mountain. The green spur descending south-west from the *llanadas* is the **Loma de Cuascadra**.

5 EL ROBLEDAL

The great oak forest of **El Robledal** to the north of **La Maroma** is such a lovely place that it seems a pity it should be the preserve of more adventurous hikers climbing **La Maroma**, hence this short, hassle-free circuit for those seeking tranquillity without the huffing and puffing and perspiring attendant on getting into the high mountains.

1	1½ H	6 km	215m / 215m	↻	0

Stroll
Arroyo de los Presillejos

Access: by car

To reach the start, take the track beside **Hotel Los Caños de la Alcaiceria** between kms85 & 84 of the A335, setting the odometer at 0. We turn right at km2.5, km4.8 (both signposted 'Zona de Acampada'), and km4.9, then park just before the next junction at km5.1.

(The bus between **Torre del Mar** & **Granada** via **Alhama** stops at **La Alcaiceria** twice daily.)

Our walk starts on the 'Área Recreativa 400m' dirt track to the right (Wp.1 0M) passing below **Cortijo del Robledal Alto** (ignore the branch climbing directly to the *cortijo*). The track divides briefly before entering the **Robledal** *área recreativa* where we bear left below the central reservoir, following a branch (initially obscured by pine needles) passing above circular shower stalls. Beyond the pine, the track enters more open woodland and dwindles to a path (Wp.2 10M) running alongside a shallow stone *acequia* amid lovely lichen-frosted oak.

The *acequia* path curves into the **Arroyo de los Presillejos** valley, passing a small catchment reservoir (Wp.3 15M). After a further 250 metres we bear left to cross the *acequia* and traverse an open field below tall pine, on the far side of which we join the **Fuentes del Robledal** dirt track (Wp.4 21M) just east of a small white pumphouse. For the stroll, bear left here to join the full itinerary at Wp.9, otherwise we turn right, crossing the stream via a concrete ford/bridge and climbing past several small *fuentes* to **Los Barracones** (Wp.5

32M), a complex of *turismo rural* bungalows built by the local authorities in 1994 but as yet unused! However, there's a barbecue hut and several picnic tables, making it a nice place for a break.

The track climbs to the right between the barbecue hut and bungalows to a reservoir, from where a forestry path leads to **Barranco Selladero** and a long pathless ascent of **La Maroma**.

The southernmost *fuente*

But in keeping with the no huff-and-puff policy of this itinerary, we retrace our steps for a little over 100 metres till, just before the southernmost *fuente*, a path doubles back on the right (S Wp.6) to a gate in the fence above the stream. Recrossing the dry bed of the **Arroyo de los Presillejos**, we pick up a faint path roughly defined by stones. The path climbs through a chicane then becomes clearer as it zigzags up through pine and

The view north from Wp.7

oak to a rocky knoll with good views over the **Zafarraya** valley and up the **Presillejos Barranco** to **Tajo del Sol**, **Puerto de Lobera** and the **Salto de Caballo** cliffs (Wp.7 52M).

The path then veers south, joining the waypoisted route to **La Maroma** 300 metres later (Wp.8 63M - Wp.4 of the **Robledal-Maroma** climb - use one or the other to avoid confusion).

Bearing left (ENE), we follow a logging track descending through stately pine, passing 'Los Corrales de Martín', now indistinguishable from the surrounding woodland apart from a sign declaring their presence. The track broadens and views open out to the north-east, after which it doubles back to the left and descends to a T-junction with the **Los Barracones** track (Wp.9 84M). Turning right, we follow this track back to our starting point.

The fire-ravaged, cistus-swathed landscape above **Sedella** can look a bit bleak in the intense flattening white light of Andalucía, but there are enough shady dells and riparian picnic-spots tucked away in obscure corners to offset the general desiccation, while the overall topography is so splendid it amply compensates for the degraded vegetation, specially on a damp winter's day when low-lying cloud hinders higher climbs. Climbing via **Río de la Fuente** to the superbly situated ruins of **Cortijo de la Junta**, we traverse **Loma de la Fuente** and return to **Sedella** via the flank of **Arroyo de la Fuente**.

The denomination of the *río* and *arroyo* is a little arbitrary, the river being rather less substantial than the stream, and different sources name or ignore one or the other more or less indiscriminately. The area further defies the mapmaker's art with a bewilderingly mutable medley of old cart tracks, more recent dirt tracks, ancient mule trails, royal ways, drovers' trails, goat paths, footpaths, hoofpaths, pathlets and firebreaks. This rich variety of ways swap identities with the fluidity of a troupe of well-practised mimics imitating one another at an impersonators' workshop, as a result of which one man's dirt track is mapped as another man's firebreak becoming another man's path and another man's nothing at all! In truth, it's impossible to say "This is a dirt track and this a path", as routes can change nature three or four times within the space of 25 metres. However, so long as you follow the general compass orientation, pathfinding is never a problem. Just bear in mind that the nature and width of any given way is liable to change abruptly.

The itinerary as a whole gets a modest exertion rating, but the steep, firebreak descent off **Loma de la Fuente** requires robust knees and either the courage of your convictions or the courage of my convictions, as the stretch between Wps.22 & 23 gives every indication of going nowhere. Rest assured, it does go somewhere, and the somewhere it goes is well worth going to.

| 3 | 3½ H | 10 km | 550m / 550m | ↻ | 3* |

| **Stroll**
Cortijo la Herreriza | | **Short Version**
Arroyo de la Fuente
(linear - in reverse) |

* in **Sedella**

Access: on foot from **Sedella**

Puente Romano

We start from the steps in front of **Ermita de la Esperanza** (Wp.1 0M) (signposted on the road from **Salares**) at the eastern end of **Sedella**. Heading north, we pass the **Colegio Público Rural** and turn right beside House No.15 onto a concrete lane passing, after 100 metres, a green sign for 'Puente Romano / Picaricos / Las

Llanadas'. Forking left at the Y-junction after **Casa La Resculadera** (Wp.2), we stay on the main track, which soon dwindles to a trail descending to the delightful stone footbridge of **Puente Romano** (Wp.3 14M).

Ignoring a faint way branching left through the oleander immediately after the bridge, we climb (E) on the remains of an ancient mule trail, winding across sheets of bare rock before climbing steadily alongside an oleander-choked gully (ENE)

The way can be a little confusing here, but staying close to the gully, we avoid all risk of straying off path. After following the gully for 100 metres, we veer right (E then S Wp.4 25M) on a narrower stony trail that soon tapers to a goat path for the final climb (N) to the ruined **Cortijo de la Herreriza** (Wp.5 31M).

Climbing away from la Herreriza

Immediately behind the *cortijo*, a confusion of ways meander through the cistus. Following a slightly oblique, north-easterly trajectory alongside a shallow gully, we soon find a clear, natural way climbing (WNW) along a runnel in the rock to a crossroads 75 metres behind the ruins (Wp.6).

Bearing right, we climb (NE) along the southern flank of a small spur tipped with a threshing circle. 50 metres east of the threshing circle, we join the very ragged remains of an old cart track (Wp.7 42M). N.B. The final approach to the 'track' splinters into a multiplicity of ways; don't fuss about getting the 'right' route, just follow whichever way seems easiest; you'll soon see the track and threshing circle.

Continuing ENE is the old *vereda* between **Sedella** and **Alhama de Granada**, which has now fallen on hard times and declined to a firebreak, part of which is used in Walk 30(b). Bearing left, we follow the equally impoverished track (N), now little more than a shabby path, climbing gently between the ubiquitous cistus and occasional clumps of oleander. A little over 100 metres later, we reach a narrow concrete *acequia* (Wp.8), which we follow toward the head of the **Río de la Fuente** valley, until the clear way crosses a miniscule concrete 'bridge' (Wp.9 53M), and climbs to join the first of two broad paths (Wp.10 58M) originating on the *vereda*/firebreak. It's at this point that our itinerary starts carrying on like a comedian with a multiple personality disorder.

Bearing left, we pass a couple of concrete-coped springs and climb to join a broader trail/track/terrace (there's really no telling) (Wp.11 64M). Maintaining direction (NNE), we soon see the fang-like ruins of **Casa Cuascuadra** on the ridge to our right, after which we climb between a scattering of fine healthy pine. Following a steady climb, the path curves right (SE) below a rough terrace lined with pine (Wp.12 80M), but soon resumes its northerly progress, bringing into view an outcrop of rock on **Loma de Cuascuadra** before joining a clear path linking the **Casas de Cuascuadra** and **de la Junta** (Wp.13 85M) Neither ruin is visible, but we can see the V-shaped watersheds at the head of **Río de la Fuente** and the broad trail on the river's right bank (our left) that leads to **Casa de la Junta**.

Bearing left (NNE), we follow the path down to the **Río de la Fuente** ford (Wp.14 96M). Ignoring a minor path climbing along the left bank, we stick with the main trail (WSW), crossing the river and climbing to a junction with a minor branch to the south (Wp.15), where we swing right (N), climbing past a threshing circle before curving onto the terraced pasture surrounding **Casa de la Junta** (Wp.16 110M).

To continue, we climb behind the ruin onto the northern end of the upper terrace (the one crowned with a thin band of shale), and take a narrow path climbing (SSW) behind twin erosion trenches onto a small platform (Wp.17 250 metres from the ruin) from were we can see **Salares** and **Sedella**. 125 metres later, the path crosses a grassy rise and disappears very briefly (Wp.18), reappearing a few metres to the west. After following a contour line across the slope and dipping into a couple of small watersheds, we climb onto a broad firebreak on **Loma de la Fuente** (Wp.19 130M).

Bearing left (S), we descend along the western side of the firebreak, looking for bulldozer tracks forking right 125 metres (Wp.20) and 200 metres (Wp.21) from Wp.19. We can take either branch (the second is slightly less steep) as they soon rejoin (Wp.22 138M) to form a narrow but steep firebreak descending to the west. We now scrunch up our toes and flex our knees for the abrupt descent along the firebreak, which is painstaking but never particularly alarming, apart from the fact that it looks like it's going to drop off a cliff. In fact, a little way below a small stand of pine, an ancient path joins the firebreak from the south (Wp.23 150M), after which path and firebreak fuse in a rough track descending (NE) to **Arroyo de la Fuente**, a lovely spot for a picnic.

Once in the valley, the track veers left (SW), passing an old limekiln before descending to a concrete ford (Wp.24 160M). Beyond the ford, we follow a good dirt track for 75 metres then fork left between two tall, charred but thriving pine onto an old cart track, now reduced to a walking trail (Wp.25). We follow this trail as it curves along a contour line, the **Arroyo de la Fuente** ravine rapidly dropping away below us, until we join a broad but rough dirt track (Wp.26 178M) above a large waterhut and a partially abandoned byre, the southern end of which is clad with a tin roof while the northern end sprouts a skeletal tangle of bent metal rafters.

The main track curves NW round the southern end of the byre, but we descend SSE below the waterhut onto a minor track leading to a large, dry reservoir, 25 metres to the west of which is a partially roofed ruin. Bearing left behind the ruin, we descend past a small house dedicated to the 'INEM Taller de Empleo Sierra Tejeda' job-creation scheme (Wp.27), in front of which the track ends and we take a narrow pomegranate-lined path descending alongside abandoned terraces. The path soon traverses better tended terraces and crosses an *acequia* (Wp.28 195M), 50 metres after which it's momentarily patched with ancient cobbling. After winding between increasingly immaculate terracing, we're suddenly confronted by **Sedella**, which we enter via a muddy farm track below a small house (Wp.29 207M).

We follow the track down to a narrow cobbled lane descending past **Casa Donna** onto **Calle Llana**. As in the mountains, so in the village: there's no 'right' way to return to the start (the organic nature of Andalusian village making - we're talking evolution here, not development - would have a professional city planner banging his head against the wall in despair) and I make no claims for this being the most direct way - it's simply the one we happened to follow. We bear left past houses Nºs 41 & 42 then turn left into **Calle del Principe**. At the first crossroads, we again turn left along **Calle Libertad** towards **Calle Jardines**, which we take to the right, back to the start of the walk.

If you're doing the Short Version

Take **Calle Llana** from the church square then turn right immediately after houses Nºs 41 & 42, the first of which is distinguished by red-painted brickwork. The house at Wp.29 has a yellow trimmed balcony, bare metal garage doors and a dry, creeper-canopied spring in front of it. The path leading to the terraces climbs between the house and the spring and is striped with a single thick black pipe.

(a) Arroyo Turbilla

Most walkers visiting the old generating plant or 'light factory', **Fábrica de la Luz**, above **Canillas de Alabaida**, content themselves with the classic walk up **Río Cueva del Melero** to **Puerto Blanquillo**, a variant of which features in Itinerary 8. However, there are many more tracks and trails round here, and this short itinerary is designed to give you a glimpse of the possibilities. It's not the sort of walk to have you gasping, either with exhilaration or exhaustion, but if you just want a quick outing with good views and largely easy walking, it's highly recommended. The proviso of 'largely' is necessary as there's a steep descent on a firebreak followed by 100 metres off path.

Best done on a late autumn or winter's afternoon when the sea is burnished by the setting sun and the hillsides picked out in golden light.

Access: by car

Short Versions
(a) descending via the track at Wp.6
(b) in reverse to **Cortijo La Parra**

To reach the start, take the road forking right at the **Competa** entrance to **Canillas de Albaida** (**'Calle Santana'**, also bearing a ceramic sign for 'Zona Recreativa Fábrica de la Luz'), setting the odometer at zero. Follow the U-bend round to the right below the **Santa Ana** chapel at 400 metres and take the tarmac lane along the flank of the valley. At km1.8, fork left for 'Zona de Acampada Fábrica de la Luz', passing the **Montosa** gravel quarry at km3. Park 750 metres later just after the first, roofless generating building.

At the far end of the car-park, concrete steps (Wp.1 0M) descend onto the riverside camping terrace, below which brick steps lead to a stepping-stone ford across the stream. Beyond the banks of oleander lining the stream, we skirt maintained terraces and take a partially paved trail climbing behind an electricity-pylon.

After passing a second pylon (Wp.2 5M), the trail veers right briefly before resuming its southwesterly climb to a third pylon (Wp.3 15M). It then winds between the pine in a northerly direction to join a dirt track on **Cerro de la Cueva del Agua** (Wp.4 26M), from where we enjoy fine views of **La Maroma**.

Bearing right, we follow this track round toward the bare dome of **Cerro de la Chapa**, bringing into view **Cerro de Rajas Negras** at the head of the **Cueva del Melero** valley. Passing an overgrown branch track (Wp.5), we climb gently between well-tended olive groves to a stand of fine cork oaks (still

La Parra just visible from Wp.6

harvested) and a junction with a track descending to **Arroyo Turbilla** (Wp.6 42M). For a short walk, turn right here and follow the track back to the **Fábrica de la Luz**. Otherwise, we continue along the main track, forking right 150 metres later at a Y-junction with a track to **Cortijo de los Llanos** (Wp.7). It's worth pausing here to look at the way down from Wp.10. The firebreak and **La Parra** ruins are clearly visible on the far side of the **Turbilla** valley. We descend off the firebreak above the second large group of pine to the upper ruin, then take the rough track to its left.

After the Y-junction, we climb steadily to the main **Canillas-Salares** track circling the **Cueva del Melero** valley (Wp.8 50M). Bearing right again, we follow this track as it curves round to the east, enjoying the easy walking and fine views. After crossing **Arroyo Turbilla** (Wp.9 71M), we pass the *cortijo* of the same name and climb to a bend where a broad firebreak descends to the right (Wp.10 84M).

The Cuevo del Melero valley

Leaving the dirt track, we descend along faint goat paths crisscrossing the face of the firebreak, favouring the right hand side when the gradient eases off. At the start of the second stand of pine on the right (Wp.11 96M), we leave the firebreak via a tiny path curving off to the right.

Descending steeply, we follow a faint, rough way along the northern flank of the pine for 100 metres onto the terraces beside the uppermost **La Parra** ruin (Wp.12). Fifty metres northwest of the ruin is a broad platform and the start of an overgrown track (Wp.13 99M) which we follow all the way down to the valley.

Passing the second ruin, we ignore myriad goat trails branching off in every direction, and stay on the main track, which writhes about like an epileptic snake, before becoming clearer and passing a picturesque cabin. Descending through delightfully bucolic landscape, we pass a 'prohibido el paso' sign (as derelict as the buildings; the goatherd who uses the land doesn't object to ramblers). Joining the main track descending from Wp.6 (Wp.14 130M), we bear left to return to **La Fábrica**.

(b) Cerro de la Cueva del Agua

Access: by car

If you don't like the sound of firebreaks and off-path antics, there's another short walk that can be done from **La Fábrica de la Luz**, all of it on good tracks and paths. Following the lane back from the **Fábrica** car-park for 750 metres, we turn right 100 metres after the **Montosa** quarry on a broad dirt track (Wp.1 15M) descending to cross the river by a bridge. We climb along this track for 2km till it's crossed by a cairn-marked path (Wp.2 62M) coming up from the river below the **Santa Ana** chapel.

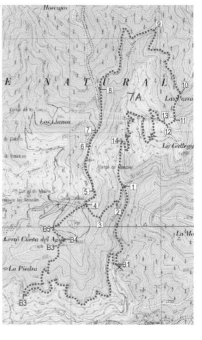

Turning right, we follow this path as it climbs in a northerly direction to cross a firebreak (Wp.3 80M). 75 metres later, we fork left at an apparent Y-junction (Wp.4) for a final gentle climb (NW) before recrossing the track we left earlier (Wp.5 85M).

Following a level trail, we skirt **Cerro de la Cueva del Agua,** rejoining the track at Wp.4 of Walk A (91M). From here, we can either descend via the cairn-marked trail on the other side of the track or via the dirt track at Wp.6.

The climb via the **Beekeeper's Cave** (**Cueva del Melero**, nowadays rather more the Goatherd's Cave) to **Puerto Blanquillo** is the classic excursion from **La Fábrica de la Luz**, and very nice, too. But in this variant, we go one step further than very-nice-too, tracing out a near perfect loop, and 'stealing' the best bit of the popular **Los Pradillos** circuit from **Competa**. It's an easy walk, but just big enough to merit the high exertion rating.

Short Version	Alternative version
Puerto Blanquillo via **Arroyo de la Cueva del Melero**	Climb to **Puerto Blanquillo** via the *arroyo* then follow the southern branch of the track round to descend from Wp.4 of the present itinerary or follow the northern branch to descend from Wp.10 of Walk 7(a).
Stroll	
Arroyo de la Cueva del Melero in reverse - easy walking until Wp.17	

Access: by car (see Walk 7)

From the southern end of the car-park at **La Fábrica de la Luz**, we take the rough access ramp (cut to traffic by a green chain) (Wp.1 0M) leading to the upper camping terraces. When the ramp divides on the terraces behind the main building, the lower terrace ending at the toilet block, we turn right on a path climbing past a fire-hazard warning sign. Sticking with the main path and ignoring minor branches onto the surrounding arboretum terraces, we climb steadily, crossing a dry *acequia* beside an empty reservoir (Wp.2 10M).

The steady climb continues on a clear path flanked by pine scrub, views opening out to the west toward **Torremolinos**, and the culminating point of **Sierra de las Nieves**, **Torrecillas**. Passing above the **Montosa** quarry, we ignore a faint way onto an old terrace wall (Wp.3) and veer left for the final 50 metre climb to the **Canillas - Puerto Blanquillo** dirt track (Wp.4 25M). (If you happen to be looking for this path in the opposite direction, it's framed by cairns and comes 30 metres west of the chained-off fork descending to **Cortijo Melero**.)

Bearing right, we follow the track through a long gentle descent, passing the enviably located **Casa la Montosa**, and bringing into view the distinctive rocky crown of **Cerro Atalaya**. After crossing a firebreak, we pass an apiarist's track climbing to the left. 250 metres later, after a kilometre and a half on the 'Canillas - Blanquillo' track, we fork left on the cusp of a U-bend (Wp.5 45M), climbing past a second apiarist's spur, from where we can see, high above us, the horizontal streak of the **Vereda de Competa** between **Cerro Gavilán** and **Cruz de Canillas**.

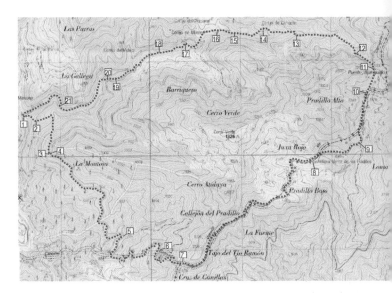

We now embark on a long slog up this preternaturally tranquil track (one half suspects some catastrophe has eclipsed the clatter of cars and lucre on the coast), passing a minor track doubling back to the left (Wp.6 70M). Staying on the main track, we continue our steady climb through a sequence of long chicanes, until we join the **Vereda de Competa** at **Cruz de Canillas** (Wp.7 86M), where the track veers right and we turn left on a trail marked with a cairn and a red bulls eye waymark.

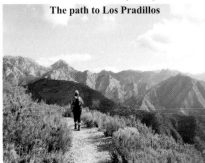

The path to Los Pradillos

If you feel like a breather, the ruined **Venta María Guerrero,** 75 metres along our trail, enjoys superb views to the south. Don't expect to have it to yourself, though. This is the finest section of the official **Los Pradillos** circuit and is popular with guided hiking parties.

After the *venta*, we follow the trail east, enjoying superb views of the **Sierra Almijara**, notably of **Lucero** and **Cerro del Cisne**, before curving round **Cerro Atalaya** and descending slightly to cross a couple of watershed gullies. We then climb a small rise, now carpeted with shrubs, but betraying a sorrier history in the charred trunks of fallen pine. Still following a clear path, we descend across more watersheds, passing an old lime kiln, 250 metres after which we reach **Venta Los Pradillos** (Wp.8 122M), also known as *Tejarillo* for the *tejas* or tiles that were baked here, fragments of which are still scattered around the ruin.

Behind the massive threshing circle at the ruin's eastern end, a slightly narrower path waymarked with red dots takes us past a second lime-kiln and another ruin, **Venta Cándido**, 175 metres after which, we pass a cairn-marked path climbing from the right (Wp.9 130M). Continuing on the main trail, we curve north into the valley of **Arroyo de Juan Rojo**, a feed stream for **Arroyo de los Pradillos**.

After crossing an affluent and climbing steadily alongside the *arroyo*, we fork left at a waymarked junction (Wp.10 141M) and start walking up the dry streambed. There's no path as such, but there are plenty of cairns and the walking is easy as we climb along the watercourse, briefly favouring the left bank before rejoining the boulder-strewn bed of the torrent for the final climb to **Puerto Blanquillo** (Wp.11 150M), where a waypost marks one of two ways across **Puerto de Competa** (an alternative access to the start of Walk 19).

Bearing left, we follow the track for 150 metres until a waypost and cairn (Wp.12) mark the start of the path descending to **Arroyo de la Cueva del Melero**. The path is steep at first (a little rock-skiing is inevitable), but soon curls round to run alongside the dry head of the stream, long stretches of sand proving wonderfully soft underfoot compared to our usual rocky paths. After passing a second waypost, we cross the watercourse (Wp.13 172M) and climb a small, rocky rise, bringing into view **Cortijo de Camacho**. Resuming our descent, we hear water in the stream and dogs in the *cortijo*, the latter avoided by bearing left below the *cortijo* on a path (Wp.14 180M) descending alongside then crossing a tiny affluent, beyond which we pass the **Camacho** *huerta*.

Continuing our descent along a narrow dirt path, we go through a bedstead gate and, ignoring a faint path along a terrace (Wp.15), fork left to stay on the main path alongside the stream, passing below a ruin (**Cortijo de la Lagunilla**) and going through a wooden gate (Wp.16 190M). Ignoring a cairn-marked path crossing a footbridge to the left immediately after the gate, we continue on the main path, fording an affluent and going through a second wooden gate onto the immaculately maintained terraces of **Cortijo Chaparral**. Passing behind a fine cork oak, we traverse terraces crisscrossed with a maze of irrigation pipes onto a winding, partially paved descent back to the stream (Wp.17 200M), which we ford three times in 300 metres before joining the end of a rough dirt track (Wp.18).

A faint path on the right descends to a silt-dam, but we follow the track for 500 metres till it runs into a U-bend on a better-stabilized track almost opposite the **Beekeeper's Cave** (Wp.19 217M). This track climbs to a junction just east of Wp.4, but we bear right, down toward **Cortijo Melero**, shortly before which, a waypost and red arrows indicate our path (Wp.20) descending below the *cortijo* to traverse terraces of almond, olive and walnut trees.

Beyond the terraces, the path cuts across mixed woodland and scrub before descending to the stream and crossing onto the right bank (Wp.21 230M). Tunnelling through oleander, we ford the stream twice before returning to **La Fábrica** via a rickety footbridge below the main building. For those doing the stroll or short version, this path starts at a waypost just before the **Arroyo Turbilla/Cortijo La Parra** track fords **Arroyo de la Cueva del Melero**.

Clichés aren't coined by accident, but reflect some fundamental truth, functioning as a shorthand for shared experience. Take, for instance, phrases praising the compact: 'size doesn't matter', 'small is beautiful', 'small but perfectly formed' … all those trite expressions, whether designed to soothe a diffident male ego, promote a minimalist ideal of business, or assert the charms of the vertically challenged, could be applied with equal veracity to this beguiling stroll along the **Río Cájula**. It's a great little walk, starting at a chocolate-box millhouse, continuing along a delightful oleander-lined stream, passing ruins that should inspire the most dismally ham-fisted DIY unenthusiast to dig out his toolkit, and enjoying views over the sort of pastoral idyll that could gobsmack even the glibbest estate agent.

| Stroll | * + 30 minutes if walking from the village |
| Cortijo Rafaeta | ** in **Canillas** |

Access by car:
Follow **Avenida de Andalucía** through **Canillas de Albaida** and fork right for 'Puerto de los Carboneros' at the junction with the **Archez** road. Park 500 metres later next to the 'Puente Romano' sign or, if the millhouse on the right isn't occupied, in the small parking area below the house.

Canillas de Albaida

Access on foot:
Follow **Avenida de Andalucía** past the supermarkets then, when it bears round to the left, carry straight ahead on **Calle Estación** to **Restaurante Almijara**. Immediately after the restaurant, turn left on **Calle Geránios** then bear right to cross a broad platform, beyond which a cobbled mule trail descends to **Puente Romano**.

The walk starts at the northern end of the dirt parking area below the millhouse at the confluence of **Río Cájula** and **Río de la Llanada**. Fording the **Río Cájula** (Wp.1 0M), we follow a path along its left bank (our right), re-crossing the stream twice in the first 150 metres. We then stroll between neatly tended terraces and partially tailored hedges of oleander, passing a breezeblock water hut below a confluence of watercourses (Wp.2 10M).

Our path curves into the valley on the right (NE), returning to the right bank 75 metres later, where a cobbled section climbs above a small waterfall before tunnelling through oleander into a wilder landscape dominated by massive blocks of rock and some overhanging crags. After fording the river twice more (the fifth and sixth crossings including the one at the start), we ignore a

faint branch on the right running alongside a fence, and follow the main, waymarked path climbing away from the river to the end of a rough dirt track below a small ruin. 50 metres short of the ruin, we turn right on a narrow path signposted 'Camino Río' (sic) (Wp.3 20M).

The path traverses terraces of avocado trees then crosses a shallow watershed and an *acequia* (now merely a partially interred pipe), entering the *Parque Natural* (Wp.4). Climbing over a small sandy shoulder, we pass a couple of boundary cairns, before descending back to the stream (Wp.5 30M) and returning to the left bank.

Ignoring a minor branch forking right 175 metres later (Wp.6), we descend to our final crossing (Wp.7 37M), after which the path climbs past the ruined **Cortijo Rafaeta**, briefly glimpsed earlier as we crossed the sandy shoulder after the avocado orchard. We now leave the **Río Cájula**, climbing along the southern flank of **Arroyo de la Minilla**, which we ford 350 metres later (Wp.8). The path then winds across largely abandoned terraces toward the semi-ruinous **Cortijo de la Parrilla**, now used for stabling. Fifty metres and four terraces below the *cortijo*, we bear left along a tree-shaded terrace (Wp.9), at the end of which we recover a clear path climbing past the ruin to a dirt track (Wp.10 52M).

Cortijo de la Parrilla

Bearing left, we follow the track as it curves round to recross **Arroyo de la Minilla** (Wp.11 62M). After a long, gentle climb with fine views towards **Puerto de Competa** and **Sierra de Játar** (the latter particularly appealing in the brief winter weeks when it's frosted with a light dusting of snow), the track curves south to a triple junction (Wp.12 73M). Forking left, we descend past a new bungalow, after which we ignore all branches and follow the main track as it descends steadily across immaculately maintained slopes of olives and vines, now increasingly maculate with new housing.

The track eventually bottoms out below a red-gated bridge leading to a cabin on the left (Wp.13 86M). Climbing steadily, we follow the main track till it veers sharp right (W) (Wp.14 96M), at which point we turn left on a minor track curving behind the unfinished **Villa Sierra**. Between the villa and a second small house, we leave the track (Wp.15) and take an old mule trail, soon passing the first patches of cobbling. After crossing the **Carboneros** road (Wp.16 105M), the mule trail descends to **Puente Romano** and a narrow path onto the road, just south of the start.

You wonder what this end of the **Sierra Tejeda** did to earn itself such ill fame. Admittedly, it's pretty arid, though a river does run through it, and I don't doubt living up here in the past wasn't always a barrel of laughs, but looking at the local names you're bound to suspect the toponymists had it in for the place.

Barranco del Malinfierno, from the south

Malas Camas, 'Bad Beds', **Barranco de Malinfierno**, 'The Barranco of Bad-Hell', **Collado de Carneros**, 'The Pass of Rams', also known as **Collado de la Orza**, meaning a 'Clay Pot' or 'Luffing', and **Collado de Sablazo**, 'Sabre wound' or in a figurative sense 'Wheedling money out of someone', neither of which is a very happy image.

Then there's **Cerro de los Majanos**, 'The Summit of A Pile of Stones', **Loma de Ningunico**, something like 'A Hillock of Nothing', **Haza del Aguadero**, 'The Ploughed Land at the Watering Hole' (inspirational, isn't it?) …there's even a place called **Añales**, which I believe is a yearling, but with so much prejudice about (whoever expected a rocky mountain to be a 'Good Bed'?) you can't help but conjecture otherwise. After a while, even something as superficially innocent as **Dos Hermanas**, 'Two Sisters', sounds a little sinister, while **Barranco del Potril**, which has no translation I can find, inevitably puts one in mind of a Shakespearian dastard. At the very least, the doleful individual that named these places wasn't worried about real estate values, which is all to the good for us, as this is one of the most neglected corners of the *Parque Natural*, despite enjoying some extraordinarily dramatic scenery and superb views. Given the dryness away from the stream, it's not recommended when it's hot, but on a cold, crisp winter's day, you'd have to go a long way to find quite such a splendid walk. Apart from a brief, optional off-path climb to the summit, the itinerary follows old dirt tracks and is suitable for any reasonably fit walker.

4 | 4H 40M * | 18 km | 800m / 800m | ↻ | 0

* but allow up to 5 hours

Short Version
Haza del Aguadero

Stroll
Río Alhama - there are several attractive plunge pools and possible picnic spots alongside the stream in **Las Cañadas**.

Access: by car
To reach the start, we take a narrow dirt track (SSW) branching off the GR141 (the old L12 between **Alhama de Granada** and **Játar**) 500 metres north of the junction with the GR-SO-15 from **Arenas del Rey**, 200 metres north of

the 'L12 9' kilometre post. If you're approaching from the north, this track starts 500 metres after another one with distinctive red gates. Our track is indicated by a milestone-style post for 'Sierra de Játar y de Enmedio, Haza del Aguadero' and a wooden GR7 signpost obscured by shrubbery. NOTE: there's a slight risk this track may be impassable after prolonged, heavy rain.

Setting the odometer at zero as we leave the road, we reach a crossroads that initially resembles a Y-junction at km0.6; we take the central track (the left fork of the apparent Y-junction), passing a house backed by a small red bullring 75 metres later. Ignoring a branch on the left at km1.7, we pass a large *cortijo* at km2.1 and park at km2.5, where a very faint track branches left and there's plenty of flat ground for manoeuvering. It is possible to drive a little further, but not terribly desirable.

From our designated parking area below the **Campiñuelas** spur of **Sierra de Játar** (Wp.1 0M), we continue (WSW) on the same track, dipping into a shallow valley and climbing over a low rise. The track levels off, passing a pothole before curving round toward the **Barranco de Malinfierno** and a 'Camino Particular Prohibido el Paso' sign (Wp.2 20M). Ignore this sign, which is directed against trail-bike and 4x4 enthusiasts. If you do happen to be challenged by the landowner (he drives a dark green Toyota pick-up), just emphasize that you're walking (*andando*) and aren't messing up his track with your car (*coche*). The gentleman in question was amenable enough when we spoke to him, but in the unlikely event of push coming to shove, you could also point out that this is a *Parque Natural* and that any track or path leading to the coast, a monument, or summit is a public right of way in Spain. Keep it friendly, though. Landowners aren't always delighted to find their property suddenly enclosed by a *parque natural* and indignant hikers blustering about the right-to-roam won't make the park authorities' job any easier.

After descending to a level stretch above the **Río Alhama**, the track runs alongside the stream and starts climbing **Las Cañadas**, the narrow mouth of **Barranco de Malinfierno**. We follow this track all the way to the **Haza del Aguadero** ruin, so what follows is merely for the purposes of pacing progress.

- After climbing steadily, the track winds through a defile (Wp.3 40M) where it's roughly patched with concrete and passes the affluent **Barranco del Potril**.
- Snaking away from the river, we climb behind a narrow, 30 metre high waterfall, above which (Wp.4 60M) the track maybe waterlogged by a series of subterranean springs.
- Crossing a bridge, we see the summit of **Malas Camas** for the first time. 100 metres later, we ignore a branch to the left (which leads to a major spring in the river) (Wp.5 82M) and follow the main track for another 100 metres to the **Haza del Aguadero** ruins, which are invisible till the last moment.

Haza del Aguadero, Malas Camas ahead

As we approach them, the destruction seems total, but in fact, there are two rooms in the more northwesterly ruin that have long been a popular bivouac with hikers doing a west-east traverse of the principal *sierras*. Nowadays the doors have been torn off for firewood and the floor's a bit mucky, but they still give adequate shelter if required.

Our itinerary continues directly behind the ruins on a rough dirt track (Wp.6 86M) climbing west across **Hoya de Gutiérrez** into a bleak but spectacular landscape of limestone and scrub. When the main track doubles back on the right (Wp.7 112M), we maintain our westerly direction on a narrower track climbing to the ridge (Wp.8 120M) between **Malas Camas** and **Cerro Albucaz**, from where we already have a quite stunning view toward **Llanadas de Sedella** and **La Maroma**.

There's no path to the top of **Malas Camas**, just a slew of stones spotted with hedgehog broom, but the trig-point is visible and it's easy to find a relatively natural way. Climbing north, just to the right of the first little hump below the summit, we gradually curve northwest, picking our way across crumbling rock onto **Malas Camas** (Wp.9 137M). Given

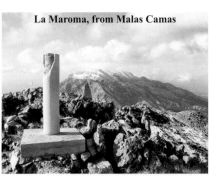

La Maroma, from Malas Camas

the outlook from the track, this may seem a superfluous ascent from below, but if you're up for the off-path bit, I guarantee the extra views make it more than worthwhile.

Taking extreme care on the loose rocks, we retrace our steps to the dirt track (Wp.8 150M). Ignoring faint branches to the west (Wp.10) and southwest (Wp.11), we follow the main track (SSE) to a junction just east of **Cerro Albucaz** (Wp.12 162M).

Bearing left toward the blunt pyramid of **Lucero**, we descend into deep, dark woods (anyone with a red riding hood would well advised to keep it to themselves), after which we join the main track descending from **Llanadas de Sedella** (Wp.13 179M). Following this track to the east along the **Cuerda de Nevazo**, we traverse a patch of pine wood so dense and dark it would have you looking askance at the most lovable granny. Emerging in the open (Wp.14 190M), we bear left, descending onto **Collado de los Carneros** (Wp.15) to join the **Malinfierno** track descending (NW) back to **Haza del Aguadero** (210M). We return to the start via the same dirt track.

The etymology of this *sierra* is uncertain. One theory claims it comes from Arabic *almijar*, literally 'the draining board', for the rapidity with which rainwater pours off the summits and floods into the sea (riverbed walkers take note). More prosaically but equally plausible, it is said to be named for its abundant fig and grape drying beds - Spanish *almijares*. In either case, there's a functional continuity: this is a place for shifting fluids, either off the mountains or out of the fruit grown on them. They are jobs for which the component sierras are eminently qualified, riven as they are with gullies and gorges, and spattered with more southern facets than a field full of heliotropes

The topography is equally apt for hiking, as this is the locus of the deepest ravines and sharpest pinnacles. Indeed, though not as high as the Sierra Tejeda, it is in some ways more spectacular.

Navachica seen from Alto de Cielo on Walk 3

The highest summit is **Navachica** (1828 metres), which can be climbed from the south via **Barranco de los Cazadores** (a rewarding but very long route), from the north via **Cortijo de Cabañeros** and **Cueva Cólica** (less of a climb, but with some obscure stretches), or from **Peña Escrita** to the east, an 'easy' route marred by the rather soulless '*parque ecologico*' at the start.

Lucero, as seen on Walk 18

But far and away the most emblematic peak in this area is **El Lucero** (1779 metres) (*lucero* means bright star in Spanish), also known as **Cerro** or **Raspón de los Moriscos**, a rather distressing term implying being abrasive with Christian-convert Moors! You can certainly see why it should be associated with sharpness.

A perfect pyramid, **Lucero** is easily distinguished all along the coast to **Málaga**, and is one of the classic ascents in the province. It's also sometimes included in a length-wise traverse of the entire chain, though I don't recommend this as the descent on the eastern side to **Puerto de Frigiliana** involves a gradient of 80%! The other classic summit here is **Alto de Cielo** (1508 metres), **Nerja**'s presiding peak and the object of an annual race from the beach, the winners of which run up those fifteen hundred metres so rapidly they make the ordinary walker look like a toddler.

The paths traversing the mountains and linking the coast with the interior are particularly important here, as the dense, spiky scrub might otherwise make the range virtually impenetrable apart from the occasional dry riverbeds. However, there is one other activity that has opened up, quite literally, the mountains in this area, and that is mining. Galena was long extracted from the mines in the **Barranco de los Cazadores** (**Minas de la Cruz**, **de la Buena Fe**, **de la Furia**, and **del Tajo**) and carried on mules down to **Playa de Burriana** for refining and shipping, and it's thanks to this traffic, which continued until the early twentieth century, that we have such a fine trail running the length of the *barranco*.

Barranco de los Cazadores

Barranco de la Higuera

The mines themselves have never tempted me, but it is rumoured that one of them, probably the **Mina del Tajo**, bores through the **Loma de Enmedio** all the way to **Barranco de la Higuera**.

Excluding the coastal towns, the best known settlement in this area is the celebrated village of **Frigiliana**. To be honest, **Frigiliana** is far from being my favourite place in the region. It's the prototype *Pueblo Blanco* in every sense with all the advantages of having been established by the Moors and being dirt poor for centuries, and all the disadvantages of being invaded by too many people like you and me. However, there's no denying the beauty of the old quarter and I recommend strolling around the **Barrio Alto**. Also worth noting are the cane-syrup factory (sometimes dubbed a 'palacio' as the original sixteenth century building was the home of the Counts of Frigiliana), the oil press processing local olives, the ceramic mural depicting the Battle of Frigiliana between Moors and Christians, and the remains of the 9th century **Castillo Lizar**.

The towns along the coast will be familiar to most holidaymakers and are fairly predictable for first time visitors, so I won't rehearse the obvious pros-and-cons of a Mediterranean tourist resort. However, I will put in a word for **Maro**, the village to the east of **Nerja**. Every second house has rooms to rent, so it isn't exactly an immaculate undiscovered gem, but if the other resorts had followed **Maro**'s example, the Costa del Sol, nay, the world would be a better place! New building has been limited, quality of life has taken precedence over cash, and it's about as near as you'll get to an authentic Spanish village on the coast.

I also recommend the virtually unknown farming towns and villages to the north of the mountains, in particular **Jayena**. A scruffy little country town that at first glance seems to be populated by rather more dogs than people, it's about as authentic as any place gets anywhere. The people are friendly, if initially a little wary (doubtless wondering what on earth tourists are doing there), it's got all the basic services, and there's some great walking in the surrounding countryside. As an index of just how unspoiled it is, you can still expect to get a free *tapa* with your drink, a phenomenon of old Spain that's increasingly rare.

This section of the book also includes what is, despite the best efforts of the road builders who are currently drilling a new motorway through the mountains, still the least spoiled stretch of the Costa del Sol. Time was when the coves tucked between the **Acantilados de Maro y Cerro Gordo** were the winter habitat of travellers in shabby vans and the summer resort of extended Spanish families camped out on the beach cooking vast *paellas* under marquees so big it looked like an impromptu bazaar had opened for the day.

Playa de Cantarriján

Nowadays, except for the routes down to **Cantarriján**, all the tracks are closed to non-residential traffic, drop-outs are discouraged, and it would be a very determined family indeed prepared to labour down to the beach with all the traditional paraphernalia.

In many ways, this is a shame, as the gregarious egalitarian muddle of insiders and outsiders was a glorious sight to behold: black-clad Spanish grannies, skirts tucked up, pop-socks sodden, paddling and nattering with perfect indifference beside the baking naked bodies of sun-worshipping northern Europeans; bow-legged granddads, soldered to smouldering Ducados, trading smoke signals with latter-day hippies wreathed in clouds of other flammable herbs; chubby, hirsute fathers carelessly wielding spear guns and watching the inert toasting flesh of *las rubias* ('the blondes') rather more closely than the darting movements of their ostensible prey; harassed mothers fanning spitting braziers through a haze of charcoal smoke, keeping themselves going with regular applications of *tinto de verano*; handsome young men edging in where fathers feared to tread, keen to promote a transient but practical demonstration of European union; sensible elder sisters dipping chortling nappy-swaddled babies in the gently lapping waves; shrieking children kicking footballs at one another and occasionally winging a passing tourist; tiny bouncing, barking Spanish lapdogs doing their level best to bully into submission the massive mongrels that panted lethargically under the travellers' vans … all in all, it created an engaging ambience that would have done justice to a Giles cartoon.

The litter, though, was something else. The sea thick with fag ends, every bush flying the pink flag of civilization, each secluded corner piled with plastic bags of rubbish, there were days when even the confirmed humanist would wonder whether people were such a good idea after all. Now that the area has been declared a *paraje natural* and cleaned up, the man-made atmosphere has declined, but the walking environment has improved immeasurably.

There are various ways to explore the beaches and cliffs of the *paraje natural*, including half-a-dozen strolls and a rather complicated linear route from **Maro** to **La Herradura**, but we've opted for one classic easy walk and two slightly more adventurous scrambles. Even if you don't walk here though, it's worth scheduling at least one day for a bathe and a meal at **Cantarriján**. Spend an afternoon lounging round on the beach and you'll begin to understand why the travellers' loved this place so much. Who knows, you may even end up buying your own van!

The first of our coastal walks in and around the **Paraje Natural de los Acantilados de Maro y Cerro Gordo**, is at once the shortest, the most pitiful looking on the map, and the most adventurous. For anyone familiar with the area wondering where the adventure lies on these largely conventional strolls, it is in the little known route linking the two via an infinitesimal path and a couple of erosion gullies where we use ropes to aid our descent. A more complete curate's egg would be hard to imagine, combining as it does two of the most secluded coves on the coast with mortuaries of tattered plastic skins shed by the ubiquitous hothouses. Don't let the hothouses put you off. The beaches are more than adequate compensation.

Access:
On foot from **Maro**

Strolls
Either beach as a linear route, excluding the ropes

* in **Maro**

The **Hogar Centro y Social Maro** (basically the pensioners' club) is strongly recommended for a beer and a sandwich at the end, as it epitomizes the deft way **Maro** accommodates the not obviously coherent communities of which it is composed, being at once a refuge for the card-playing, domino-clacking old boys for whom it was built, while also welcoming tourists and the more marginal residents of the cabins and encampments seen in the *barranco*. The walk crosses private land. If there's anybody in the cabin at Wp.7, ask permission to pass. And take care not to tread on the irrigation pipes between Wps.11&13.

We start from the **Hogar Centro y Social** (Wp.1 0M) at the western end of **Maro**. Taking the road toward **Nerj**a, we bear left after 75 metres, following a bend of the old road round to a junction with a track accessing hothouses (Wp.2).

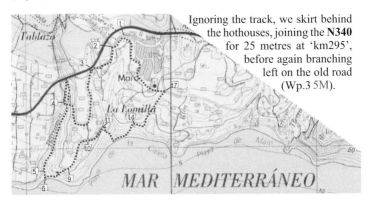

Ignoring the track, we skirt behind the hothouses, joining the **N340** for 25 metres at 'km295', before again branching left on the old road (Wp.3 5M).

Puente de Aguila aqueduct

The road descends between tropical orchards, melon patches, hothouses and, unhappily, the general debris of industrial farming, passing two tracks branching south before curving round to cross the old bridge over **Barranco de Maro**, a little way below the new bridge and the spectacular **Puente de Aguila** aqueduct. Immediately after the bridge, we turn right on a dirt track (Wp.4 15M) heading north before descending into **Barranco de Maro** and doubling back to the south, passing under the old bridge.

After passing a small house, the track dwindles to a path burrowing through the bamboo down to a triple junction (Wp.5), where we fork right, climbing above the final growth of bamboo before emerging in the delightful little cove of **Cala Barranco de Maro** (Wp.6 25M). From the easternmost of the two small beaches, another path climbs to a cabin (Wp.7). Bearing right and passing in front of the cabin (ask permission if it's occupied), we find a narrow, precipitous path climbing across two old terraces (burned and abandoned). Behind the second terrace, a rough, naturally 'stepped' way climbs steeply to the east, passing a slightly vertiginous stretch before disappearing below bare rock. Scrambling across the rock, we pass a tiny sluice gate at the end of a natural *acequia* (Wp.8), after which we traverse a field of smooth volcanic rock, joining the end of a dirt track (Wp.9 35M) back in plastic-land.

Following the track, we pass a vine-draped cabin before reaching a Y-junction (Wp.10) just 100 metres from our outward route. If you don't like the sound of what follows, take the branch on the left. Otherwise, we bear right then fork left 25 metres later, bringing **Playa de la Caleta** into view as we descend toward a concrete reservoir. Just before it bottoms out below the reservoir, we leave the dirt track, doubling back on the right on a tiny irrigation path (Wp.11 45M).

The path descends through dense vegetation for 50 metres to an avocado terrace, from which we drop down steeply (a bit of Tarzan-like tree hanging helps), going through a gateway of bamboo draped with *Dama de Noche* (L.*Cestrum Nocturnum*) before emerging in the open on an abandoned terrace. We descend off the first terrace via a steep erosion gully (Wp.12) to a second terrace where, slightly to your right, you'll find the first rope (Wp.13). At the time of writing, these ropes are new and well-tethered. However, this is hardly an official route so I make no claims for their condition in future years. Be it on your own head! In fact, the gully with the first rope could be negotiated unaided, the gradient being such that I walked down face first, merely using the rope as a 'bannister'. Ten metres after the first rope ends, a second slightly more vital rope helps us down a shorter but steeper patch of erosion to a gap in the bamboo fringing the beach, where we slither down on our bottoms onto **Playa de la Caleta** (60M).

The chances are you'll have this privileged spot to yourself, though I should point out that the day I recorded this walk, I emerged from the sea, more than ordinarily exposed in all my sagging dangling middle-aged glory, to be greeted by a dismayed party of holidaying nuns picking their way down the main path. Buñuel would have made much of it. I made my excuses and left.

To return to **Maro**, we take The Nuns' Way, the obvious path two-thirds of the way along the beach, climbing alongside a wire mesh fence. The path is rough at first, but soon becomes smoother as it passes below a small house to join a dirt track (Wp.14 66M), once again, the inevitable harbinger of plastic-land. Climbing along the track, we ignore a first, major branch to the left, then, in the crux of a second left hand branch (Wp.15), take a tiny path climbing along a partially tailored drainage gully to join the concreted end of another track (Wp.16) leading to the **Playa de Maro** road. Turning left then left again onto a dirt path climbing alongside the sugar factory ruins (Wp.17), we arrive in the **Plaza de la Iglesia de Maro**, from where we simply follow the balcony road, **Virgen de las Maravillas**, back to our starting point.

11(b) TORRE DE MARO

The Martello towers dotted along the Costa del Sol betray an uneasy history of clashing cultures, strategic imperatives, and good old-fashioned piracy. In this short itinerary, we visit one of the best preserved of these towers with the option of extending the walk down to a wonderfully isolated stretch of coastline. There's a risk of vertigo on the extension.

*	3 including the extension
**	+ 1km (return) for the extension
***	+ 100 metres for the extension
****	in **Maro**

Stroll
(see text)
Extension
(see text)

Access: on foot from **Maro**

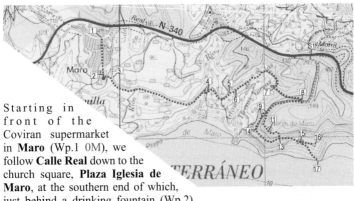

Starting in front of the Coviran supermarket in **Maro** (Wp.1 0M), we follow **Calle Real** down to the church square, **Plaza Iglesia de Maro**, at the southern end of which, just behind a drinking fountain (Wp.2), steps descend onto a dirt path that skirts the sugar factory ruins before joining the **Playa de Maro** road (Wp.3 5M). We follow the road for 650 metres till it traces a U-bend round the **Río Maro** and begins its final descent to the beach.

Immediately after crossing the stream, we fork left on a rough concrete track (Wp.4 15M) climbing between orchards of custard-apples, figs, and oranges.

Ignoring three access tracks branching right, we follow the main track till it curls north to a mini-*meseta* topped by a plastic hothouse, at which point we fork right on a minor track (Wp.5 20M) descending to another hothouse in the valley. Fifty metres from the turn-off and 50 metres before the track ends, we bear left on a well-trodden path (Wp.6) skirting the flank of the mini-*meseta*, passing behind a cabin and below a small house, where the path runs into a dirt track.

Following the track round to the southeast, we continue straight ahead at a crossroads (Wp.7 25M), climbing for nearly 200 metres to an inverted Y-junction (Wp.8) where we double back to the right. After crossing a broad platform, the track descends and we fork left on a clear path (Wp.9 31M), forking left again 50 metres later at a Y-junction (Wp.10) for the final stepped climb to **Torre de Maro** (Wp.11 35M).

Torre de Maro, Nerja in the distance

For a very short car-based stroll to the *torre*
Follow the main road for 1.3km from the eastern entrance to **Maro** then fork right on a dirt track at km297 of the N340 (signposted 'Torre de Maro'), parking 100 metres later at the signposted start of the 'Sendero de Torre de Maro' (Wp.S1). From here, we simply follow the broad trail south then southwest to the *torre*.

To continue the main walk
We follow a faint path to the east, curving behind the safety-rail to a blue waymark on a rock (Wp.12) 75 metres from the *torre*. Bearing right, we descend into a rough gully then follow the watershed to the south for 75 metres till we glimpse the ruin of a cabin lower down to the east (Wp.13 45M), at which point we have a choice of routes. For the main walk, simply turn right and follow the path as it curves round the south of the *torre* to join the end of a dirt track above a small house (Wp.14 50M). At a junction with a U-bend in another track, we bear right to rejoin our outward route at Wp.9. If you're doing the stroll, you could also incorporate this loop, continuing to the north at Wp.8 to return to your starting point.

For the extension
Turn left at Wp.13 and follow a rough path curving round a vertiginous bend (don't go too fast as it drops away rather abruptly). The path then drops down to clearer, easier walking. At a Y-junction (Wp.15), we can either fork left to picnic at the ruined cabin (Wp.16) or take the clearer fork on the right descending across a succession of ancient terraces to the sea (Wp.17 60M) and some good rock-bathing opportunities if the swell isn't too high. Return by the same way to rejoin the main walk at Wp.13.

Cantarriján is the last of the *playas* in the *Paraje Natural* the general public can reach by car and is an essential Costa del Sol outing, boasting a great beach, grand landscape, clear waters, and two of the coast's finest *chiringuitos*, **La Bola Marina** and **La Barraca**. Even if you don't want to walk, a day lounging round the beach, floating in the limpid waters, and stuffing yourself rigid with fresh fish is compulsory. That said, the experience will be all the better if it includes the walk. Despite increasingly invasive ribbons of tarmac being strewn along the coast like so much tickertape, this is a grand little wilderness, so infrequently visited we've even seen *cabra montés* rambling about a mere 100 metres from the Mediterranean! Though the traverse of **Cerro Caleta** itself is off-path, orientation is easy as we simply follow the ridge till it descends to the **Cañuelos** dirt track. Long trousers are preferable for pushing through the scrub on the ridge. There's a slight risk of vertigo. Even if you don't mind heights, stay well away from the clifftops.

| 1 | 2H | 5 km** | | 250m / 250m | ⚠ | ↻ | 5 |

Access: by car

> **Stroll**
> **Torre Caleta** (see text)

To reach the start, take the dirt track for 'Playa de Cantarriján' from the La Herradura Costa Tropical provincial limit on the N340. The walk starts on a spur doubling back on the right 1.1 kilometres from the road. If you're arriving from the east, it's safer to descend to the beach via the **Cerro Gordo** road then take the track north. Wp.1 is 350 metres from the entrance to the *chiringuito* car-park.

The spur (Wp.1 0M), which is only a few metres long, leads to **Arroyo de Cantarriján**, where GR-style red-and-white waymarks direct us onto a narrow but clear path doubling back to the left (S) and climbing steadily amid dense vegetation to a Y-junction within sight of the sea (Wp.2 5M). We stay on the main path as it veers round to the right and climbs (SW) past some tiny caves, 50 metres after which it levels out (Wp.3 10M), three metres before a clump of *palmetto* round which the path briefly divides.

For the stroll, continue on the waymarked path past the *palmetto* and turn left at Wp.13. For the main walk, we leave the waymarked path, taking a very faint way on the right toward the cliffs of **Cerro Caleta**, clearly visible to the northwest. The faint way meanders through the pine and across the rocks, disappearing altogether as it emerges from the trees 100 metres later (Wp.4) on an open slope blanketed with *esparto* grass. Bearing left (NW), we scramble up the patches of bare rock protruding from the *esparto* grass, aiming for the higher cliffs while remaining a prudent distance from those immediately to our left. A brief but very steep climb (the only reason this diminutive walk merits such a high exertion rating) brings us onto the southern tip of **Cerro Caleta** where, at the time of writing, a single stone like a miniature menhir endeavours to pass itself off as a cairn (Wp.5 30M). This is not actually the summit, but it's the best viewing point and one of the most remarkable *miradores* along this stretch of the coast. There are other places with comparable views, but none quite so inclusive of outlook and exclusive of access.

Staying well back from the cliffs, we pick our way along the ridge, stepping from rock to rock, taking extreme care as the shrubbery is singularly malign, leaping out to trip you up just when you're poised midway between rocks. Though the ridge is pathless, it appears to have entertained a convention of striptease artistes, and is 'waymarked' with discarded clothing. After crossing **Cerro Caleta** and a second small summit (Wp.6 43M), we descend to the northwest, pushing our way through cistus and retama, slightly favouring the southwestern flank of the ridge - a largely redundant piece of advice as the northeastern flank soon resolves itself into a cliff! Beyond the final rise, **Los Caracolillos** (Wp.7 50M), we reach a comparatively clear way descending through the pine and scrub, crossing a couple of tiny retaining walls and passing a large carob tree, below which we find a shrine to 'San Judas Tadeo' and a clear path leading to the **Cañuelos** dirt track (Wp.8 62M).

Turning left and ignoring all branches, we follow this track down to **Playa de Cañuelos** (Wp.9 77M). We then stroll along to the eastern end of the beach where, improbable though it seems as we approach, a tiny GR-waymarked path (Wp.10 82M) climbs steeply onto crumbling terraces behind **Cala de Cañuelos**, at the far end of which we pass behind the ruined coastguard's cabin on **Peñon del Fraile** (Wp.12), overlooking one of the finest little coves on the coast.

Torre Caleta

Several paths curve behind this cove, but given the erosion, it's best to climb via the higher path, passing a couple more mini-caves before skirting round the erosion gully separating us from **Torre Caleta**.

After the gully, we come to a waymarked junction (Wp.13 97M). For **Torre Caleta**, follow the minor path to the south. Otherwise, we bear left, staying on the waymarked route as it curls its way through dense vegetation. The path soon climbs into the pine and crosses a patch of bare rock before rejoining our outward route at Wp.3 (110M).

We step back in time for this long, exhilarating walk, following the route of the former mule trail crossing **Puerto de Frigiliana**, one of the principal trading routes (sometimes called a *via pecuaria*, though properly speaking that refers to a drovers' trail) linking **Granada** with the coast, and consequently lined with the *ventas* or inns servicing the muleteers. Fast food it was, too, or rather fast drink, former teamsters recalling how they would nip into each bar and knock back a quick brandy before hurrying out to catch the mule train as it continued unsupervised up the trail. Despite its populous history, **Puerto de Frigiliana** is now one of the sierra's more recondite corners and the grand landscape below it feels agreeably remote. The *puerto* itself is nothing very spectacular, but the approach is extraordinary: anyone who fails to be impressed by the final climb should consult a doctor, as several vital nerve endings must be disconnected - either that or you've stopped in one *venta* too many.

Most of the walk is on dirt track, much of it driveable, as result of which the main loop (excluding the final climb past **Venta Panaderos**) is suitable for mountain bikes. However, the accumulating effects of erosion and benign neglect on the part of the park authorities, who want to discourage motorized traffic and plan to cut access below **Collado de Páez Blanca**, mean this track, the old 'Ruta del Acebuchal' driving itinerary, is gradually returning to its original state. One can at present drive an ordinary car to Wp.4, but there are long, narrow stretches where negotiating the stand-off if you came head to head with another vehicle would involve the delicacy of a bomb-disposal expert. The walk is not recommended in hot weather, but is otherwise easy enough to be suitable for novice walkers.

* depending on which options you take on the return

Stroll	**Short Versions**
Venta Cebollera	**(a) Collado Blanquilla**
	(b) El Carrascal - stay on the dirt track at Wp.10 to do the loop round the **Higuerón**.

Access: by car

To reach the start, take the **Pedregal** concrete track from the **Frigiliana - Torrox** road, 3.4km from **Plaza Ingenio** in **Frigiliana** or 500 metres west of **La Posada Morisco**. Setting the odometer at zero as you leave the road, bear right at **Cuatros Caminos** (km1.6) for 'Acebuchal'. 200 metres later, when the concrete track veers left and descends steeply to the west, maintain direction (NW) on a rough dirt track. At km2.3, fork right at a Y-junction (the branch on the left descends to the hamlet of **Acebuchal**) following a very narrow track for 600 metres to an abandoned marble quarry. There's ample parking to the left of the track.

Setting off from the quarry (Wp.1 0M), we continue along the track as it follows a contour curving along **Umbria del Fuerte** (the shady side of **El Fuerte**, the mountain overlooking **Frigiliana**), soon bringing into view the remaining rooftop of the **Venta Cebollera** ruins and the conical summit of **Lucero**. After a little over half-an-hour, we pass a steep branch to the right (Wp.2) and a first, overgrown trail up to **Venta de Cebollera** (Wp.3 34M).

Staying on the main track, we descend toward **Arroyo del Acebuchal**, crossing a path (Wp.4 41M) between the hamlet of **Acebuchal** and the *venta*, which an information board calls 'Venta de la Jara o Cebollera', established some three-hundred years ago and operational until the last century. The board also identifies **Cerro Verde** (the scrub-clad summit directly ahead of us) as the site of skirmishes between the *Guardia Civil* and *la Gente de la Sierra*, 'the people of the sierra', a catchall phrase used indiscriminately for the assorted republicans, idealists, bandits, accidental outlaws and dedicated thugs (the boundaries between the categories weren't always clear) who took to the hills after the Civil War.

Staying on the track, we descend into the sandy bed of **Arroyo del Acebuchal**, passing below a couple of fangs of scorched masonry. Thirty metres after a more substantial ruin, **Hito 14** of the *Ruta del Acebuchal*, we fork right at a Y-junction (Wp.5 45M), staying in the streambed and leaving the dirt track, which continues to **Cortijo del Daire** and, eventually, **Competa**.

Ignoring an old trail doubling back on the right 75 metres later and, 200 metres after that, two cairn-marked gullies on the left (Wp.6), we follow the increasingly rocky watercourse up to a Y-junction (Wp.7 62M), where we fork right on a trail climbing above the former torrent.

The trail climbs steadily, dipping back into the watercourse twice, before rejoining the dirt track at **Collado Blanquilla** (Wp.8 75M), within sight of the lopsided summit of **Cerro del Cisne**, reputedly the toughest walk up in the region.

(NB The 'Ruta del Acebuchal' signboard identifies this point as 'Puerto Blanquillo', but we've opted for the *collado* option to avoid confusion with the better known **Puerto Blanquillo** visited in Walk 8.)

Continuing along the dirt track to the north, we enjoy grand views over **Barranco del Higuerón** and pass a traffic control panel which, with fine irony, stipulates a 30kph speed limit. 200 metres after crossing **Barranco del Marmol**, where there's a dry *fuente*, we fork right at a Y-junction (Wp.9

86M), soon passing the small, circular ruin of **Venta Camila**, and bringing into view **Venta Panaderos**. The track crosses a succession of meagre springs and watercourses before bridging two substantial streams in the **Barrancos del Bartolo** and **Atajo** (aka **Caracolillo**), which define the **Venta Panaderos** spur. The literal meaning of *atajo* is a 'shortcut' and there are indeed ways climbing into the watercourse toward Wp.11, but they're all badly overgrown. Instead, we leave the dirt track 50 metres after **Barranco del Atajo**, taking a broad cairn-marked trail doubling back to the left (Wp.10 117M).

Lucero

The trail soon dwindles to a path, climbing steadily between invasive clumps of cistus and broom, bringing back into view **Venta Panaderos** and the daunting crags draped along the southern flank of **Lucero**.

The path levels off briefly before a longer gentler climb brings us back to the **Atajo** watercourse and the 'junction' (Wp.11 127M) with the *venta* path - now so badly overgrown it's barely visible.

The first defile at Wp.12

Swinging right, we climb away from the watercourse (SSE) amid less invasive scrub, soon traversing a narrow defile (Wp.12). It's at this stage that one starts to appreciate why the muleteers needed quite so many *ventas* to keep them fed and 'watered'. These people weren't strolling along a nice neat dirt track admiring the fine views, soaking up the sun and enjoying the general tranquillity, but toiling up tough trails, day after day, with bandits popping up from the rocks like so many ducks at a fairground shooting booth. The name of the next ravine says it all: The Gorge of Anguish.

The trail dips down briefly, crossing **Barranco de las Angustias** (Wp.13 135M) before skirting the hillside toward **Cerro del Cisne**. Just when you think it can't possibly be going to the *puerto*, it veers sharp left (NNW) and starts a stunning climb, winding between natural 'walls' of rock. After passing through another, broader defile (Wp.14), we dip down into an unnamed affluent of the **Barranco del Higuerón**. Climbing along the watercourse, we ignore an apparent path branching right (Wp.15) and follow a rubble strewn way back into **Barranco de las Angustias** beside the wall of an ancient ruin (Wp.16 146M).

After an agreeably level stroll, amid a silence so total it suggests God has depressed the 'Loudness' button, a final climb winds along the course of the *arroyo* to **Puerto de Frigiliana** (Wp.17 163M) where we join the dirt track climbing from **La Resinera**. There are routes to the west up **Lucero** and east up **Navachica**, but neither are suitable for a publication like this, so unless there's some kind person prepared to meet you near **La Resinera**, we retrace our steps to the dirt track below **Venta Panaderos**.

Once back on the dirt track, we can either return to **Collado Blanquilla** via the same route or, if you can face an extra 75 metres climbing, continue along the dirt track to the south. After passing a branch to the left, the track snakes its way down to a confluence of watercourses. Veering south, it approaches a hairpin bend, on the cusp of which a cairn marks the start of the path up **Cerro del Cisne** (Wp.18), which I contemplated, but only very briefly: even the beginning is overgrown and the final climb looks plain grim.

We continue descending on badly eroded track, where all but the most gung-ho mountain-bikers will have to dismount, before re-crossing the stream. Immediately after the **Higuerón** helipad and firefighting reservoir, we pass the start of a path traversing the southern flank of **Cisne** to **Puerto de los Umbrales** and **Río Chillar** (the traverse is clearly visible from above, but the path is said to be overgrown toward the end) (Wp.19). We then climb back to Wp.9 and **Collado Blanquilla** (Wp.8 85 minutes from **Puerto Frigiliana**), where once again we have a choice of routes, either descending via **Arroyo del Acebuchal** or continuing along the track toward **Collado de Páez Blanca**.

In the second instance, as we round a bend within sight of the junction of dirt tracks on the *collado*, look for two cairns framing a faint path dropping down to the left (Wp.20 100M). The first couple of metres are very steep, but the gradient soon eases off as the path (indiscernible from a distance but reasonably clear step-by-step) winds between the scrub, curving south to pass a young pine (Wp.21) before descending to rejoin our outward route via either of the two gullies at Wp.6 (110M).

Like most practising adults, I generally take 'infantile' to be a pejorative adjective, but when it comes to messing about in rivers, I'm all for a rapid regression to childhood, even for the most august grown-ups. If you suffer a lurking urge to splash your way through that puddle or have fond memories of paddling in streams during your nonage, then this is the outing for you, following the largely pathless course of the **Río Higuerón** - named for the fig tree said to grow at its source. Unlike its counterpart in the **Chíllar**, where seemingly incessant wading can lose some of its charm, the criss-crossing of the **Higuerón** is a constant pleasure. Despite the pathless nature of the route, most of it is very easy and suitable for walkers of all ages and capacities, always presuming there's something of the child skulking about inside you. However, after Wp.5 the route becomes increasingly rough and the end is only recommended for the most agile, as an amusing time hopping from stone to stone becomes a hell-or-high-water scramble (a dunking is virtually guaranteed) up the chutes, waterslides and cascades of the *cahorros*, the straits toward the head of the river.

Under no circumstances attempt this walk after, during, or when there is a threat of heavy rain. Walking sandals or trainers preferable after Wp.5 and essential after Wp.7. GPS coverage is poor to non-existent.

*	for the Short Versions, 4 to the end of the *cahorros*
**	in **Frigiliana**

Short Versions
(a) to the bend in the river below **Cortijo de Conca**
(b) to the confluence with **Barranco del Marmól**

Stroll
To the **Pinarillo Espeso** *Área Recreativa*

Access: on foot from **Frigiliana**

If arriving by car from the coast, fork left for 'Frigiliana Casco Historico' on the approach road and park in one of the car-parks at the bend in the road where the wall is emblazoned with ceramics. From the car-parks, we walk up the slope to **Plaza Ingenio** below the old sugar-syrup factory, **Palacio de los Montijanos**. The walk starts on the narrow lane descending to the right of the **Unicaja** bank (Wp.1 0M). The lane curves round behind the bank to a right hand bend where it passes, opposite **Villa los Molineros**, the slip path of the alternative climb back from the river (see Wp.9).

Fifty metres above the riverbed, we fork left along the concrete wall of an *acequia* (Wp.2 5M), though you could equally descend directly to the riverbed and follow the waterlogged track to Wp.3. The path briefly drops off the *acequia* but rejoins it after fifity metres, curving round to a large reservoir, **Pozo Batán**, which is used as a swimming pool during the summer. 75 metres later, we pass the start of the **Limán Trail** (Wp.3 20M), signposted 'Sendero de la Fuente del Esparto'.

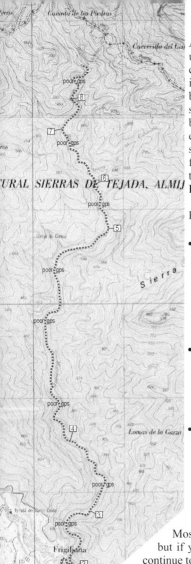

And that's all you really need to know until Wp.5, as we now simply follow the course of the river, making use of intermittent stretches of track and path, but on the whole, hopping from side to side of the watercourse and winding between clumps of oleander, banks of esparto grass and reeds, below the gaunt, scorched crags of **El Fuerte** and the pine forested flank of **Sierra de Enmedio** - 'in the middle' because it's between the **Ríos Higuerón** and **Chíllar**.

For the purposes of pacing progress …

- After skirting a first, largely abandoned *área recreativa* and ignoring a second path (doubling back on the right behind a cairn and a twin-trunked pine) up to the **Limán Trail**, we pass a lime kiln and come to the well appointed **Pinarillo Espeso** *área recreativa* (Wp.4 40M).
- A little over half-an-hour from **Pinarillo Espeso**, the summits of **Lucero** and **Lucerillo** come into view and the valley widens, passing two dry affluents descending from the west, **Barrancos del Almirez** and **del Arco**.
- Below the ruins of **Cortijo del Conca** (camouflaged by the surrounding rocks), the river narrows between low cliffs then curves left toward the head of **Acequia de Lisar** and a first waterhut (Wp.5 90M).

Most people will be happy to turn back here, but if you care to elevate the drama, you can continue to Wp.7 and, if you really want to ratchet up the commotion, onto the *cahorros*. In either case, now's the time to put on whatever soakable footwear you've got. If you do continue, bear in mind that timings become ever more relative, varying according to the level of water and your own agility.

The river becomes steeper and rougher as we pass below the invisible ruins of **Cortijo de Roma** (identifiable from the riverbed by a protruding waterpipe). A second, smaller waterhut (Wp.6 106M) precedes the first narrow stretch by 75 metres. To avoid this, there's said to be a path starting behind the hut, but it's so badly overgrown, I recommend sticking with the river, taking care as the rocks in this section can be slippery. 500 metres after these first mini-straits we come to a junction with the broad, dry **Barranco del Marmól** (Wp.7 137M). If you continue, expect to get wet.

..distressingly friable looking rock..

Bearing right, we follow the **Higuerón** toward the southern face of **Cerro del Cisne**, climbing more steadily, passing some delightful little jacuzzis and several high pinnacles of distressingly friable looking rock. 400 metres after the convergence of the two *barrancos*, a very approximate way climbs to the left (Wp.8 151M), skirting the *cahorros* and eventually leading to the dirt track below **Puerto de Frigiliana** (see Walk 12). We, meanwhile, push 'infantility' into the realms of 'imbecility' and continue upriver, entering the extraordinary *cahorros*, clambering over six small and not so small waterfalls.

Don't worry if you lose count, you'll know when you can go no further, without a shadow of doubt. Bear in mind that what's tricky on the way up is trickier on the way down.

- **Fall Nº1** can be skirted by slippery rocks on the right.
- **Nº2** is awkward; passage is greatly facilitated by long, spidery legs and arms.
- **Nº3**, immediately after Nº2, is a doddle.
- **Nº4** is high but dry (on the left) and has piled stones to help the climb.
- **Nº5** is passed by a very rough way over the rocks on the left (N.B. Take the same way back. The central oleander-aided slither is only for Lex Barker and other proto-simians).
- **Nº6** is torrential, but using a boulder on the left, still passable, after which we see graffiti on the walls (a dedication to been-there-done-that vandalism one has to admire).
- **Nº7** (173M) Stop!

Preparing for a dunking

We return by the same route save for near the end, where walkers with a good head for heights can fork right, 250 metres after **Pozo Batán**, on a cairn-marked path climbing from the *acequia*. After crossing a mildly vertiginous ledge, we pass a spectacular little cave, then climb across bare rock striped with the remains of ancient tailored steps. A faint, south-westerly traverse (again slightly vertiginous) brings us to the slip path behind the house passed at the beginning, identifiable from this side by green railings round the terrace.

Though not the sort of itinerary to gratify your more gung-ho, give-me-derring-do hiker, this pleasant outing from **Frigiliana** is a good exploratory loop, giving an idea of the lay of the land for several other excursions, and taking in some superb views en route. In particular, the modern quarter of **Frigiliana**, which looks a bit bland on the spot, is revealed in an altogether different light, only a shade less organic and picturesque than a traditional Andalusian village developed over centuries rather than decades.

The middle section of the itinerary follows the same path as Walk 16 in reverse, but the outlook is sufficiently different to merit doing the route both ways. The path along the southern end of the **Sierra del Enmedio** ridge is faint, but reasonably easy to follow so long as you stick to the ridge, skirting to the right of the rougher and more precipitous rises.

Frigiliana from Cuesta de Sordo

3 · 2H · 6½ km · 350m / 350m · ○ · 4*

* in **Frigiliana**

Access: on foot from **Frigiliana**

We start in **Frigiliana** as per Walk 13 (Wps.1-3), descending into the **Río Higuerón** and the beginning of the **Limán Trail** (Wp.3 20M), signposted 'Sendero de la Fuente del Esparto', which we take to the east.

The trail, which is perfectly clear and offers no opportunity for straying off path, climbs steeply, the gradient easing on gentler traverses and levelling out briefly before passing an overgrown (so overgrown it's easily missed) branch on the left (Wp.4). 100 metres after this branch, we come to a clear, wayposted junction on the crest of **Sierra de Enmedio** ('in the middle' because it's between the **Ríos Higuerón** and **Chillar**) (Wp.5 40M), which is where we join Walk 16 in reverse.

The Higuerón valley from the Limán Trail

Turning right, we follow a clear path to the south for a little under 100 metres till we

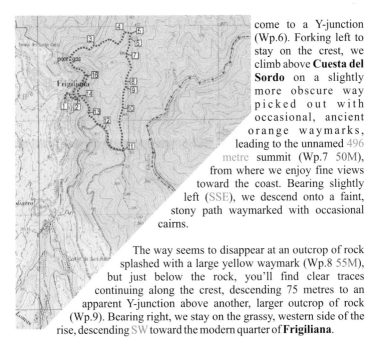

come to a Y-junction (Wp.6). Forking left to stay on the crest, we climb above **Cuesta del Sordo** on a slightly more obscure way picked out with occasional, ancient orange waymarks, leading to the unnamed 496 metre summit (Wp.7 50M), from where we enjoy fine views toward the coast. Bearing slightly left (SSE), we descend onto a faint, stony path waymarked with occasional cairns.

The way seems to disappear at an outcrop of rock splashed with a large yellow waymark (Wp.8 55M), but just below the rock, you'll find clear traces continuing along the crest, descending 75 metres to an apparent Y-junction above another, larger outcrop of rock (Wp.9). Bearing right, we stay on the grassy, western side of the rise, descending SW toward the modern quarter of **Frigiliana**.

Taking care to follow the cairn-marked way, we wind through scrub and esparto grass, passing a large, flat-topped pile of stones (Wp.10 65M). Our descent continues, meandering between dense cistus and rosemary, and a scattering of young pine, eventually passing the cairn-capped stump of an old electricity post (Wp.11 74M), 50 metres short of a new, metal pylon, visible from Wp.7.

Bearing right (W), we drop down onto a clear path heading back towards **Frigiliana**. The path follows a contour line before traversing a shallow valley and passing the ruins of **Corral del Pinto** (Wp.12 86M). It then descends (NW), winding between broom and rosemary before crossing cobbling and bare rock into the **Río Higuerón** (Wp.13 95M).

Fording the river, we bear right, following a narrow path then a stony way along the right bank (our left), briefly taking advantage of a faint path along a terrace of avocado trees. At the end of the terracing, we re-cross the **Higuerón** (Wp.14 101M) onto the left bank, picking up a narrow path initially bisected by a black pipe. 45 metres later, after passing a lime kiln, we join the track (Wp.15) from **Frigiliana**. The ford here is quite deep, so if you don't want to splash straight across, continue upstream for 225 metres, dipping in and out of the watercourse, until an easy ford brings us back to the *acequia* path (Wp.16 105M).

The **Río Chíllar** is one of Sierra Almijara's most celebrated beauty spots and the walk up the river, most of it in the river, and through the metre wide straits known as *cahorros,* is perhaps the most spectacular excursion accessible to non-dedicated ramblers. However, it can be hard work, so despite being relatively short and involving a very moderate ascent, this classic walk gets a high exertion rating. The rocks are rarely slippery, but after a while, wading through the water resembles one of those fiendishly clever exercise machines seen in gyms dedicated to reproducing the sort of drudgery generations of our forebears did their level best to escape.

We've done the walk twice, once ankle-to-calf deep and once, as recorded here, calf-to-thigh deep. It makes a difference. If you happen to visit when the water is low, you may find the walk correspondingly easier. Whatever the effort though, it's worth persevering, as there are some lovely spots further upriver and (subject to the warning in the text) the return route is a perfect contrast, a high, airy stroll along a canalization wall overlooking the valley and enjoying fabulous view of the high mountains.

Short shorts (not pedal-pushers) and walking sandals or trainers are essential; a towel, dry socks and walking boots desirable. Do not enter the river after, during or when there's a threat of heavy rain. The full walk is only recommended for experienced walkers, but the Short Versions (depending on conditions) are suitable for everyone. GPS coverage is poor to non-existent in the riverbed.

*   but in view of the variability of conditions in the river, allow up to nine hours including stops.

	Stroll	Short Versions
Access: by car and (adding 4.5km return) on foot from **Nerja**	**Central Eléctrica del Chíllar**	(a) Los Cahorros (b) Wp.4

To reach the start, take the old **C340** from Maro to **Nerja** and, at the first roundabout (signposted 'Centro de Salud' & 'Barriada Los Poetas'), get into the bus alley/residential lane alongside the main road, then take **Calle Picasso,** the first turning on the right (100 metres before the flashing pharmacy cross), setting the odometer at zero. 300 metres later, fork left at a Y-junction (the right-hand branch has a no entry sign) and follow a roughly asphalted lane down to a dirt track along the **Río Chíllar**. At km1.4 we pass under the motorway bridge. At km2.2 we pass a cement factory and the main track, now concreted, crosses the river. We park below a single, tall eucalyptus between the cement works and a huge quarry.

N.B. The first two kilometres of the walk to the *Central Eléctrica* (the **Chillar** hydroelectric plant) are driveable in an ordinary car. However, the track is subject to flooding, and manoeuvering at the end on a busy day can be complicated. Starting the walk from the cement factory avoids any potential problems.

From the eucalyptus (Wp.1 0M), we follow a stony track (N) along the **Río Chíllar** valley, which narrows and becomes more attractive after we pass the quarry. Winding in and out of the water amid increasingly rich vegetation, we eventually come to the end of the riverbed track at the *Central Eléctrica*, where we pass the path used for our descent along the turbine tube at the end of the walk (Wp.2 30M). After climbing a concrete ramp (a mini-race when the river's in spate, and sometimes slippery), we start walking in the river.

And that, essentially, is all you need to know. Reliable GPS reception soon disappears, easily identifiable natural features are few and far between, and given that you're going to be knee deep in water for the next couple of hours, you really don't want to be fumbling about with anything not 100% waterproof. I've therefore reduced description to a minimum.

There is nowhere to go wrong as the only option is to follow the watercourse, taking advantage of intermittent paths on either bank. These paths are gradually disappearing in brambles, so regard this as a water walk with only very occasional patches of dry land. Also bear in mind that the last stretch of river-walking seems to go on for ever, but it is worth pushing on to the 'W' waterfall at the 165 minute point.

- 55M The first and least spectacular *cahorros*.
- 65M The first real *cahorros* - you'll see why they needed a special name for them.
- 80M The second spectacular *cahorros*

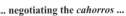

... negotiating the *cahorros* ...

- 95M A succession of dirt paths switch back and forth from bank to bank before re-entering the river on a narrow stretch fretted with overhanging bamboo.
- 125M 50 metres after a cliff (on our left) sculpted to Gaudiesque effect with mineral deposits, the river divides briefly round a small island; we follow the course to the right.

After passing a felled but still vital fig tree hanging over the stream (140M), the patches of path increase both in frequency and length, though there are still several deep pools (some superb natural jacuzzis among them) and leg-stretching rapids to be negotiated before we come to a series of small waterfalls (160M). At this stage, the hitherto rather redundant blue waymarks suddenly become very useful, guiding us through rocks on the left bank of the stream (our right) past a succession of cataracts to a large blue 'W' painted on a rock beside one of the finest little waterfalls and plunge pools on the river (165M). Even if you don't do the full loop, it's worth persevering until this superb spot. The only drawback is that, in early summer, horseflies reckon it's a superb spot, too.

You must now decide if you want to do the full walk or return by the river. The circuit involves another thirty to forty minutes in the river followed by a brief but steep climb then a gloriously level walk along the old *acequia* feeding the *Central Eléctrica*.

WARNING: Though never manifestly dangerous (the most vertiginous sections have been fenced) the *acequia* is not for everyone as we walk on a narrow concrete wall (never more than a foot wide, sometimes as little as six inches) passing occasional unprotected drops of up to five metres. Even the most carefree alpinist has to take it one step at a time, literally watching every step and stopping to enjoy the views. There is a strong risk of vertigo. Do not do the *acequia* after heavy rain as there are stretches prone to rockslides. And don't do it on your own. If anything went wrong, help could be a long time coming.

Just beyond the waterfall, there's an old landslide which can be crossed either by a clearly trodden way initially doubling back to the east, or by following the blue waymarks along the river. Both routes rejoin five minutes later, at which point progress is apparently blocked by a dense wall of oleander. In fact, pushing on into the oleander, you will find a natural way, almost immediately bringing us back to splashing up the river. Once again, we crisscross the river, this time with one or two longer stretches of path.

A brief trodden way leads us onto a rockslide (180M), after which three blue waymarks guide us back into the river above a small waterchute. We now wade up the river till we pass a dry affluent *barranco* descending from the west, 30 metres after which, large blue arrows indicate obscure ways onto both banks of the river (200M). Bearing left here leads to the **Limán** trail to **Frigiliana** and the continuation of the **Río Chillar** path to **La Presa**. We, however, turn right, passing a wooden post and red waymarks before pushing through dense reeds onto a dry path climbing south-east.

After a steady climb on an increasingly clear path lined with broom, cistus and palmetto, we cross a small landslip gully and, 75 metres later, join the *acequia* (Wp.3 210M), which we follow to the south. As with the river, there is no way to lose yourself, so the main purpose of a guidebook is for timekeeping and deciding if it's the sort of walk you want to do. If you've come this far despite the warnings above, the assumption is that airy heights don't disturb you.

If, however, you reach the first vertiginous, fenced section (Wp.4 220M) and (a) decide it's not really for you or, (b) find that the fencing has deteriorated and is no longer safe, TURN BACK. Under no circumstances continue if the wires have gone or the moorings of the fencing posts do not look absolutely firm. If you do turn back, you can either return via the river or continue climbing from Wp.3 to **Collado de los Galgos** (aka **Apretaderos**) then follow Walk 16 back to the *Central Eléctrica*.

Approaching the first fenced section of the acequia

As I say, description is strictly redundant, but for the purposes of time keeping:
- At Wp.6 250M the third stretch of fencing coincides with a spectacular overhang.
- At Wp.7 280M we pass the fourth and fifth stretches of fence. Take particular care ten minutes later as the coping of the wall is crumbling and unstable underfoot.
- After widening for 100-metres, the *acequia* ends at the head of the *tubería* (Wp.8 295M), the turbine tube descending to the power station.

We continue along a stony path to the south for 100 metres, bringing **Nerja** into view, then veer right (NW), zigzagging back to the *tubería* (Wp.9 305M). After a straight stretch, tighter zigzags descend alongside the pipe, steepening as loose stone gives way to a dirt path leading to concrete steps beside the upper building of the *Central Eléctrica*. A few metres below the upper building, we bear left (don't follow the steps down to the lower buildings, which are fenced in) on a rough path rejoining our outward route at Wp.2 (320M).

Think BIG. This is walking on a large scale in every sense: grand scope, grand views, grand effort, and grand fun. But it's not for the faint of heart. Falter for a moment, and you may begin to wonder why you ever took up rambling in the first place. It's a roller coaster, with more ups and downs than a manic depressive toying with a yo-yo, but if you can cope with the lows, the highs will have you gasping with as much wonder as fatigue. Not suitable as a first excursion, but highly recommended as the definitive tour of this superb landscape.

Access: by car and (adding 4.5km return) on foot from **Nerja**

To reach the start, take the old **C340** from Maro to **Nerja** and, at the first roundabout (signposted 'Centro de Salud' & 'Barriada Los Poetas'), get into the bus-alley/residential lane alongside the main road, then take **Calle Picasso,** the first turning on the right (100 metres before the flashing pharmacy cross), setting the odometer at zero. 300 metres later, fork left at a Y-junction (the right-hand branch has a no-entry sign) and follow a roughly asphalted lane down to a dirt track along the **Río Chíllar**. At km1.4 we pass under the motorway bridge. At km2.2 we pass a cement factory and the main track, now concreted, crosses the river. We park below a single, tall eucalyptus between the cement works and a huge quarry.

From the eucalyptus (Wp.1 0M), we take **Camino de los Almáchares**, the concrete track climbing away from the cement works onto **Cerro del Pinto**. Ignoring all branches, we climb past a succession of villas and *cortijos* until we come to a T-junction (Wp.2), where we turn right, forking right again at a Y-junction (Wp.3 20M) 40 metres later, passing **Villa Los Tres Pinos** and **Villa Almachares**.

After passing a concreted branch climbing on the right to a reservoir, we leave the housing behind and are confronted by a quadruple junction of minor tracks amid the pine (Wp.4 31M). We take the second branch from the right, which is waymarked with a cairn. 100 metres later, we fork right at a Y-junction (Wp.5), on a track that soon dwindles to a trail, climbing gently amid peaceful pine scrub along the *Parque Natural* limit, bringing into view first **Lucero** and the new quarter of **Frigiliana**, then the **Tajos del Sol** and **Almendrón** above the **Río Chillar**. After curving NE and passing a lime kiln, we reach the first of two Y-junctions within 40 metres of one another. We fork left at the first (Wp.6) and right at the second (Wp.7 62M), where the trail narrows to a path.

Skirting to the left of a rocky rise, we dip down briefly before climbing to the cairn-capped stump of an old wooden electricity post (Wp.8, 125 metres from the second Y-junction) from where we can see the path descending alongside the **Chillar** *tubería*, which we follow at the end of our walk. Our present objective is the small summit with a spoon-like southern face which we can see to the north.

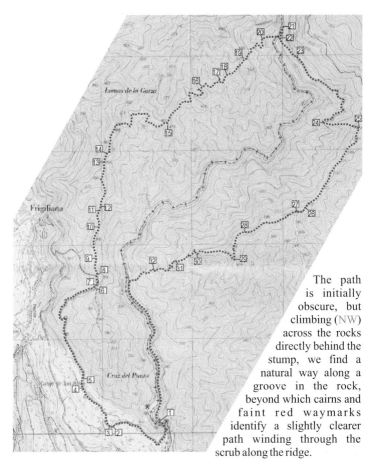

The path is initially obscure, but climbing (NW) across the rocks directly behind the stump, we find a natural way along a groove in the rock, beyond which cairns and faint red waymarks identify a slightly clearer path winding through the scrub along the ridge.

After skirting to the right of a partially uprooted pine (Wp.9 69M), we continue among cistus, rosemary and young pine. Looking ahead, the path is indiscernible, but clarifies itself each step of the way, soon traversing a stand of more mature pine and passing a large, flat-topped pile of stones (Wp.10 80M).

The climb steepens for 50 metres before easing off and skirting to the left of the next pine-clad rise, beyond which we ignore a faint way (Wp.11) curving SE round the rocks. Our path becomes obscure again, but maintaining a northerly direction for 75 metres, we pass a large rock daubed with two yellow waymarks (Wp.12). Behind the rock, a reasonably clear way climbs over the unnamed 496 metre summit, from where a very narrow dirt path descends through the pine (NE). Maintaining a northerly direction, we snake down to a broader, stonier section, crossing an outcrop of rock and passing a branch doubling back to the left (Wp.13), 100 metres after which we join the wayposted **Limán Trail** at the top of its climb from the **Río Higuerón** (Wp.14 106M).

The **Limán Trail** is clear, unmistakable, and waymarked or wayposted at regular intervals, so after that necessarily but unhappily wordy start, you may care to put the book away now and just enjoy the path till it descends to the **Río Chillar**. For the purposes of time-keeping:

- Turning right, we follow the trail along **Sierra del Enmedio** (N) then veer east to traverse the dry slopes of **Loma de la Garza** (aka **Garzón**) before climbing to a small *col* (Wp.15 131M).
- Descending into a more verdant landscape, we dip up and down across a succession of watersheds, terminating in a brief, steep, partially cobbled climb (Wp.16 150M).
- At a Y-junction (Wp.17 155M), we fork right, ignoring a waymark on the left and staying on the main path.
- After a corridor of rock so smoothly sheared it looks tailored, we reach a second cobbled stretch (Wp.18 160M) leading into a gully, above which we climb steeply to the final *col* overlooking the **Chillar** (Wp.19 166M)

The corridor of rock at Wp.18

This is a good place for a break and to decide which of the alternative return itineraries you wish to take. On a fine day and if you're equipped with walking sandals or trainers, you might like to descend via the **Río Chillar** (Walk 15). If you've not done it before and it seems appropriate (see 'Warning' in Walk 15), you could follow Walk 15 to the end of the *acequia*, clearly visible on the far side of the valley. If you don't want to get your feet wet and don't like heights, follow Walk 17 from the *acequia* up to the **La Presa**-**Pinarillo** track, rejoining the present itinerary at Wp.25. The full-blown 'BIG', which I recommend, follows the *acequia* for a little over 1km then takes a narrow path, just visible from here, up to the *collado.* We then wind along the crest before descending to the end of the *acequia*.

The *acequia*

- Having contemplated the options and enjoyed the views, we zigzag down **Cuesta Jiménez**, passing a couple of redundant shortcuts. After crossing a watershed (Wp.20) and traversing a very slightly vertiginous section, we join the path (Wp.21 180M) that climbs to **La Presa**. Bearing right, we descend alongside the river, weaving between large boulders and low cliffs down to a ford (Wp.22 185M).

River-walkers turn right, *into* the stream, everyone else cross the **Río Chillar** and follow the wayposted path up to the *acequia* (Wp.23 200M).

Personal phobias and weather conditions permitting, we bear right, following the *acequia* for 1100 metres. At a stretch of new concrete slabs covering the *acequia*, just before a couple of red waymarks on its lip, we turn left on the narrow path seen from the far side of the valley (Wp.24 226M). This path climbs steadily to steeply (E), joining the **La Presa-Pinarillo** track at **Collado de los Galgos** (aka **Apretaderos**) (Wp.25 242M).

Two paths head south along the crest, one skirting a small summit, the other going over the top, before rejoining 180 metres later. This pattern is repeated several times. In each case, I recommend following the lower route skirting the summits, partly because you won't want to be doing any superfluous climbing by this stage of the walk, but more importantly because the crest splits after roughly a kilometre and the OTT option takes you onto the south-easterly **Cerro Mangüeno** fork, *away* from our descent.

Taking the non-OTT options, we pass to the east of the third summit (Wp.26 260M), essentially a discrete mini-crest composed of several tiny tops, identifiable by a path branching <u>right</u> onto the first of the tiny tops. This is a useful point of reference as the next OTT branch, forking left 75 metres later over the 603 metre top, the highest along the crest (Wp.27), is the one we really have to avoid, skirting its western flank in order to join the westerly branch of the ridge, where the path more or less levels out (Wp.28 275M).

300 metres later, the path veers right (NW) between two small cairns (Wp.29 280M) to run along the southern flank of a westerly spur, within sight of the quarry at the start of the walk. The path crosses onto the northern flank, curving along the tapering spur from where we enjoy stunning views of almost the entire circuit. After bearing left onto a small promontory (Wp.30 291M) overlooking the end of the *acequia*, we zigzag into a steeper descent, briefly interrupted by the tip of the spur before dropping down to the end of the *acequia* (Wp.31 296M).

The end of the *acequia*

Our path heads south for 100 metres then doubles back to the right (NW), zigzagging down to the *tubería* (Wp.32 307M). After a straight stretch, tighter zigzags descend alongside the pipe, steepening as loose stone gives way to a dirt path leading to concrete steps beside the upper building of the **Central Eléctrica**. A few metres below the upper building, we bear left (don't follow the steps down to the lower buildings, which are fenced in) on a rough path descending to the bed of the **Río Chillar** (317M), which we follow (S) back to the start.

Tucked away at the head of **Río Chillar** under the towering cliffs of the **Tajos del Sol** and **Almendrón**, **Cortijo Imán** is one of the region's most recondite and evocative ruins. The extent of the ruins suggest that, in it's day, it must have been a major commercial nucleus: further up the valley there's even a former tobacco factory, the **Fábrica de Imán**, though what they thought they were doing curing tobacco up there is anybody's guess - the *Imán* must have nurtured a serious nicotine habit. Nowadays, nothing could be more remote, and the idea that **Nerja** is less than 10 kilometres to the south, would elicit delirious incredulity if you didn't know it to be a fact. *Imán* means both 'imam' and 'magnet'in Spanish, but given the location and the ruin's classic Moorish combination of stone and brick, I would guess the *cortijo* is named for a Moslem cleric; which is entirely appropriate, as the setting could scarcely be bettered for having you dropping to your knees in deference to some entity bigger than yourself. Perched on the only patch of flat land in the entire valley, surrounded by jagged mountains, you feel very small indeed.

(N.B. Some maps identify the **Barrancos de Coladilla** and **Contadero** as 'Colailla'and 'Contaero', a consequence of local truncated pronunciation.)

Long sleeves and trousers are recommended for pushing through the broom on the final climb, while walking sandals are useful but not essential for fording the river. There's a slight risk of vertigo en route to **La Presa**, the source of the water used to turn the turbines of the **Chillar** *Central Eléctrica*, and a strong risk if you take the *acequia* option on the return. Pathfinding is tricky and vital after the 85 minute point. Unfortunately, GPS reception is poor to nonexistent in the riverbed, so some attention to the text is necessary. If you don't want to do a long walk, Short Version A is particularly recommended. You'd have to go a long way to find such a splendid spectacle for so little effort. The sheer drama of the landscape can even be a little intimidating.

| 4 | 5H | 14 km | | 750m / 750m | ⚠ two-way | ↔ | 0 | 🍴 |

Access: by car

Strolls	Short Versions
(a) Barranco de Coladilla	(a) Barranco Contadero
(b) Fuente del Esparto	(b) La Presa

To reach the start, follow the signs from the motorway for 'Cuevas de Nerja' then, just before the entrance to the *cuevas* car-park, turn left on a track signposted 'Área Recreativa El Pinarillo 5km'/'Fuente del Esparto', setting the odometer at zero. Park in the main *área recreativa* car-park at km4.7.

Starting from the car-park (Wp.1 0M), we follow a minor track descending (N) into **Barranco de Coladilla**. After crossing the *barranco*, we fork left at a Y-junction (Wp.2) and continue straight ahead when the main, right hand branch curls back to form a crossroads (Wp.3 5M). The track to the left at the crossroads ends at an affluent of the **Coladilla** below **Cerro Mangüeno** and is a pleasant two-way stroll (Stroll A). Carrying straight on at the crossroads, we climb through a sharp bend before joining the main **Fuente del Esparto** track (Wp.4 10M). For Stroll B, turn right here and follow the track past **Fuente del Esparto** until it loops back to the *área recreativa*. For the main walk, we bear left and follow the track up to **Collado de los Galgos** (aka **Apretaderos**) (Wp.5 15M).

Three paths branch off to the left here, two following the crest, one descending to the **Chillar** *acequia*, but we stay on the track as it veers right (N), passing a 'No Pasar' sign (!) directed against cars rather than walkers and warning of rockslides. We now simply follow this track till it ends, passing en route the wayposted path climbed on our return (Wp.6 30M). After a long, gentle climb, the track curves north, bringing into view the high mountains ringing the source of the **Chillar**, and dwindling to a broad trail (Wp.7 41M).

We descend along the trail, passing and hopefully not provoking some of the rockslides warned about at the *collado*. After passing fearsome overhanging cliffs, the trail crosses an affluent of the **Chillar**, **Barranco Contadero** (Wp.8 55M), and dwindles to a path leading to the neck of a rocky spur. From here it starts its long, winding, occasionally precipitous descent to the river and the power station *acequia* (70M), 50 metres south of **La Presa** ('the dam') and the roofless sluice-keeper's cottage, the terrace of which is a good place for a break.

... fearsome overhanging cliffs ...

Ignoring a path climbing to the main sluice, we ford the **Río Chillar** just west of the northern end of the ruin, climbing through thorny scrub on the far side of the river then almost immediately descending into a generally dry stretch of riverbed, where a clear, partially tailored way takes us to the left of the dam wall. 50 metres after the dam, we cross back onto the left bank (our right) and take a clear way winding between banks of oleander. A little over 500 metres later, we return to the right bank (85M), which is where pathfinding becomes slightly tricky.

A clear way traverses a flat field of stones just below the confluence of the **Chillar** and **Barranco de los Pradillos** (aka **Barranco de la Cueva de Parra**), the first major affluent since **La Presa**. When the obvious way climbs slightly to cross the mouth of the **Barranco de los Pradillos**, look for a cairn (100 metres from the last river crossing) on your right indicating a pathless way back to the river and an easy crossing onto the left bank. If you miss this cairn, the clear way crosses the confluence, passing a line of stones blocking another path into **Barranco de los Pradillos** before ending back at the river beside a large fallen pine, another potential ford, but much wider and deeper.

Once across the river, we continue to the north, without the benefit of a path but passing occasional cairns. Five minutes from the recommended ford, just beyond the confluence and more or less opposite the end of the clear path at

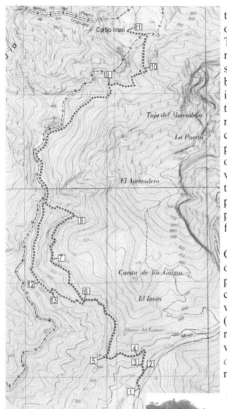

the fallen pine, we fork right on a narrow dirt path (95M). The path soon descends to re-cross the river in order to skirt a massive clump of bamboo, after which we immediately cross back onto the left bank to recover the narrow dirt path, which climbs away from the river, passing under a massive overhanging rock (100M), at which point you can relax, as there's no longer any possibility of missing the path, despite the fact that it's frequently overgrown.

Climbing steadily, we push our way through invasive patches of spiny broom, crossing a shoulder tipped with a distinctive outcrop of (from a distance) triangular rock (Wp.9 126M) from where we can clearly see the *cortijo* and the line of our remaining climb.

The cortijo

After crossing a watershed, **Barranco Almendrón**, below the appalling cliffs of **Tajo Almendrón**, we climb steadily to steeply, skirting behind the bluffs (Wp.10 150M) separating the **Almendrón** watershed from **Barranco del Imán** (aka **del Cerezo**).

An easy stroll leads down to **Barranco del Imán**, after which a brief but rough climb takes us across a small rise to the **Cortijo Imán** (Wp.11 160M). The path branching north 50 metres east of the *cortijo* is said to climb to the **Fábrica del Imán** and the track passing **Puerto de Frigiliana** and descending to **La Resinera**, but I've not walked it so can't say what state the path is in. The bread oven at the southern end of the *cortijo* is big enough to provide shelter for a couple of people if necessary.

We return via the same route with the option of taking the *acequia* from **La Presa** then climbing **Cuesta de los Galgos** to rejoin our outward route. The

Galgos path is clearer than the **Contadero** route up to Wp.8, but the *acequia* is narrow and, despite stretches of fencing which the Spanish call *quitamiedos* ('fear-removers'), sufficiently vertiginous to paralyze anyone who dislikes heights. As a point of comparison, this stretch of the *acequia* is far 'worse' than its continuation, which we follow in Walk 15. Whatever your relationship with vertigo, great care is required as the wall is narrow and not all the major drops are protected. Anyone with a tendency to trip over should go back the same way.

From **La Presa** (229M), we follow the *acequia*, passing a first stretch of fencing and, shortly thereafter, an unprotected 5 metre drop. A long, largely covered section of *acequia* leads to the second stretch of fencing (the most vertiginous section), overlooking the descent of the **Limán Trail** and the path climbing along the river (235M). The next fenced section is also vertiginous, after which stone steps (240M) descend onto a path skirting a section of *acequia* channelled under overhanging and rather friable looking rock - nip past the end quickly! We soon see the path climbing from the river, but before we join it, we pass a stretch of exposed gold piping and an old metal conduit laid with duck-boards, where it's best to descend below the two of them rather than walking on the boards.

When the *acequia* crosses the clear wayposted path climbing from the river (Wp.12 250M), we turn left and begin our steep climb back to the dirt track. After dipping down briefly, the path resumes climbing, doubling back to the left at a junction with a minor path (Wp.13 255M) descending to a roofless cabin. We then enjoy/endure the final slog up to rejoin our outward route at Wp.6 (270M).

Some outward bound publications give the impression wild places are the preserve of athletes constructed on a monumental scale with legs like professional footballers', hearts the size of a European principality, and the sort of lung capacity that could happily inhale enough Peruvian marching powder to keep a Hollywood power brunch high for a year. Discovery Walking Guides like to suppose otherwise. In this spectacular tour of the high valleys behind **Torrox** and **Cómpeta**, we visit a landscape that couldn't be wilder in terms of natural architecture, but which is accessible to anyone accustomed to climbing your average English hill. Better still, it begins and (rather more importantly) ends at the Hotel **Casa de la Mina**, aptly identified at its entrance by a sign saying *'Para todos comidas'* ('Meals for everyone') and run by Carmen, who proudly asserts that she has no timetable - you turn up, she'll feed you, and well.

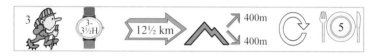

> **Stroll/Short Version**
> **Arroyo de los Pradillos**

Access: by car

To reach the start, take the tarmac road off the MA102 **Cómpeta-Torrox** road at **Venta de Palma** just above **Cómpeta**, signposted 'Hotel Casa de la Mina' (N.B. not the dirt track immediately east of the *venta*, signposted 'Casa de la Mina'; we join this later), setting the odometer at 0. Following the signs for the hotel, we turn right at 500 metres on a concrete lane then left on the dirt track at km1. This track's something of a Home Secretary: it's firm, forbidding and a bit rough on strangers. Prospects for getting through without a very expensive vehicle, look dim at the outset. But, confirming the Home Secretary analogy, it's also well-maintained and hard enough to resist erosion. Don't expect a smooth ride, though. Ignoring a minor branch on the left at **Puerto del Collado**, we park just before the green gates of the hotel at km5.3.

From the hotel gates, we continue along the same track, signposted 'Venta de Panaderos' (Wp.1 0M), almost instantly curving into the *vistas panoramicas* promised by a signboard on the approach. The deep, distant indentation in the valley where you can see the white speck of a waterhut, is **Arroyo de los Pradillos**, sometimes called **Arroyo de Juan Rojo** above the dirt track. Our itinerary climbs the eastern flank of this stream. After an eroded branch descending on the right to the **Casa Montilla** ruin (Wp.2 5M), we see up to our left the ruins of **Venta Maria Guerrero**, passed toward the end of the walk.

The track dips in and out of the contours with nothing to distract us but stunning views, until we pass a second minor track descending to ruins on the right (Wp.3 34M). 250 metres later, we ford **Arroyo de los Pradillos** and, 75 metres after that, we leave the track, forking left on a microscopic path barely

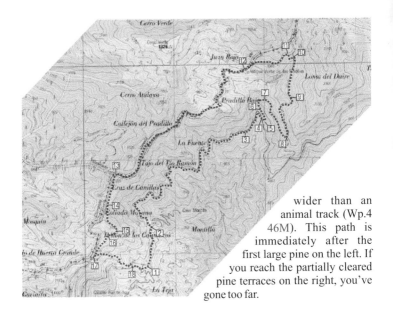

wider than an animal track (Wp.4 46M). This path is immediately after the first large pine on the left. If you reach the partially cleared pine terraces on the right, you've gone too far.

The path climbs steeply (SE) for 50 metres to a small gully where it veers back to the north (Wp.5), levelling off briefly before climbing a gentler gradient toward a stand of eucalyptus below **Venta Los Pradillos**. After crossing a rocky watershed above the *arroyo* (Wp.6 55M), we wind into a second steep climb and the path broadens, soon doubling back to the right, away from a high waterfall below the eucalyptus, and zigzagging up to a crossroads with a canalization path (Wp.7 64M). Turning right, we follow the canalization path (SSE) for 400 metres until it climbs between pine to a second crossroads (Wp.8 76M), where we turn left.

This path winds along the flank of the mountain, dipping down briefly before climbing through cistus onto a small platform behind a natural 'terrace' wall (Wp.9 90M) from where we can see the **Venta Candido** ruin. We then descend (N) into **Arroyo de Juan Rojo**, on the far side of which a rough path (Wp.10 95M) climbs (W then N) to the old *vereda* between **Cómpeta** and **Granada**, also used in Walk 8 (Wp.11 100M).

Turning left, we skirt behind **Venta Candido** (the terraces in front of the ruin are a good spot for a break) and descend past a lime kiln to the picturesque ruin of **Venta Los Pradillos** (Wp.12 112M).

Threshing circle at Venta Los Pradillos

Contrary to what some maps suggest, there are no longer any branch paths off this *vereda*, so it's time to put the book away and just enjoy one of the finest stretches of walking in the region, descending through the pine to the west of the *venta* before climbing round a small spur, crossing a succession of watersheds below **Cerro Verde** and the more distinctive rocky outcrop of **Cerro Atalaya**. 75 metres after the **Venta Maria Guerrero** ruin, we join a dirt track at **Cruz de Canillas** (aka **Portichuelos**) (Wp.13 150M), within sight of **La Maroma**.

The track descends on the right to **La Fábrica** and **Canillas de Albaida** (see Walk 8), but we turn left, forking left again at a Y-junction 300 metres later (Wp.14) to climb onto **Cerro Gavilán**, easily identifiable by its firewatch hut and one of the finest *miradores* in area.

Lucero from Cerro Gavilán

N.B. It's also possible to follow the main **Cómpeta** track curving round the western flank of the summit, climbing less and enjoying correspondingly poorer views. After a steady climb, the distinctive yellow block of **Hotel Casa de la Mina** comes into view (Wp.15 161M).

On the southern side of **Cerro Gavilán**, shortly before the summit and the end of the track, we turn left on a narrow path (Wp.16) heading north and descending along a ridge to a Y-junction of the main **Cómpeta** track and the minor track climbing from **Puerto del Collado**. From the Y-junction, we double back to the left (E) on a narrow path marked with a small cairn (Wp.17 170M). After a gentle easterly descent, the path swings right and zigzags down to join the **Casa de la Mina** dirt track (Wp.18 185M) 100 metres west of the hotel.

19 LUCERO FROM RAMBLA DE LA MOTA

Dominating the skyline east of **Málaga**, the distinctive triangular peak of **Lucero** (also but less well known as **Raspón de los Moriscos**), can stake a strong claim to being the *Parque Natural's* emblematic mountain. **La Maroma** may steal *malagueño* hearts as the province's highest summit; **Alto de Cielo** may quicken -even break- the hearts of athletes from **Nerja** competing in the annual race to the top from the beach; **Navachica** may pride itself on the longest approach; **Cerro del Cisne** may muscle its way in among the big boys by being tougher than all the others; but when it comes down to it, **Lucero** elicits the most frequent plaudits from the "Cor-look-at-that!" brigade rolling by on the motorway. And much the same sensation prevails when you're standing on the summit, only multiplied tenfold. Simply put, it's one of the wildest and most dramatic peaks in the area. And it's one of the easiest to climb. As for the views, well, all I can say is, any more birds-eye and you'd be a fish-finger. In short, essential walking. Of course, there's a catch. The long drive to the start is not for nervous passengers, still less for nervous drivers, and there's a risk of vertigo on the walk itself, but if you're game for those challenges, it's not to be missed.

* but allow 3 hours minimum if you're not accustomed to high mountains

Access: by car

> **Short Version**
> **Coladero de los Mosquitos**

To reach the start, take the road from **Fornes** to **Arenas del Rey** and, at km2.4, turn south on the *Parque Natural* dirt track to 'Vivero La Resinera 2.5km', setting the odometer at zero. After 1km we pass an *área recreativa* and, on our right, the GR7 path to 'Arenas del Rey'. At km1.6 in front of the **La Resinera** chapel, where there's a sign for 'Puerto de Cómpeta 16km', fork right then right again 150 metres later - the main track on the left at the second junction is signposted 'Vivero La Resinera', our branch, somewhat more flimsily, 'Crta. Blanco Ibérico'.

We now simply follow this track, which is well-maintained as it's the access to a working quarry (beware tell-tale clouds of dust heralding a lorry weighted with several tons of marble and a gradient in its favour!), all the way to the signposted start of the walk, ignoring the occasional and very minor branch tracks. After two kilometres on this track, we traverse a long plateau then climb into the most spectacular stretch of the approach (watch those knuckles whitening!), curving round **Cerro El Cenacho**, where the track becomes slightly rougher. Twelve kilometres from the turn-off, we pass a small hut on our right, and reach the signposted path 650 metres later. There's room to park at the start and alongside the track in the preceding 500 metres.

The path begins on the far side of **Rambla de la Mota**, the dry watercourse behind the signpost (Wp.1 0M), and is as spectacular and as clear as the approach track. After climbing gently in an easterly direction, bringing into view the Sierra Nevada and, more significantly, some superb karstic formations in the immediate vicinity, we curve into a southerly orientation, climbing more steadily. The path divides briefly before crossing a broad shoulder below **Cerro de Rajas Negras,** where we pass a waypost (Wp.2 15M) in front of the fabulous little summit of **Cerro de la Mota**, dominating a classic karstic landscape suggesting God had rather more of Gaudi in him than did Gaudi of God, a proposal that would please neither party, but the nearest I can get to evoking the spectacle.

After a very brief descent, we resume our stony climb, crossing two small rises, from the first of which we see the main summit, identifiable by the ruined *Guardia Civil* post on top, and looking considerably more daunting than it did from the track.

Lucero, from above
Collado de la Perdiz

Descending from the second rise, we cross **Collado de la Perdiz** (aka **Puerto Llano**), a broad pass within sight of the sea, where a couple of pathless routes join our itinerary, climbing from **Cortijo del Daire** to the south, and crossing the *llanos* to the northeast to a mini-col between the **Carretera Blanco Ibérico** and **Río Cacín**.

Despite it's name (*perdiz* = partridge), the *collado* is a good place for observing *cabra montes* on a quiet day.

Sticking to the main trail, we pass a small boundary marker for Málaga Province ('MP') (Wp.3 34M), bringing into clearer relief the final zigzagging path to the top. Ignoring a couple of shortcuts, we climb toward the mini-summit just west of **Lucero**, variously called **Cerro de la Venta Panaderos** (after the *venta* below it) or, more engagingly, by the diminutive **Lucerillo** ('little bright star').

A little way below the summit of **Lucerillo**, the path more or less levels off for an easterly traverse to the tiny col between the two summits, **Coladero de los Mosquitos** (Wp.4 51M). If things seem a bit too airy for your tastes at this stage, turn back now, as it gets considerably airier on the final climb and even more so on the way back down. The *coladero* is already a fabulous spot with superb views of the coast, **Cerro del Cisne**, and the *tajos* above **Río Chillar**. Otherwise, it's simply, if such things ever are simple, a matter of slogging your way up those final, tightening zigzags to the peak of **Lucero** (Wp.5 65M).

View from the ruin

The ruin (welcome shelter when there's a wind, which there often is, but be wary of the crumbling walls) is an old *Guardia Civil* outpost constructed, so it's claimed, thanks to a little mild military extortion, muleteers crossing **Puerto de Cómpeta** having their goods impounded until they'd lugged a couple of sacks of cement or builders' supplies to the top. From this eyrie the soldiers would survey the *maquis* based on **Cerro del Cisne**, whose movements they would signal with a mirror to their colleagues on **Balcón de Europa** in **Nerja**.

Local mountaineers occasionally descend the eastern flank of **Lucero**, but then people are prone to all manner of madness and an 80% gradient is hardly consistent with our 'leisure walking' brief. We return by the same path, taking particular care on the more exposed bends at the beginning.

Navachica, the Sierra Almijara's highest summit, is also among its most inaccessible, either involving a very long climb, an excessive amount of off-path walking, a 4x4 vehicle, or some very hairy acrobatic antics on precipitous ridges. All of which means it's a must do for a certain type of hiker, among whom, regrettably, I must count myself. We've opted for the long climb from the south, which is the classic route. It's a great walk and, if you're up for the apparently endless scrambling up the *barrancos*, and what seems like an even longer descent, it's highly recommended. The silence is so absolute it borders on the lonesome, while the views are stupendous, definitive sitting-on-top-of-the-world stuff, the only drawback being that the top of the world tends to be a bit windy, so you probably won't want to be sitting there too long - come prepared. Otherwise, one vital piece of equipment - stamina.

GPS coverage is poor to non-existent in the *barranco,* hence the paucity of waypoints for the first part of the walk. Unless you're suddenly seized by a compelling desire to climb a sheer cliff or go down a mine-hole, this is not a problem, as there's nowhere to go wrong. Pathfinding above **Barranco del Rey** can be difficult, especially on the way back down. The last section of the walk should not therefore be undertaken without a GPS receiver when visibility is poor. Not recommended on your own - at least make sure somebody knows exactly where you're going.

	Stroll & Short Versions
	Barranco de los Cazadores - suitable turning points would be the end of the dirt track (25 minutes), the *mirador*
Access: by car	at Wp.3, **Mina de la Furia**, or the **Tajo del Águila** confluence of *barrancos*.

To reach the start, follow the signs from the motorway for 'Cuevas de Nerja' then, just before the entrance to the *cuevas* car-park, turn left on a track signposted 'Área Recreativa El Pinarillo 5km'/'Fuente del Esparto', setting the odometer at zero. We pass the Cortijos de la Civila dirt track at km2.9 and the *área recreativa* at km4.7. Park a kilometre after the *área recreativa*, when the track curves round to cross the dry watercourse, at which point **Barranco de Coladilla** becomes **Barranco de los Cazadores**.

We set off up **Barranco de los Cazadores** (Wp.1 0M), passing a path on the right into **Barranco de la Higuera** and a track doubling back on the left toward **Fuente del Esparto** (Wp.2 10M). We stay in the *barranco*, which we follow all the way to its confluence with **Barranco la Charca/del Rey**, some 4km and 600 metres climbing later. Passing some of the largest and best preserved of the *barranco's* troglodytic dwellings, the track becomes steeper and narrower and increasingly rough as the cliffs close in around us, before finally tapering away altogether (25M) at the foot of a clear path climbing a rockslide, already a supremely dramatic destination for a stroll/short version. The path climbs steadily, veering right at a shallow sooty cave (30M) then right again at what should be a T-junction with an old mining path (35M), though the branch to the left has long been cut by the rockslide.

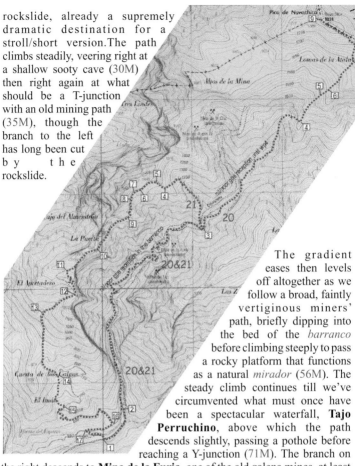

The gradient eases then levels off altogether as we follow a broad, faintly vertiginous miners' path, briefly dipping into the bed of the *barranco* before climbing steeply to pass a rocky platform that functions as a natural *mirador* (56M). The steady climb continues till we've circumvented what must once have been a spectacular waterfall, **Tajo Perruchino**, above which the path descends slightly, passing a pothole before reaching a Y-junction (71M). The branch on the right descends to **Mina de la Furia**, one of the old galena mines, at least one of which, probably **Mina del Tajo**, tunnelled so deep it is said to stretch all the way to **Barranco de la Higuera**.

Forking left and ignoring an apparent second left hand branch 40 metres later, we climb through lush scrub, after which the trail levels out and enters the bed of the *barranco* for a second time. We now stay in the bed of the *barranco*, soon passing a patch of path shored up with rocks, immediately after which, two large cairns, one in the bed of the *barranco* one on the left, mark the path to **Tajo Almendrón** (Wp.3 80M), which is where the present itinerary and Walk 21 diverge.

We continue along what is perhaps the most agreeable section of the **Barranco de los Cazadores**, a flat-bottomed valley, the slopes of which were partially cleared in spring 2004, leaving young oaks space to spread amid the pine, resulting in pleasant, open, airy, and above all easy walking, an interlude for which you'll shortly be grateful. We soon see a small summit ahead of us, **Tajo del Águila**, which separates **Barranco de los Cazadores** from its neighbour, **Barranco de los Caños del Rey**, more often known as **Barranco del Rey**.

Reaching the obvious confluence of *barrancos* at the foot of **Tajo del Águila** (96M), we bear left, following a clear, cairn-marked path into **Barranco la Charca**, while the **Barranco de los Cazadores** (sometimes called **de la Encina** or **de la Loma de la Encina** in its upper reaches) continues to the right. Our path follows **Barranco la Charca** for 75 metres before veering right into **Barranco del Rey** (though you probably won't notice the difference as the continuation of **La Charca** is veiled with thick undergrowth).

The walking gets rougher, then gets gruelling, as we follow an uneven but obvious way, far wilder than anything encountered so far, but reassuringly marked with regular cairns. After a little over five minutes and some 350 metres from **Barranco de los Cazadores**, we come to our first, modest scramble over bare rock. The vegetation becomes denser, though our way, following the dry watercourse, is never less than clear. Climbing between slopes carpeted with oak scrub, we cross two more bare rock scrambles (111M), after which the patches of path disappear and it's just a question of keeping on keeping on, clambering across the rock so frequently that counting the scrambles becomes pointless.

After a couple of hundred metres of this, we skirt to the right of a five metre high wall of rock (122M), immediately returning to the watercourse (cairns mark a way climbing higher to avoid the next series of rock scrambles, but it serves no great purpose as they're easily passed). Less than 100 metres from the five metre wall, we skirt to the right of a second, almost entirely white three metre wall and immediately climb a long but easy 'stepped' chute. Just as the clambering seems to be assuming a faintly unforgiving quality (you can't help feeling a certain kinship with poor old Sisyphus, forever pushing his boulder up a hill), the *barranco* becomes choked with rosemary and broom, 30 metres from a fifteen metre high wall (137M). This is where we leave the *barranco* on a clear way climbing to the right (ESE).

Tajo Almendrón seen from Baranco del Rey

The trodden way climbs a steep stony slope, almost immediately passing the first of three cave-like mine holes, the first of which is a good place for a break and adequate emergency shelter if necessary. Keeping the mine holes to our left, we labour up the slope, bringing **La Puerta** and **Tajo Almendrón** into view behind us.

After the third cave/mine, the way becomes more obscure and we have to take care to follow the cairns, leading us through the scrub onto the tip of a ridge running along a NE-SW axis (Wp.4 152M), from where we have fine views of all the summits and ridges surrounding **Barranco de los Cazadores**, including the bare eastern face of **Navachica**, though the top is some way to the west of the visible summit.

Bearing left, we climb more gently along the line of the ridge (NE), essentially off path, but following a reasonably clear way winding between the oak scrub and passing frequent, often large cairns. Climbing steadily into an increasingly bare and rocky landscape, we skirt to the left of the ridge's culminating point and pass two massive waist-high cairns, after which we aim for a large, solitary pine (unmistakable from below, but less easily identifiable on the way down). From the pine (Wp.5 170M), which is further distinguished by a wooden post tipped with fading yellow paint, we continue to the northeast, on the featureless slopes of **Loma de Atalaya**.

After a final waist-high pile of stones (Wp.6 176M), the cairns become smaller and less frequent, often the case when they're most vital, but you can appreciate that even the most constructive spirit would be a bit weary by this stage of the walk. We orient ourselves by following the shallow indentation of a watershed and, high above us on the horizon behind **Navachica**, a pole carrying a diagonally divided black-and-white plaque marking the provincial frontier.

Views to Sierra Nevada from the summit

Beside a small and rather precarious cairn, we cross a distinct fold in the rock (Wp.7 186M), the first of a series of long shallow shelves sweeping off the small summit to our right (E) and descending to the plateau south of **Navachica** (W). We now negotiate our way through denser clumps of prickly oak scrub, emerging on the ridge just to the left of the black-and-white plaque (Wp.8 197M) where fine views open out to the north, including (just a stone's throw away, it would seem) **Sierra Nevada**. We now simply bear left (NW) and, passing a small sinkhole after 75 metres, climb across the bulbous swell of the summit to the trig-point (Wp.9 207M).

The walk can be extended on a number of pathless routes; west via **La Cadena** to **Puerto de Frigiliana**, south via the **Tajo del Sol** to **Tajo Almendrón**, south-east via **Lomas Llanas** to **Barranco de los Cazadores**, or south-south east via **Cuesta del Espartal** to **Alto de Cielo**. None of them though are really suitable for a book of this sort. The only option I might recommend to experienced walkers would be to extend the walk into a linear traverse, descending via the **Casas de la Monticana** (where there's a spring and plenty of shelter for an overnight bivouac) before continuing north to **Jayena** (see Walk 26).

For a first excursion though, it's wiser to return the same way. The **Loma de Atalaya** can be disorienting on the way down. GPS users should keep their GPS receivers turned on. Otherwise, retrace your steps as closely as possible, taking great care to locate the solitary pine at Wp.5. There is another, slightly larger pine to the NW which isn't obvious on the way up, but can easily be mistaken for our pine on the way down. It's essential to get back on the cairn-marked route below the pine. Likewise take care descending from Wp.4 into the *barranco*, as once again it's easy to stray off what is already a sufficiently precipitous 'path'. And finally, watch your step in the **Barranco del Rey**: in descent, the scrambles are what the French call *casse-gueule* - basically 'gob-breaking'.

Superlatives come easy when trying to evoke the **Sierras Tejeda** and **Almijara**, but the sheer drama of this particular landscape defies description … any more dramatic, and it would be overacting. All I can say is go there, see, gasp, then go again. There's a strong risk of vertigo, but if you can possibly overcome the phobia, do so. Essential walking.

N.B. The **La Puerta** pinnacle is sometimes called 'Almendrillo', in which case the narrow plateau to its south is dubbed 'La Puerta'. For once, toponymy, frequently so intriguing, is superfluous. This is a landscape beyond mere name-calling.

Short Versions	**Stroll**
Barranco de los Cazadores (see Walk 20)	**Barranco de los Cazadores** & **Fuente Esparto**: take the track doubling back on the left at Wp.2 of Walk 20 to rejoin the present itinerary at Wp.19

Access: by car

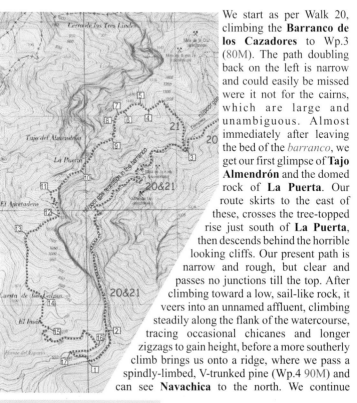

We start as per Walk 20, climbing the **Barranco de los Cazadores** to Wp.3 (80M). The path doubling back on the left is narrow and could easily be missed were it not for the cairns, which are large and unambiguous. Almost immediately after leaving the bed of the *barranco*, we get our first glimpse of **Tajo Almendrón** and the domed rock of **La Puerta**. Our route skirts to the east of these, crosses the tree-topped rise just south of **La Puerta**, then descends behind the horrible looking cliffs. Our present path is narrow and rough, but clear and passes no junctions till the top. After climbing toward a low, sail-like rock, it veers into an unnamed affluent, climbing steadily along the flank of the watercourse, tracing occasional chicanes and longer zigzags to gain height, before a more southerly climb brings us onto a ridge, where we pass a spindly-limbed, V-trunked pine (Wp.4 90M) and can see **Navachica** to the north. We continue climbing steeply until, roughly 200 metres from **Collado Nido del Buitre** ('Vultures Nest Pass', the dip in the ridge just south of **Tajo del Sol**), we turn left on a narrow path marked with a large cairn (Wp.5 120M) (the path we've been following so far peters out below **Tajo del Sol**).

The branch path climbs (WSW) on a gentler gradient, gradually levelling out, inasmuch as the terrain allows, before crossing a small rocky shoulder (Wp.6 125M), the culminating point of the walk (in altitude if not emotion) though we do have a little more climbing to do. After heading west for ten metres, we begin curving south, cautiously traversing virtually pathless rock and debris dotted with cairns. 200 metres later, we reach a first rockslide (Wp.7) across which a clear trodden way descends to a stand of oak, immediately running into a second, much longer rockslide, composed of big boulders interleaved with brief intervals of trees and trodden ways. A clear way then winds down to a third, less stable rockslide (Wp.8), beyond which we continue descending to a rocky spur, where the path is recognizably path-like, and **La Puerta** comes back into view.

La Puerta

Following the clear rough path (it may not match everybody's definition of a path, but after the rockslides it looked pretty pathlike to me - when in doubt look for the cairns), we zigzag down to a small platform of rock (Wp.9 139M), not easily described or distinguished visually, apart from the fact that it overlooks the clear and very spectacular path passing below **La Puerta** and climbing to the trees silhouetted on the horizon.

La Puerta, Navachica in the background

This path is vertiginous, but not nearly so bad as it looks from this perspective. Descending very carefully even if you don't suffer from vertigo (perhaps especially if you don't suffer from vertigo - anyone who does will be taking infinite pains not to make a mistake), we pass below **La Puerta**, enjoying perhaps the most extraordinary views yet over **Barranco de los Cazadores**, then climb to the left of the pines seen silhouetted against the sky (Wp.10 156M). It's worth leaving the path here, either cutting directly through the trees or 50 metres further along to enjoy stunning (and stunningly vertiginous) views over the head of the **Río Chillar**.

After enjoying the views, we continue on the main path, climbing sligh sticking to the higher traces, as far back from those appalling possible, overlooking the tiny ribbon of track climbed at the start On the whole, the cliffs are some distance from the path, but there of points where they're only five metres away, so stick with th until the path begins to descend, when it's best to follow the cairn-marked route, as the way becomes increasingly faint. 50 metres below a straggly line of pine (Wp.11 160M), large cairns indicate where we veer left, back towards the cliffs and a pronounced dip where we can see a clear reddish dirt path. Carefully following the cairns, we descend across scree and scrub, taking extreme care in the last 50 metres, as the path comes briefly (which is quite long enough) within a couple of metres of the clifftops.

From the pronounced dip (Wp.12 170M), we follow the clear path, which is rather more stony when you're on it than it looks from above, as it descends (SW) alongside and then in (Wp.13 181M) a shallow watershed. After 50 metres in the actual watercourse, it swings left, becoming increasingly well surfaced and stable underfoot, as it crosses otherwise rather bleak terrain where sightings of *cabra montes* are virtually guaranteed.

Eventually, it joins the end of a dirt track (Wp.14 200M), where we have a choice of routes, either following the dirt track immediately, or bearing right on a faint cow path cutting a long bend in the track before rejoining it 350 metres later (Wp.15 210M). In either case, we follow the end of the track down to a T-junction (Wp.16) with the track climbing out of **Barranco de los Cazadores** at Wp.2. We turn right here then left 325 metres later, at the junction with the **Fuente del Esparto** track (Wp.17) to return to our starting point.

dly and
cliffs as
the walk.
are a couple
higher traces

arquía 111

quía

This attractive tour round (we don't actually go to the top) **Tajo de los Bueyes**, a small summit behind **Maro**, makes use of two classic *barranco* paths, one climbing the **Barranco Sanguino**, the other descending **Barranco Coladilla**. In between, we get great views, wild countryside, and a picturesque ruin. A good walk for getting your bearings on the first day, but take plenty of water, as the middle section is dry and exposed.

| 3 | 3H 40M | 14 km | 500m / 500m | ↻ | 3* |

* in **Maro**

Short Versions
(a) **Barranco Sanguino** (see text)
(b) **Barranco Coladilla** in reverse (see text)

Access: on foot from **Maro**

Our itinerary starts at the eastern exit from **Maro**, where we cross the N340 and go through a tunnel under the new motorway (Wp.1 5M), immediately after which we bear slightly left to take a dirt track, passing behind hothouses and in front of a row of bungalow farm buildings. The track ends after the bungalows (Wp.2 9M) and we follow a path alongside an olive grove, dipping into the dry watercourse after 50 metres before skirting a second, abandoned olive grove. We then cross the watercourse and curve round a bend, where the last rumour of the roads disappears, and we enter **Barranco de Sanguino**, soon passing a fire-blackened cave (Wp.3 15M).

We follow the watercourse up the *barranco* for the next fifty minutes.

Carrying straight on at a cairn-marked crossroads with a narrower path (Wp.4 26M), we climb gently, our trail hedged with box, oleander, dwarf palm, pine and holly-oak, and patched with shambled soil churned up by foraging boars. The *barranco* gets wilder the higher we go, smooth boulders of dry falls and the traces of boars increasing in both frequency and size, while the vegetation becomes marginally more invasive. Twenty minutes from the cave, the trees recede briefly and we

skirt to the right of a particularly large boulder.

Traversing a stand of tall pine, we see the eastern cliffs of **Tajo de los Bueyes**, at which point we leave the bed of the *barranco*, bearing right on a clear path flanked by large cairns (Wp.5 64M).

If you're doing Short Version A
- it's possible to continue along the watercourse for at least 300 metres to a confluence of feed streams (Wp.6). You may be able to go further, but it gets increasingly overgrown, and even to reach this point you have to bend double under a tunnel of oleander.

Barranco de Sanguino

The path to the right at Wp.5 climbs steadily, burrowing between pine, broom and overblown bushes of rosemary, gradually revealing itself to be an affluent watershed. At a pronounced bend, the path leaves the watershed (Wp.7 70M), and we wind through chest-high rosemary, bringing the roofless walls of **Cortijo Almáchar** into view.

Nerja in the distance, from Almáchar

Our winding climb continues up an increasingly stony spur, eventually emerging at a T-junction (Wp.8 94M) with the main path from the old campsite and **Nacimientos de Maro** (if you're looking for this junction from the top, it's picked out with vivid mauve waymarks).

Bearing left, we continue climbing on a less scratchy (in every sense of the word) path to a second junction (Wp.9 110M), 50 metres east of **Cortijo Almáchar** - a good place for a break; the old threshing circle to the west of the ruin is a particularly pleasant spot for a picnic.

Continuing on the main path from the junction, we traverse a young pine wood behind the *cortijo*, initially on the level then descending slightly to a dry watershed. The path levels off again and curves round to the west, crossing two small rises before joining the **Cortijos de la Civila** dirt track beside a garage-like building (Wp.10 126M). The 'garage' is a bit grubby, but it is open (largely because one door has been torn off its hinges to 'metal' the track) and provides adequate shelter in an emergency.

We turn left, passing at the first pronounced bend a crossroads of paths (Wp.11). The path on the left passes a pluviometer before petering out behind some impressive little pinnacles. The path on the right is the one used at the end of Walk 23. We stay on the dirt track, taking advantage of three cairn and wayposted shortcuts, until it emerges on the main **Pinarillo** track (Wp.12 154M), 2km from the *área recreativa*. Turning right, as if for the *área recreativa*, then left 175 metres later (Wp.13), we follow a rough track (blocked to traffic by boulders) into **Barranco de Coladilla** (Wp.14 166M). If you're doing Short Version B, it's possible to continue up the *barranco* after this point, passing the next high dam wall by a vertiginous, stepped route on its left. The high dam after that is rather more complicated.

We, meanwhile, set off down the delightful, eucalyptus-lined *barranco*, passing innumerable overhang caves, which are occasionally occupied by weekend campers. After a little over twenty minutes in the *barranco*, the track along its bed becomes more distinctively track-like, and we pass a cairn-marked path (Wp.15) and a waymarked scramble (Wp.16 189M) both of which climb to the left, rejoining the main **Pinarillo** track some 500 metres from the **Cuevas de Nerja**. We stay on the *barranco* track, following it as it climbs out of the **Coladilla** 50 metres later (the *barranco* itself is soon blocked by debris, broken-glass, brambles and dams). The track crosses an abandoned builders' tip before descending onto an old road alongside the **Cueva de Nerja** exit of the motorway (Wp.17 200M).

This is the starting point for Short Version B
- and is identifiable by an *ayuntamiento* 'Prohibido El Paso' sign 30 metres along the track (directed at fly-tippers rather than ramblers). To get here by car, turn right 300 metres west of the **Maro-Nerja** roundabout on a track signposted 'Horsin' Around', setting the odometer at zero. Follow the track as it curves round to the right of then behind the sugar factory (unmistakable with its distinctive tall chimney), turning right at km0.9 to pass under the link road between the A and N340s. Turn left 100 metres later to go under the motorway and park 100 metres after that.

To return to **Maro** from Wp.17, we turn left, passing under the motorway, then turn right and take the tunnel under the A/N340 link road, bearing left to pass behind the sugar factory. After cutting across the wasteland to the east of the sugar factory, we take the dirt track curving left in front it to join the **Maro-Nerja** road, which we follow back to **Maro**.

Not so long ago, **Nerja**'s mountain of choice, **El Alto de Cielo** was a comparatively easy ascent beginning at **Cortijo de la Civila**. Nowadays, the track to the *cortijo* is only suitable for 4x4s (even then it calls for some deft driving) and the walk has been transformed into one of the region's big climbs. The classic waymarked itinerary from the south via the *cortijo* remains popular and can be crowded at weekends, but the **Barranco de la Higuera** route is rarely used and takes us up one of the most tranquil mountainsides in the area. That 'up' is the key word, though. It's very arduous, possibly the steepest climb in the present publication, nigh on 1000 metres in under four kilometres counting the zigzags, more like two as the crow flies. Moreover, the last 300 metres (height, not length) are off-path and only recommended for experienced hikers. And as if that wasn't enough, the full loop via the **Molinero** ridge tacks on yet another 300 metre climb just when you least want it (the reasons for this are explained in the text) and is only for the very fit. All these provisos notwithstanding, it's a grand walk, largely because **Cielo** is the first high summit in the chain, making it one of **Sierra Almijara's** finest *miradores*, enjoying great views of the coast, all the major peaks in the park and, on a clear day, North Africa

To avoid that final 300 metre climb, I recommend coming as a two car party if possible, leaving one vehicle at km2.9 of the **Pinarillo** dirt track. Otherwise, there's the 'Short' Version, which is as strenuous as the full walk, but 'easier' because it follows a clear, wayposted and waymarked path all the way to the top. The walk is not recommended on a hot day, though the summit is immeasurably improved by clear skies, when we can properly appreciate the superb views. The western slopes of **Alto de Cielo** are said to be home to many vipers, so watch your step.

*   but allow at least 7 hours including stops
**   including the ascent from Wp.17

Stroll
If you squeeze through the undergrowth for 50 metres when the main path curves round toward Wp.3, it's possible to continue up the **Higuera** for a while.

Short Version
Alto de Cielo via **Cortijo de la Civila** (linear two-way)

Access: by car or (adding 6km return for the Short Version) on foot from **Cuevas de Nerja**

To reach the start, follow the signs from the motorway for 'Cuevas de Nerja' then, just before the entrance to the *cuevas* car-park, turn left on a track signposted 'Área Recreativa El Pinarillo 5km'/'Fuente del Esparto', setting the odometer at zero. We pass the **Cortijos de la Civila** dirt track at km2.9 (leave one car here if you're in a two-car party) and the *área recreativa* at

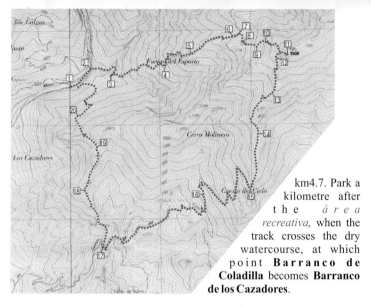

km4.7. Park a kilometre after the *área recreativa,* when the track crosses the dry watercourse, at which point **Barranco de Coladilla** becomes **Barranco de los Cazadores**.

We start on the rough track up **Barranco de los Cazadores** (Wp.1 0M), passing the first of several troglodytic dwellings, some of which were inhabited within living memory. After 250 metres, we bear right into the eucalyptus-lined **Barranco de la Higuera** (Wp.2 5M). Following a clear path, we climb along the **Higuera** for another couple of hundred metres, after which the path bears right climbing steadily (S) onto a broad spur, defined by the **Higuera** and an unnamed affluent, where it recovers its easterly direction and we begin the big climb (Wp.3 15M) up the slope known as **Cuesta de la Luna**.

The views (notably of **La Puerta** and **Tajo de Almendrón**) are already excellent and improve steadily, which is just as well, since we need some distraction from the unremitting climb during the frequent and inevitable stops to catch our breath. The path is clear and passes no junctions, so it's simply a matter of keeping on keeping on, winding through the switchbacks, and taking your time. After almost a kilometre, the path veers left for a longer northeasterly traverse (Wp.4 49M), crossing a shallow watershed gully. We then skirt a small outcrop of rock, visible for most of the climb so far, bringing into view the summit of **Alto de Cielo** (Wp.5 80M), topped with a cross currently sporting a natty fluorescent orange waistcoat.

We continue northeast on the back of the spur behind the small outcrop of rock, the gradient easing then levelling out altogether for 50 metres below a wall of rock, after which we traverse the first patch of sparse woodland, composed mainly of pine but incorporating a few holm oak, too. Beyond the trees we pass below a large bulbous rock, visible from Wp.5. The path then levels off again as it approaches an affluent watershed of the **Higuera**, before which there are two cairn-marked ways onto the ridge behind the bulbous rock (Wp.6 and Wp.7 95M), the second just before the watershed. Beyond the watershed, the clear path winds through a final chicane then crosses a shoulder before eventually petering out at the head of the **Higuera**. We, however, leave the path at Wp.7, taking the second of the cairn-marked ways (the two ways merge at Wp.8, but the second has more cairns). The remainder of the climb is off-path. Timings are very relative, but include pathfinding.

Following the cairns, we pick our way through oak scrub, climbing south for 75 metres to a large, fire-scorched pine (the one with the thickest trunk) (Wp.8) behind the bulbous rock. At the scorched pine, we veer east on an increasingly clear rocky way - sometimes a little too clear so you still need to keep an eye open for the cairns to avoid meandering round aimlessly amid the increasingly meagre scrub. There's no single way here and conflicting cairns frequently vie for our attention, but 175 metres from the scorched pine, we cross a narrow spine of rock (Wp.9 114M) and bear left to follow the line of the spine (NE).

At the end of the spine (Wp.10, 100 metres from Wp.9), we resume a more easterly direction, aiming towards the summit cross. The cairns are less frequent now that the cross is visible again, so we zigzag back and forth, pretty well making it up as we go along, seeking the path of least resistance (they're all fairly resistant!), and bearing in mind that it's easier to approach the top from the northwest.

After traversing slopes of debris patched with oak scrub, we join the waymarked route climbing from the south for the final brief climb to the **Alto de Cielo** trig point (Wp.11 145M). The cross just beyond it is said to have been erected by a German sailor grateful for escaping (presumably as the result of some rapid negotiations with his God) an apparently inevitable shipwreck; hence the mirrored face looking out to sea.

The cross on Alto de Cielo

Looking west from the top

To descend, we take the blue-waymarked route to the south. The way is well-trodden and clearly waymarked, with only two moments of critical choice, but the initial descent is rough, steep and very unstable underfoot, so some care is required. Immediately after passing the first waypost (Wp.12 150M), we ignore a fork to the right and continue our delicate descent (S), down to the foot of the summit and a long ridge (Wp.13 165M) punctuated midway by a small, triangular peak. After skirting to the right of the triangular-peak, we fork left at a second Y-junction (Wp.14 175M), staying on the back of the ridge, bringing into view **Cortijo de la Civila** and its dirt track.

Toward the end of the ridge, the path winds through a small chicane and, 100 metres later, at a waypost (Wp.15 187M), veers sharp right for the first of the long traverses descending to the *cortijo*. During the descent, we can see the path climbing over the **Molinero** ridge, which looks considerably easier from above than from below. Toward the end of the descent, our path divides twice, in each case the two branches rejoining a few metres later, the second time running into the end of a rough dirt track (Wp.16 211M).

We follow this track, which again divides briefly, circling a roofless, green, breeze-block building, before descending past the partially ruined **Cortijo de la Civila**, so named, it is said, because it used to be inhabited by a woman given to wearing a *Guardía Civil* uniform. How she came by the uniform and what happened to its original occupant is not specified. Continuing along the dirt track, we pass a garage-like building, where we join Walk 22. 100 metres later, the track crosses a minor path branching left and a cairn-marked path climbing to the right (Wp.17 230M).

If you've been able to come with two cars, follow Walk 22 down to Wp.12. If you've come with only one car and can't face anymore climbing, do likewise and follow the **Pinarillo** track back to the start, though I strongly recommend avoiding this as the **Pinarillo** track is long, dry, dusty and much driven, especially at weekends, often as not by people who haven't entirely grasped the potential of the brake pedal. If you've got one car and can cope with another 300 metre climb (these are big Ifs), turn right on the cairn-marked path.

The path climbs steadily to steeply for five minutes, then levels out before resuming its steady climb. It divides briefly below a knoll (Wp.18 250M) then climbs onto the **Molinero** ridge overlooking the **Pinarillo** *área recreativa*. After two more steady climbs curving round the southern side of the ridge, it finally levels off (Wp.19 269M) 75 metres short of a distinct westerly spur of ragged rocks. The way behind the rocks is momentarily overgrown, but almost immediately clears as we begin our descent across the **Umbría del Lobo**.

This slope is crisscrossed with replantation paths dotted with tens of thousands of saplings protected by tubes of green mesh, but there is only one instance in which a re-plantation path could be mistaken for the main path and since that is a fork climbing to the right, there's little chance of mistaking the way - only a helium filled hiker would be ready for more climbing at this stage of the day. This is where we get our reward for the stiff final climb, as the views of the **Barranco de los Cazadores** are among the best to be had from anywhere.

Winding down the mountain, we bring into view the faintly distressing line of the path climbed in the morning (from this perspective it looks insane), shortly after which we pass the helium-hiker's right-hand branch (Wp.20 285M), and maintain an easterly direction toward the morning's path, still a couple of hundred metres above our starting point. The path then veers round to the west, resuming its rapid, winding descent, finally running alongside the southern lip of a deep, red erosion gully, emerging 50 metres north of our starting point.

The **Peñón de los Castillejos** used to be a substantial little walk, following a dirt track climbing above **Río de la Miel** via the **Cortijos de los Nacimientos** hamlet, but since this track has been asphalted (2004), it's just a little walk (almost absurdly short - a dedicated walker would barely notice it at all), leaving us in the peculiar situation of having a stroll (Version B) that's longer than the main walk and a main walk (Version A) that's as easy as the stroll! But the **Peñón** is such a superb *mirador* that visitors ought to be notified of its location even if it was a mere ten steps from the car. As it happens, it's a few more steps than that, many of them pathless, but it's still far and away the shortest itinerary in the book. The views are superb, but even more striking is the strategic location, of which both its name and the scant Moorish remains on top are a consequence. Despite it's brevity, do bear in mind that the rudimentary reasons for building a fortress here haven't changed - there's essentially only one way up and if you get it wrong you fall off the edge! That said, the climb itself is never vertiginous unless you go out of your way to make it so and, once the path is found, progress is not a problem.

For those discouraged by thoughts of sketchy paths and sheer drops, Version B is a pleasant stroll round the base of the **Peñón** and its sister summit, **Cerro de los Gigantes**. The views are almost as good as from the top (though not quite, the scramble is worth it) and it's a particularly pleasant outing between November and February, when golden autumn light gilds the brittle leaves of the vines and the clean clear air crystallizes the views to the east. Behind **Cerro de los Gigantes** one can often see a large herd of *cabra montes*, including an unusually large number of bucks.

The only drawback to all this is that a major forest fire has devastated **Barranco de los Gigantes**. It's a bit bleak, but the *barranco* retains a certain rugged grandeur, and the flora is already recovering, thin shoots of broom threading their way through the spindly black limbs of retama and bright green dwarf palm providing splashes of colour. Given a couple of years, I'd imagine the only reminder of the fire will be the protruding fingertips of burnt retama and the odd scorched pine.

(A) Peñón de los Castillejos   (B) Barranco de los Gigantes

two-way

*	(A) 1 hour 5 mins	(B) 1 hour 40 mins
**	(A) 3.2km	(B) 5km
***	(A) 200 metres	(B) 100 metres

N.B. Refreshments: nothing on the spot, but bearing in mind that both walks can be done in a single morning still leaving time to reach **Cantarriján** and have a swim before lunch in one of the *chiringuitos*, 5

Access: by car

To reach the start, take the turning north at the bottom of **Cuesta Anamaria** (the long eastern descent on the N340 from **Maro** to **Playa Molino del Papel**), signposted (after the turning!) **'Rio de la Miel'**. Setting the odometer at zero at the turn-off, we get our first sight of the **Peñón** at km2 and fork left at km4, on the newly and narrowly asphalted lane. After 9km, we cross the **Cortijos de los Nacimientos** hamlet. Park at km11.5 where, at the time of writing, the tarmac ends and a double-headed track branches North. After the walk, drive south on the **Loma de las Cuadrillas** dirt track, which eventually runs into tarmac, descending to the N340 a little way to the west of the **Playa de Cantarriján** turning.

We take the track to the north (Wp.1 0M), forking left at the Y-junction 150 metres later (Wp.2). After climbing steadily between two large reservoirs, we ignore three minor branches to the left, the second two mere access tracks to the vines. The fourth branch, a rough but obvious track doubling back to the left between olive trees, is where the two versions diverge (Wp.3 15M).

For Version A, the short full-walk

We turn left and climb (SW) along the track for 175 metres, till it veers sharp right and a cairn (Wp.4) marks a faint way through the shrubs to the west. Hereafter, the waypoints are so close together, I give distance from the preceding waypoint rather than time. The rough way curves round onto the western side of a small spur, bringing the **Nacimientos** hamlet into view before disappearing in the undergrowth.

Admiring the view below Wp.5

Picking our way between the rocks and prickly scrub (N), we find a clear trodden way (Wp.5 50 metres), climbing (E) past the remains of a wall before bearing north. There are two ways to the north, one obscure, marked with a cairn and easier to follow on the way up, another a few metres to the west, clearer but unmarked and easier to follow on the way down.

View from above the ill-made boot

In both cases, the way passes to the left of the first small outcrop of rock, which resembles a very ill-made boot, crossing a small retaining wall, immediately behind which there's a small pit-like structure (Wp.6 100 metres) left from the Moorish fortress.

Again there are two onward routes, the more easterly way identified by a couple of cairns and easier to follow on the way up, the westerly route clearer on the way down, the two separated by a mere 15 metres. The easterly route skirts to the right of a small head of rock then immediately veers away from the cliffs. The two ways merge in a reasonably clear trodden way leading to the summit of **Peñón de los Castillejos** (Wp.7 40M).

For Version B, the long-stroll
We simply continue along the main track at Wp.3, skirting below the **Peñón** and **Cerro de los Gigantes**, passing several minor branches, most of them giving access to the vineyards and almond groves on our right. The second branch to the right, effectively a Y-junction (Wp.8 25M), descends to the ruins of **Cortijo de las Bovedas**, which are thought to conceal a seventh century Visigothic chapel. We, however, fork left, the white buildings of the **Peña Escrita** zoological park visible high above us. It's now that the landscape deteriorates, ravaged by recent wildfires. The damage intensifies as we curve round into the bleak but still grandiose valley behind **Cerro de los Gigantes**, passing two more branches on the right (the first likely to disappear when the vegetation recovers), before our track ends at a small waterhut (Wp.9 50M) syphoning off the sadly subterranean waters of **Barranco de los Gigantes.**

25 PICO DE LOPERA via the 'BACK DOOR'

Easy walking, lovely countryside, stunning views, good food. What more could you want from a day out? Doubtless quite a few things, but nothing within the scope of a walking guide. Enjoy.

Short Version

Take the signposted track at the **Termino Municipal de Otivar** (500 metres south of the main itinerary, 7km north of the **Mirador de la Cabra Montés** petrol station) joining the described route (in reverse) at Wp.12. A simple, linear walk within sight of the summit throughout.

Access: by car and bus

The walk starts from the **Meson Los Prados** restaurant on the **Carretera de la Cabra Montes** (more prosaically the SO2) linking **Almuñécar** with **Granada**, of itself one of the most remarkable excursions from the coast. The restaurant is 7.8km from the **Jayena** turnoff, 7.6km from the **Mirador de la Cabra Montés** petrol station.

From the restaurant (Wp.1 0M), we take the **Huerto Alegre** lane, forking left after 250 metres (Wp.2) through the large green gates of **Cortijo de los Prados** onto a stony track. The track is soon joined by the green-wayposted **Via Pecuaria Venta de la Lata** (the old drovers' trail starting 50 metres south of the restaurant and nowadays serving no great purpose other than irritating the farmer by cutting a swathe across his ploughed field), at which point we pass the first of two large *cortijos* within the **Los Prados** estate, guarded by several large, loose and friendly dogs.

650 metres later, we pass a branch doubling back to the left (our return route) (Wp.3 15M). Continuing on the main track, we pass a minor shortcut track forking left and the second large *cortijo*, after which two paths fork off to the left. Sticking to the stony track, we curve round onto **Cuesta de las Pulgas** (Flea Hill!), where our track is rejoined by the shortcut and comes to a staggered crossroads (Wp.4 29M).

Climbing towards the second cortijo

Ignoring dirt tracks to right and left, we continue along the main track, forking right at a Y-junction 250 metres later (Wp.5). Crossing attractive, rolling arable land spotted with pine, we pass a very faint track branching left (Wp.6) and a clearer but still rough track to the right cutting across fields behind a ruin (Wp.7). We then go through a shady stand of pine, after which we turn sharp left at a major junction within sight of the high summits to the west (Wp.8 45M).

250 metres after the junction, we leave the main track, which continues to **Cortijo de Cabañeros** and eventually **La Resinera**, and fork left on a branch climbing to the south (Wp.9). Enjoying fine views of the **Sierras Tejeda** and **Almijara** (notably the central peak of **Lucero**), we climb steadily, soon curving round to the east and crossing a firebreak, shortly after which views open out of the **Sierra Nevada**. Resuming our southerly climb, we pass a junction with a track coming in from the left (Wp.10 69M), a couple of hundred metres short of the **Pico de Lopera** trig-point (Wp.11 75M) and firewatch hut, from where we have some great views over the **Sierra Chaparral** and **Río Verde** basin.

If you haven't seen any on the way up, there's a good chance of spotting *cabra montes* to the south of the firewatch hut. Amateurs of toponymy will enjoy the delightful juxtaposition to the west of **Cerro de las Monjas** and **Mojón de las Diferencías**: The Nun's Summit and The Mount of the Differences! Make of that what you will.

Great views of the Sierra Chaparral

To return, we retrace our steps to Wp.10 and turn right, descending to a wayposted junction with the Short Version (Wp.12 91M). Turning left then right 100 metres later (Wp.13), we follow a minor track meandering among small oak until it doubles back to the left and the oak give way to pine, at which point two minor branches (not marked on other maps) continue to the east (Wp.14 105M). We take the clearer branch passing to the right of a grassy hummock and descending through the pine to join another track linking the Short Version with the full walk (Wp.15 110M), where we bear left, rejoining our outward route 300 metres later. **Meson los Prados** is a grand little country restaurant, but if you're visiting on a Sunday in autumn, pray that it's not been fully booked by hunters.

26 BARRANCO BACAL & CUEVA DE LOS MORROS

This scandalously neglected route (as far as I know, it appears in no other publication though is promised in future editions of a Spanish book) is a real joy and very versatile. The waymarked route up the *barranco* (sometimes called **Río Grande**) to **Cortijo Corzola** is a grand excursion for adventurous families while the full walk extends the official itinerary into a simple but arduous loop suitable for your more *Sturm-und-Drang* sort of hiker. The walk is also recommended for anyone fond of tracking animals; a variety of spoors are found alongside the river.

The full loop is long, dry and not recommended when it's hot. The exertion rating refers to the two options, the linear route to the *cortijo* and the loop. Timings for the walk in the river, which we ford sixteen times (if I didn't lose count), are more than ordinarily subjective, given that some people will skip across the sketchy stepping stones with the giddying insouciance of a gadfly, while others will lumber about like hippos playing hopscotch; thus I cite 'moving times' between crossings, adding a global time at the junction with the **Cortijo de Corzola** dirt track to give a realistic idea of timing.

Frequent fords also make a mockery of description; happily, once we're on trail, the way is relatively clear and frequently wayposted. I therefore recommend putting the book away after the twenty minute point and not opening it again till the **Cortijo de Corzola** dirt track. All references to left and right banks of the river are opposite to the direction walked. A stick or walking pole is useful. Long trousers or pedal-pushers are preferable to shorts as there are some overgrown stretches. GPS reception is poor in the riverbed.

*	or 4 (see introductory note)
**	to **Cortijo Corzola** (one-way); allow a similar time for the return 4½-6 hours for the full circuit (see introductory note)
***	to **Cortijo Corzola** (one-way); 16km for the full circuit
****	to **Cortijo Corzola**, 350 metres for the full circuit

<table>
<tr><td>

Alternative Stroll

Stay on the access track at km2.2 for another 600 metres till it fords the river. Park on the grassy platform on the left bank then walk the GR7 dirt track (drivable, but a bit rough) for 2km as it climbs through the attractive **Barranco Orihuela** woodland. When the track doubles back to the left to climb away from the woods, a path continues up the *barranco*. I haven't explored this path, but it may go all the way to **Cortijo Corzola**.

</td><td>

Short Version

Barranco Bacal, turning back when you've had one crossing too many.

Stroll
To Wp.4

</td></tr>
</table>

Access: by car or (adding 8km return) on foot from **Jayena**

To reach the start, follow the signs for 'Bacal' through **Jayena**, setting the odometer at zero when you leave the village and cross a bridge onto a dirt track. Turn right at km2.2, signposted 'Zona de Acampada El Bacal', fording the **Arroyo Turillas** 150 metres later and doubling back to the west. Fork right at the Y-junction at km3.2 for 'Area Recreativa' and left 50 metres later to cross the **Río Grande** via a bridge leading to the camping/picnic area.

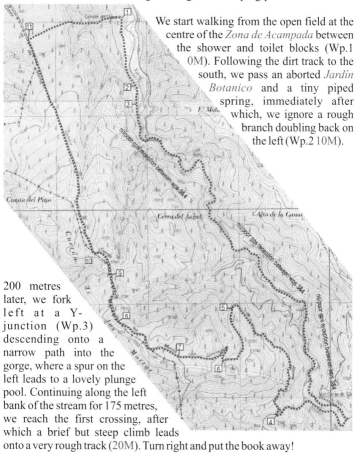

We start walking from the open field at the centre of the *Zona de Acampada* between the shower and toilet blocks (Wp.1 0M). Following the dirt track to the south, we pass an aborted *Jardín Botanico* and a tiny piped spring, immediately after which, we ignore a rough branch doubling back on the left (Wp.2 10M).

200 metres later, we fork left at a Y-junction (Wp.3) descending onto a narrow path into the gorge, where a spur on the left leads to a lovely plunge pool. Continuing along the left bank of the stream for 175 metres, we reach the first crossing, after which a brief but steep climb leads onto a very rough track (20M). Turn right and put the book away!

For the purposes of pacing progress …
- The track dwindles to a path, then widens again briefly before a narrow path traverses a tiny island then crosses onto the left bank (25M).
- After a third length of overgrown track, we follow a dry lateral channel (30M) for 75 metres then ford the stream via a slippery causeway and scramble onto the right bank.
- Two crossings later, natural stone steps lead onto a clear path 5-10 metres above the river.
- Four crossings after that, we have to walk in the stream for five metres (49M).
- After another four straightforward crossings, we fork right at a Y-junction with an old dirt track, which the path rejoins 100 metres later. The next crossing (No.13 if I didn't miscount!), brings us back onto the left bank, where we ignore faint tracks climbing to the left and stroll along the level riverbank.

- When we cross back onto the right bank, the path climbs high above the river, passing above **Pozo Romance** (76M), a gorgeous plunge pool, strongly reminiscent of that scene in *Manon des Sources* when the spectacle of Emanuelle Béart skinny-dipping in a mountain spring wreaks irremediable emotional havoc on Daniel Auteuil's peeping-Tom.

75 metres later, we cross onto the left bank for the last time and the path broadens to a trail climbing to join a grassy track after another 75 metres. Maintaining direction (SE), we stroll amid mature pine, fording the river for the last time 400 metres later. After the tumbledown ruins of a shack, the track bears west through denser woodland, passing a first signless signpost before reaching a second at a crossroads with a major dirt track (90M). <u>Allow 1¾ -2¾ hours to reach this point.</u>

Cortijo Corzola

Cortijo Corzola is a few hundred metres up the track to the left. It's an attractive picnic spot, but stay clear of the crumbling, unstable walls. Allow 15-20 minutes for the round trip. For the full circuit, return to the 90M point and continue on the main track as it crosses the river (by a bridge this time!).

A little under fifteen minutes later, we bear right at a major junction of tracks (Wp.4) and begin the long steady climb onto **Cuerda de los Morros**. Again, description is redundant, as we simply stay on the same track, ignoring all branches until Wp.11. So put the book away again and enjoy the unfolding views of the **Sierra Nevada** to the northeast, **Lucero** to the southwest, and to the north the piebald fields of pale soil tessellated with ranks of olive and almond.

For pacing progress....
- The track levels off and curves between metal chain posts (Wp.5 145M) then traces a long detour round a *barranco* and behind the 1292 metre top, passing a minor branch to the left at the head of the *barranco* (Wp.6 160M).
- After another long, gentle climb, it levels off again, passing a second faint branch to the left (Wp.7 170M).
- The track now descends, passing a wayposted path into the **Río Cebollón** (Wp.8 180M).
- After crossing a firebreak, we descend onto the broad spur of **Los Morros**. Ignoring minor branches to right and left (Wps.9&10), we continue descending, crossing a second firebreak, after which we come to a long straight stretch resembling a roman road with a conspicuous grey patch in the distance.

Halfway along the track, we pass a branch doubling back to the left and, at the end of the grey patch, a very faint branch on the right that crosses a field of stone and sand. 300 metres after the grey patch, we turn right on a broad firebreak (Wp.11 229M). We follow the reddish firebreak track till it ends 400 metres later. We then continue along the firebreak, which is rough and rocky but not distressingly steep, till it emerges among the picnic tables just short of our starting point (250M).

Maximum wilderness for minimum effort, a gorgeous walk tramping alongside a lovely stream with plenty of tempting plunge pools. Comparable to the preceding itinerary only less so (we cross the river a mere five times! six if you do the extension). Ideal for all the family and feasible throughout the year. Apart from getting there and finding the second ford, description is superfluous, so don't waste time studying the text, just walk. Take a towel. GPS reception is poor.

NOTE: the official version of this itinerary is a circuit including the **Cuerda de los Morros** (see Walk 26). However, the start of the path climbing the *cuerda* is invisible and the track along the *cuerda* has been cut by a locked gate and mesh fence encircling the fire-fighting landing strip (incidentally cutting the GR7, too). Doubtless this can be climbed or otherwise circumvented, but there seems little point complicating an otherwise perfect stroll with a frantic dash across an airfield. If you want something more arduous, the extension turns the linear walk into a long but relatively simple circuit.

Access: by car

Stroll	**Extension**
To the IARA waterfall	See text

To reach the start, take the road from Fornes to Arenas del Rey and, at km2.4, turn south on the **Parque Natural** dirt track to 'Vivero La Resinera 2.5km', setting the odometer at zero. After 1km, we pass an *área recreativa* and, on our right, the GR7 path to 'Arenas del Rey'. At km1.6, in front of the **La Resinera** chapel, we fork left at a Y-junction. Our track, which is followed by the GR7, descends via a branch signposted 'Pista de Aterizaje' to a ford across the **Río Cacin**. If this is chained off or the river is in spate, park in front of the chapel and take the footbridge over the river, adding 5km (return) to the walk distance. Ignore turnings on the right at km2, km2.7, and km3.2. Park at the km4 junction, where there's an information board explaining the resin extraction process.

Amid the pines

Ignoring a waypost indicating this is not the GR, we take the track on the right (Wp.1 0M) heading south and crossing a spring a kilometre later. 50 metres short of abandoned farm buildings, the track passes a waypost and curves round between a riverside plantation of poplar and a stand of densely planted pine (Wp.2 24M). The route is drivable to this point, though there's always a risk someone might padlock the chain 200 metres after Wp.1.

The track fords the river 50 metres after the waypost, but it's quite deep, so if you don't want to take your boots off, cut through the reeds on the left and try island-hopping to the other side. In either case, we continue along the poplar lined track on the far side of the river. Five minutes later, the principle track curves round to the right (Wp.3 30M) and climbs to **Mirador de Masajate** (where it joins **Camino de Plancha**, part of the track linking **La Resinera** and **Lopera**), but we maintain direction (SE), following a grassy track parallel to the **Río Cebollón**.

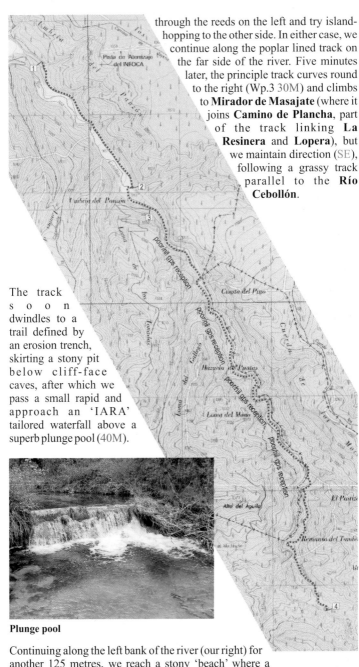

The track soon dwindles to a trail defined by an erosion trench, skirting a stony pit below cliff-face caves, after which we pass a small rapid and approach an 'IARA' tailored waterfall above a superb plunge pool (40M).

Plunge pool

Continuing along the left bank of the river (our right) for another 125 metres, we reach a stony 'beach' where a small cliff forces us onto the right bank. There are two stepping-stone fords here. The higher one, nearer the cliff, goes nowhere. The lower one, which is narrower and composed of larger rocks, leads to a broad, clear path climbing along the right bank. When this path approaches an apparent ford 175 metres later, we veer left, climbing across loose stones. We ford the river 125 metres later, taking an obvious path (50M) that almost immediately re-crosses onto the right bank.

The path dips up and down, traversing a grassy stretch below a grotto of boulders, after which we negotiate a couple of very slightly vertiginous sections. After meandering through a stand of pine, we pass a confluence of affluent watersheds and *barrancos* at **Hazuela de Puntas** (64M).

Winding between fine mature pine and passing numerous shallow plunge-pools, we come to our final crossing, where a large felled pine forms a precarious (and rotting!) bridge across the river (75M). We now trace a long curve between banks of bracken and more conventional Spanish scrub, until dense, tufty grass heralds our return to the river and a final plunge-pool/jacuzzi (85M), which is where most people will want to turn back. However, if you want more …

The precarious 'bridge'

Extension

75 metres later, we ford the river for the sixth time. After a marshy patch at the foot of a major, unnamed *barranco*, a steady climb on a clear trail takes us across the wooded rise of **El Pastizal** onto a balcony trail high above **Barranco Culebra** and other watersheds feeding the **Cebollón**. The trail then descends toward the rising bed of the river, gradually becoming a rough dirt track, which eventually joins the main track crossing the high sierra (Wp.4 115M). Turning right (I've walked this route but haven't mapped it, which is why it isn't described in detail) one could make a long, straightforward loop (comparable to Walk 26) climbing via the **Cortijos Machiche** and **Masajate** to the dirt track descending from **Mirador de Masajate** to Wp.3. Bear in mind though, it's long, dry, and not recommended on a hot day. If you just want to extend the base walk to the main track, allow an hour for the return trip.

28 THE WATERFALL OF PETRIFIED WOOD

I hadn't even heard about the Waterfall of Petrified Wood until I started researching this book, which just goes to show that even familiar landscapes can still throw up surprises. I suspect many people shared my ignorance prior to its sign posting by the park authorities and it's a walk that still hasn't appeared in print elsewhere. The natural phenomenon (it really is phenomenal) whereby lime sediment petrifies logjams in **Barranco de las Cabrerizas** (aka **de los Chortales**) is now cultivated by the addition of extra trunks to the falls, so we can see the progressive accretion of mineral deposits. Unfortunately, the official itinerary (see map diagram at the start of our walk) is a horseshoe loop returning to the road two kilometres from the start. We've therefore worked out an alternative route, reducing the road walking to 450 metres. Easy walking, but bear in mind all the climbing is at the end. Although the outward path looks alarming from the road, it is only intermittently and then very mildly vertiginous. Not recommended in hot weather.

3	3H	9.3 km		350m / 350m	⚠	↻	0

Access: by car	**Short Version** To the falls and back by the same path	**Stroll** The **Cerro Martos** '**Mirador**' (Wp.4)

The walk starts from a lay-by on **Carretera de la Cabra Montes**, 12km from the **Jayena** turn-off, 3.5km from the **Mirador de la Cabra Montes** petrol station, and is identified by a mapboard for 'Sendero del Río Verde' and two waypost.

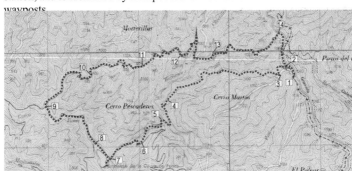

Ignoring a path climbing directly from the lay-by (Wp.1 0M), we descend round the bend in the road to the wayposted start of another path (Wp.2). Our path crosses a small rise and passes a branch to the left (Wp.3 150 metres from the road), after which it embarks on its extraordinary serpentine progress along the northern flank of **Cerro Martos**, squirming over every hump, bump and rise breaking the gradient of the slope. Apart from the minor spur at Wp.4, there are no branches, so forget description and just enjoy the views over the convolute **Sierra de Chaparral** and, from this angle, the rather grand looking **Pico de Lopera**.

The white track on the far side of the valley is our return route. It looks desolate from above and doubtless you'd be a bit desolate yourself if you did it on a hot day or got dusted down by the quad-bikes that apparently pass that way. Otherwise though, it's considerably more agreeable than it looks from above, certainly preferable to the track followed by the official route, and a good place for spotting wildlife; we surprised several *cabra montes* then got surprised right back by a viper sunbathing beside the track.

After a good 25 minutes' walking, we traverse a broad ledge-path defined by low cliffs, and emerge on a neck between the main *barranco* and an affluent gully (Wp.4 30M), where a spur to the left leads onto a slightly vertiginous natural 'mirador' (only for the sure-footed). The main path zigzags down to the affluent gully and veers SE to climb across a rocky shoulder below impressive cliffs. It then descends steeply onto roughly hewn steps leading to the petrified waterfall (Wp.5 51M). I won't even begin chucking the adjectives about - just go see for yourself; and don't neglect to climb the branch path to the right of the falls where more marvels await.

The Waterfall

Crossing the pools below the falls, we follow a good path over a small, very slightly vertiginous rise, before descending to cross **Río Nacimiento** (aka **Barranco del Pito**) and join a dirt track, visible since Wp.4, in front of a notice board listing the norms for canyoning (Wp.6 60M). This is where we leave the waypointed route, bearing right to re-cross the stream below **Fuente de las Cabrerizas**, after which a steady climb brings us to a path branching left (Wp.7 70M) onto the **Embalse de la Cueva de Funes** dam wall, a pleasant place for a break.

Returning to the track, we continue to the northern end of the *embalse*, where the main track crosses a bridge and climbs to the **Cortijos de la Cueva del Umbría** and **de la Almijara**. Just before the bridge we bear right on a minor, initially waterlogged track (Wp.8 75M) up **Barranco de la Cueva de Funes**. The track crosses onto the right bank of the watercourse 75 metres later, where you may have to take your boots off, though it is possible to pick your way round to the right of the ford without getting your feet wet.

After the next, easy ford, we pass a small field and approach a fine karstic pinnacle backed by the ragged little summit of **Cerro de las Monjas**. Following a second easy crossing of the watercourse, we curve behind the pinnacle to a third and final shallow ford, beyond which we reach a semi-troglodytic cabin and a junction of tracks (Wp.9 90M). The main track, again waterlogged, climbs to the **Umbría/Almijara** *cortijos*, but we bear right to begin our long steady ascent back to the road, its dentate crash-barriers soon visible below the antenna-topped summit of **Cerro de la Cruz**.

After crossing and briefly following a firebreak (Wp.10 110M), we wind along the **Morterillas** hillside to a cutting (Wp.11 125M), within sight of our outward path. The track descends past a scattering of beehives before climbing to a second pass (Wp.12 135M). It then loops round an affluent *barranco*, bringing into sight a spectacular cleft in the cliff below our outward path, before descending into the dry bed of **Barranco de las Cabrerizas/Chortales**, which we cross at a junction of feed streams (Wp.13 150M).

Recrossing the watercourse 100 metres later, we embark on our final 800 metre trudge back to the road, a somewhat irksome climb alleviated by a spectacular perspective on a citadel of pinnacles passed 700 metres into the outward leg. We rejoin the road (Wp.14 170M) five minutes from our start.

The final trudge

There's a lot going against this itinerary, ranging from the logistical hassles of taking two cars to the fact that we cross a large tract of private land managed by a cooperative that tolerate ramblers but at a cost - literally on one of the best known ways into the gorge, which now charges a parking/access fee. The described route by-passes the present paying arrangement, but does involve a brief off-path section. Nonetheless, set against these drawbacks the walk boasts so many pluses the book would have been incomplete without it: wonderful waterfalls, superb plunge pools, fabulous rock formations, spectacular suspension bridges, a serpentine canyon, a cavernous ravine, and a superbly tailored path for which the park authorities deserve every credit, make this essential walking.

The paying version (feasible as a linear two-way route using only one car) is administered by **Restaurante El Capricho** (T: 958-644-132 www.rebalae.com/elcapricho) in **Otívar**. The gates (see below) are open from mid-June to mid-September from 8am to 7.30pm, otherwise ask for the key in the restaurant (closed Mondays). The charge is €5 for parking plus €5 per person, up to four people, after which the car is free.

*   but allow 5 hours including bathing stops and enjoying the sights)
**   Mike Casdi, who was kind enough to ferret out details of the paying access, gets a faintly glazed look in his eye when recalling the *pollo a la manzana* (order at least 3 hours in advance) served by **Restaurante El Capricho**. I haven't tried it myself, but given the look that steals over Mike when he describes it, I suspect it merits a refreshment rating of 5 if you're doing the paying version and returning the key in time for lunch.

Access: by car

Short Versions
(a) **Las Chorreras** (see text)
(b) **Junta de los Ríos** from **Cazulas** (in reverse)

My apologies for the access details, which amount to an itinerary description in themselves, but believe me, the walk's worth it. To reach the 'end' (bearing in mind that this is a two-vehicle walk), take the GRS02 or **Carretera de la Cabra Montes** North from **Almuñécar**, setting the odometer at 0 as you pass the **Lentegi** turn-off above **Otívar**.

If you're doing the longer, non-paying version
Turn left at km3.8 for 'Palacete de Cazulas' and park at **Venta de Cazulas**, a large and largely ruinous building on the right 900 metres from the main road, identifiable by several ceramic plaques ('Almacen' / 'Oficina' / 'Sede Social') and a more prominent, modern nameplate, 'Vicente Zamora'. Given that this is private land, make sure you're not blocking any tracks or interfering with the flow of traffic on the main lane.

After parking the first car, return to the **Carretera de la Cabra** and continue north. The walk starts at km13.7 (from the Lentegi turn-off), 1.5km after the

Mirador de la Cabra petrol station, on a major track descending west from a large 'Parque Natural' sign, a 'Mapa de uso publico' mapboard, and a board describing the norms for canyoning ('Zona para la practica de descenso de barrancos'). There's room for half-a-dozen cars in a rough lay-by to the east of the road and at the start of the dirt track.

If using a taxi
Ask for "Venta de Cazulas" (end of the walk) and/or "Pista forestal para las cascadas de Los Chortales y Las Chorreras" (start of the walk).

If you're doing the shorter, paying version
Access is via the second track on the left, 1km after the **Cazulas** turn-off. N.B. NOT the 'Sociedad Co-operativa Andaluza del Campo Agricola y Ganadera de Cazulas' track at km4.3, which also leads to **Junta de los Ríos**, but is now cut by locked gates after a couple of kilometres. At present it's possible to drive to **'Junta de los Ríos'** in an ordinary car, but it's best to check in the restaurant for up-to-date information. It's then a relatively simple matter of fording the **Chorreras** watercourse and following the tailored path upstream.

Setting off from the **Carretera de la Cabra** (Wp.1 0M), we follow the track as it descends gently across the scrub swathed slopes of **Las Cabrerizas**, crossing a dry watercourse and passing a double-headed track on the left to **Llano de los Cabanitos** (Wp.2 15M). After passing an apiarist's spur branching right (Wp.3 29M), the main track also veers right and starts zigzagging down toward the **Chortales** waterfall of petrified wood (see Walk 28), at which point we take a minor branch on the left (Wp.4 35M). This branch descends to a wayposted junction with a path on the right (Wp.5 45M), which passes to the east of the **Las Chorreras** waterfall, a remarkable accretion of convolute mineral deposits resembling the cold clumped wax of many candles.

For a short walk involving a climb of a little over 300 metres, turn right here, just touching Walk 28 at Wp.6, then follow the track back to Wp.4 of the present itinerary. Otherwise, we bear left, staying on the minor track, now little more than a trail, as it descends to the first of the day's plunge pools in **Barranco de las Chorreras**. This is another potential objective for a short version (there are several larger plunge-pools just upstream), this time involving a return climb of nearly 400 metres. For the full walk, we ford the torrent (Wp.6 55M) to recover the trail as it climbs steeply to the south, before levelling off and curving southwest below menacing cliffs - not recommended after heavy rain: the path is studded with several fallen boulders and scores of smaller rocks big enough to fell Goliath.

After a second, briefer and gentler climb, we round a corner (WSW) and see a narrow path snaking back down to the torrent. At the **Barranco del Lagarto** watershed (Wp.7 70M), we leave the broad trail (which is in any case overgrown here), and take the narrow path (SE). Ignoring a branch to the right 150 metres later (Wp.8), we zigzag down alongside the watershed before crossing onto its left bank (Wp.9 80M). The path levels off briefly then descends to a junction with a spur leading to the first and perhaps finest of a succession of large, swimmable plunge pools (Wp.10), beyond which GPS reception is poor until we emerge from the gorge.

Our path continues along the right bank, initially amid dense shrubbery before

The first bridge

traversing bare rock and reaching the first suspension bridge, 150 metres from the junction above the plunge-pool, and bouncy enough to catapult impetuous walkers into the torrent. Immediately after the bridge, we ignore a path on the left and bear right on a stepped descent passing an even deeper plunge-pool.

We then climb away from the torrent, crossing a spur where two of the posts supporting a hand-cable have broken away from their moorings. This poses no difficulty, though there's a very slight risk of vertigo on the path immediately afterwards, beyond which we descend to the second bridge (94M). Bridge No.3 is a conventional wooden footbridge, solid and sagging, but stable enough to get us back onto the left bank, where a spring has made the rocks a little slippery.

Climbing away from the torrent, we pass a small *mirador* (105M). 125 metres later, we cross an area of rough paving (either an old threshing circle or an aborted *mirador*) and descend back towards the river, passing a second *mirador* before crossing Bridge N°4 (115M), possibly the bounciest of them all and the site of the last major plunge pool.

Chorreras ford

We then ford the **Chorreras** stream twice and another watercourse once to reach the end of a dirt track at the union of the **Barrancos de las Chorreras** and **Mina Rica**, otherwise known as **Junta de los Ríos** (120M).

The *acequia* starting here is the one we follow at the end of the walk. Unfortunately, the first stretch is apt only for water and water-born amphibians, so we follow the track as it descends along a broadening and deepening canyon below (briefly right under) the fabulous cliffs of **Los Charquillos**, which in places bear more than a passing likeness to a pile of melted elephants. After passing the ruin of an old mill, we cross a bridge into the **Cazulas Sociedad Co-operativa** 'Finca Particular', where we come to a curving T-junction with a bend in another track (Wp.11 145M).

If you were to bear right here you'd come to a ford, after which a long laborious climb leads through the **Cortijo de la Toma** avocado orchards onto various alternative routes to **Cazulas** and **Otivar** (the latter long, complicated and frequently slippery). We, however, take the track to the left, climbing steadily till it crosses the **Junta de los Ríos** *acequia* (Wp.12 160M), where we turn right to walk along the *acequia*. This *acequia* is not alarming unless you suffer very acute vertigo. The wall is broad and, toward the end, largely covered with slabs of concrete. Nonetheless, you still have to watch your step as there are several stretches where the surface is either uneven or has been narrowed by mini-landslips and curved concrete coping.

- After traversing a hillside of farmed olive trees, we cross a dirt track (Wp.13 173M), beyond which the cultivated land returns to scrub.
- Below a second cultivated area we pass a cabin (Wp.14 194M), home to several large, extremely noisy and extremely loose dogs that look and sound distinctly antagonistic as you approach. However, on hearing a kind word, antagonism turns to an agony of affability and they become so very soppy daft, the only danger is that they'll want to come home with you.

We then curve round to the north, bringing into view Otivar and, down to our right, **Palacete de Cazulas** with its distinctive tower, at which point the *acequia* burrows under crags and becomes impassable.

Forking left, we follow a rough path (Wp.15 200M) climbing behind the crags, where we skirt an immaculately maintained olive grove below a cottage. Staying on the edge of the olive grove, we cross a gully onto a faint way, soon essentially off-path, leading to a second gully below a rusty mesh fence (Wp.16 205M).

Following the fence to the right, we traverse a shelf of rock, 50 metres northeast of which, at the end of an overgrown terrace (Wp.17 210M), we descend to the right (S) alongside a succession of abandoned and partially abandoned terraces to recover the *acequia* (Wp.18).

Bearing left, we follow the *acequia* to a bridge spanning an overflow sluice, 50 metres after which we join a rough dirt track (Wp.19 215M). Leaving the *acequia*, we follow the track down to the right and, ignoring a fork on the left after 50 metres (Wp.20), emerge on the **Cazulas** road 300 metres later (Wp.21 225M), 50 metres above **Venta de Cazulas**.

Without in anyway scraping the bottom of the barrel, this miscellany does bear a faint resemblance to the end of a family tin of Quality Street, in that it contains those hard, dark confections that have been passed over by hands trawling for soft-centres. But the hard ones are always somebody's favourite and for more ambitious walkers these alternative itineraries may well be the grandest rambles in a grand rambling land.

The two main walks extend our **La Maroma** ascents into linear traverses of the **Sierra Tejeda**. Neither itinerary is objectively difficult, but 30(a) takes a long time and could involve finishing in the dark, while 30(b) crosses rough ground and effectively ends off-path. In both cases, I recommend doing a linear two-way ascent of **La Maroma** first. <u>Do not attempt a full traverse when visibility is poor</u>. For less robust tastes, 30(c) adapts two very spectacular paths used in longer, more arduous itineraries, into a shorter, easier walk suitable for anyone who doesn't suffer from vertigo.

(a) Traverse of the Sierra Tejeda: El Alcázar to Canillas de Aceituno descending from La Maroma (Walk 3) via Camino de la Casa de la Nieve.

Two of the three classic **La Maroma** routes combine into a magnificent excursion that compares favourably with … well, with any walk anywhere. The **Camino de la Casa de la Nieve**, the old snow-gatherers' path from **Canillas**, is the best made path up **La Maroma** and probably the most spectacular. It's the one used in summer when a moonlit pilgrimage takes place, climaxing with sunrise on the summit. Even this route involves several hundred metres off-path in featureless landscape and, as an ascent, seems long enough to encompass a lengthy stretch of evolutionary history.

Taken as a descent though, it perfectly complements the climb from the north and amply compensates for the logistical hassles, either requiring two cars or, preferably a night in **Canillas**, returning to **Alcaucín** on foot the following day via Walk 1 then following the **Alcázar** dirt track to pick up your vehicle. If returning to **Alcaucín** on foot, Wp.13 of Walk 1 can be reached by following the main road (W) out of **Canillas** and, at the large roundabout just outside town, turning right for 'Cueva de la Fajara'. Bearing right at each major junction, follow the asphalt lane down till the tarmac gives way to concrete, at which point you can either take the path to the right or, for easier walking, stay on the track (Walk 1 Wps.13-1). See Appendices for details of *casas rurales* accommodation. A GPS is very useful for finding your way down from **La Maroma** to the top end of the **Casa de la Nieve** path.

5	2½-H	16½ km	1400m	one-way	4 ***

*   from **La Maroma**, but allow up to 9 hours for the full traverse
**   including the climb to **La Maroma** from **Alcázar**)
*** in **Canillas**

> **Short Version**
> **La Rabita** in reverse

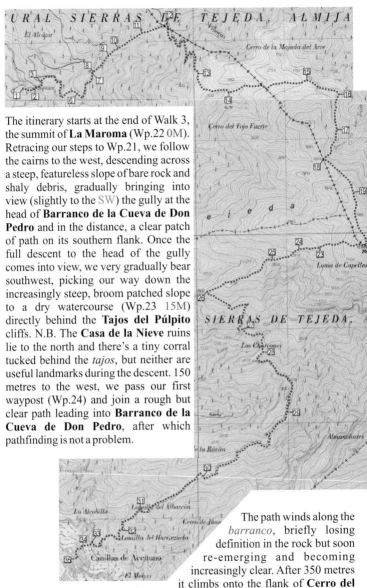

The itinerary starts at the end of Walk 3, the summit of **La Maroma** (Wp.22 0M). Retracing our steps to Wp.21, we follow the cairns to the west, descending across a steep, featureless slope of bare rock and shaly debris, gradually bringing into view (slightly to the SW) the gully at the head of **Barranco de la Cueva de Don Pedro** and in the distance, a clear patch of path on its southern flank. Once the full descent to the head of the gully comes into view, we very gradually bear southwest, picking our way down the increasingly steep, broom patched slope to a dry watercourse (Wp.23 15M) directly behind the **Tajos del Púlpito** cliffs. N.B. The **Casa de la Nieve** ruins lie to the north and there's a tiny corral tucked behind the *tajos*, but neither are useful landmarks during the descent. 150 metres to the west, we pass our first waypost (Wp.24) and join a rough but clear path leading into **Barranco de la Cueva de Don Pedro**, after which pathfinding is not a problem.

The path winds along the *barranco*, briefly losing definition in the rock but soon re-emerging and becoming increasingly clear. After 350 metres it climbs onto the flank of **Cerro del Luche** (Wp.25 25M), the rise defining the gully's southern side, following the clear stretch of path first spotted on the descent from the summit. The *barranco* drops away to our right and we maintain altitude until the path curves left (S), descending gently to a waypost and large cairn before apparently dropping off the edge of a cliff just short of the **Proa del Barco** crags (Wp.26 40M).

Happily, the drop is only apparent as the path doubles back to the left (SE) for a surprisingly gentle descent, enjoying spectacular views over **Barranco de Tajos Lisos**. As the **Sierra Almijara** and the southwestern face of **La**

Maroma come into view, the path starts zigzagging down alongside the first of the **Charcones** watersheds which we eventually cross (Wp.27 55M), bringing into view off to our right a path descending from **Collado de los Charcones** toward **Péñon Grande** (an alternative way down, arriving in **Canillas** via the football field track). 150 metres after a second, larger watercourse, we cross **Collado de los Charcones** (aka **de la Gitana**) (Wp.28 65M), ignoring the **Peñon Grande** branch on the right.

The path narrows briefly as it enters a third zigzagging stretch, at the end of which we pass and probably miss (it was never any great shakes in the first place and is now dry) the tiny **Fuente Agrìa** spring. After a very brief climb we cross the neck of a spur, swinging south with fine views over **Barranco de los Almanchares**. 300 metres along the spur we pass a narrow path doubling back to the left (Wp.29 85M), circling the head of the *barranco* to join paths above **Sedella**. **Barranco de los Almanchares** is an important refuge and breeding ground for local fauna, so this path is best ignored, but it is worth pausing to look back and admire the fine fluted cliffs to the south of **La Maroma**, the **Tajos de Capellania**.

After a winding descent off the end of the spur we curve away from **Barranco de los Almanchares**, descending across a slightly bleak, fire-damaged landscape (SW) to a stand of pine, sheltering the cave-like entrance to a Roman mine (**Cueva de la Rábita**, also spelled **Rávita** - said to be the burial place of four Moorish saints), a tiny limekiln, and the reliable spring of **Fuente La Rábita** (Wp.30 110M). After the *fuente*, the path traverses a broad sheet of rock, beyond which it resumes its clear descent, crossing patches of ancient cobbling. Descending between fields of broom and intermittent stands of pine, we zigzag across **Lomilla del Albarcón** (Wp.31 125M) onto the back of **Lomilla del Huertezuelo**, at the end of which we wind through a small rock garden (Wp.32 130M), bringing the village of **Canillas de Aceituno** into view.

350 metres later, we pass a *Parque Natural* signboard for 'Sendero Casa de la Nieve' and join a dirt track (Wp.33 140M) 30 metres to the east of a confluence of dirt tracks. Ignoring the major tracks climbing to the right and doubling back on the left (north and south), we take the minor central track, passing between whitewashed farm buildings, where it dwindles to a partially concreted, stepped mule trail descending to an alley (Wp.34). At the bottom of the alley, just below **Calle Sierrecilla**, we bear right then left at the corner defined by houses No's. 40 & 42. We continue descending at each major junction until the narrow pedestrian alley, **Calle Calleja**, debouches on **Plaza Maestro Francisco Gallero Badillo** in front of the Unicaja bank (Wp.35).

(b) Traverse of the Sierra Tejeda: El Robledal (Walk 4) to Sedella via Tacita de Plata and Llanadas de Sedella

We traverse one of the wildest corners of the sierra before descending via the *via pecuaria* linking **Sedella** with **Alhama de Granada**, an ancient royal way that is nowadays merely ancient, the regality and wayness of it having long since faded away. Although it's waymarked and follows intermittent patches of path, it is essentially off-path, requiring excellent pathfinding skills, a ready familiarity with the mountain and, preferably, GPS proficiency. It is only for the experienced and determined few. That said, I'm sure the small number of you who are equipped to undertake this route, will remember it as one of your most satisfying days rambling in the region.

* in Sedella

**Short Version
Tacita de la Plata**

Access: by car and, (adding 5km), bus

After following Walk 4 to Wp.12, we take the very faint way climbing to the east. The way disappears altogether in the grass on the ridge between the two obvious outcrops of rock, but bearing left, we pass to the right of a reasonably tall cairn (250 metres from Wp.12). To the northeast, in line with the summits of the Sierra Nevada, we can see the tips of some pine trees, which indicate the location of **Fuente Tacita de Plata**.

As we descend (NE), the tips of the trees disappear, but picking our way across patches of grass and small outcrops of rock, we head for a stand of four small pine trees where we pass the low walls of a windbreak (Wp.17). Maintaining direction (NE), still off path but on reasonably clear walking land, we bring the tips of the taller pine back into view, and can see a clear path continuing to the east. We pick our way down toward the taller pine, 50 metres behind which there's a damp cave (intermittently inhabited until a few years ago). 30 metres south of the cave is the meagre **Fuente Tacita de Plata** spring (Wp.18 130M), which has always had a trickle of water when I've visited, but should not be relied upon. 75 metres to the south of the *fuente*, we pick up the clear path seen from above, which is a little less clear once we're on it, but easy enough.

Ignoring a fork climbing to the right 75 metres after the start of the clear path, we follow a contour line below the crest, soon curving round to pass a large red waymark and the upper corner of a small fenced area (Wp.19 140M). The next crest, immediately after the fence, can be passed either to the south or the north, the latter being rougher but less vertiginous. Following a faint path on the northern flank, we climb a grassy rise, bringing **Sierra Almijara** back into view and, 75 metres below us, a clear path rounding a northern spur. Ignoring the lower path, we stay on the heights skirting the crags, at the end of which there are two metal poles, one with a diagonally divided green-and-white shield (Wp.20), beyond which we see another clear path climbing along the northern flank of the next crest. Picking our way across the rocks to the south, we join the goat path traversing the southern flank of the crest at a second green/white shield (Wp.21), from where a rough but obvious way descends to the *collada* at the start of the clear path (Wp.22, a little under 2km from Wp.12). You have to watch where you're placing your feet here, so it's worth pausing once in a while to enjoy the fabulously sculpted land to the northeast.

Taking the clear path, we climb to the spectacularly jagged eastern tip of the next crest, where a natural gateway (Wp.23 160M) leads down to a mini-col below a final, hitherto invisible outcrop of rock. It's tempting to descend here or follow one of the heavily pelleted ways used by goats round the southern face of the outcrop, but for us mere bipeds it's easier to climb directly across the top, very slightly favouring the southern side, before descending to the first small patch of pasture (Wp.24 170M). We then cross a tiny spine of rock (barely worth mentioning in view of what's passed in the last forty minutes) and join the end of a dirt track skirting to the right of a grassy knoll on the **Llanadas de Sedella**. We follow this track for 400 metres till it dips into **Hoya del Pico,** a shallow depression shortly before two large plantations of pine, where we find a flat stone with a double-headed red arrow painted on it (Wp.25 180M). We now leave the dirt track, doubling back to the right (SW) on the unregal cow paths descending along the **Loma de Cuascuadra**.

These paths are at first faint and intermittent, then multiple and indistinguishable one from the other, so it's simply a case of staying on the heights and maintaining a southwesterly direction along the *loma*, enjoying the easy walking and fabulous views of **La Maroma's** southeastern face. Sticking to the centre of the spur we descend across a succession of boulder fringed steps and the pasture deteriorates to scrub as we approach the first clear landmark, a distinct grassy dome crowned with a coronet of rock

blocked in with rough patches of wall (Wp.26 200M). 100 metres below this makeshift corral, and invisible till we go round onto the far side, are the ruins of **Casa Cuascuadra**, but before you descend it's worth pausing to fix in your mind the shape of the land below.

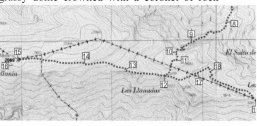

Of the two villages at the end of the *loma*, the one on the left is **Salares**, the one on the right with the large sports centre, **Sedella**. The track descending into the valley below **Sedella** is the one we take from **Puente Romano**. Descending to the left of **Casa Cuascuadra**, we follow a faint path picked out with occasional red waymarks as it descends alongside the remains of a wall. Keeping the wall and the embankment that is its natural continuation to our left, we descend along an increasingly clear cow path onto a narrower stretch of the spur where the path splinters.

Sticking to the main traces on the eastern flank of the spur we descend to a minor *col* just before a small knoll topped with a dense clump of oak, 40 metres before which there's a Y-junction marked with a long flat red-waymarked stone (Wp.27 215M), unfortunately, eminently moveable.

he junction can also be identified by a large bush of retama immediately north of it, a small fan of retama a few metres along it, and after that a red waymark on a stone set in the path. This is where the pathless descent becomes tricky. The narrow path winds through the scrub, almost immediately descending into a shallow

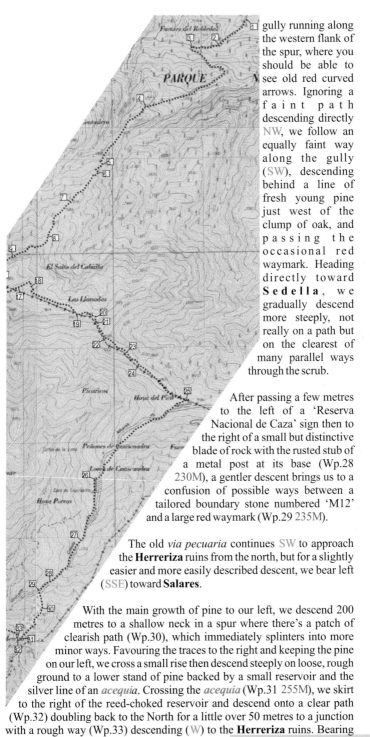

gully running along the western flank of the spur, where you should be able to see old red curved arrows. Ignoring a faint path descending directly NW, we follow an equally faint way along the gully (SW), descending behind a line of fresh young pine just west of the clump of oak, and passing the occasional red waymark. Heading directly toward **Sedella**, we gradually descend more steeply, not really on a path but on the clearest of many parallel ways through the scrub.

After passing a few metres to the left of a 'Reserva Nacional de Caza' sign then to the right of a small but distinctive blade of rock with the rusted stub of a metal post at its base (Wp.28 230M), a gentler descent brings us to a confusion of possible ways between a tailored boundary stone numbered 'M12' and a large red waymark (Wp.29 235M).

The old *via pecuaria* continues SW to approach the **Herreriza** ruins from the north, but for a slightly easier and more easily described descent, we bear left (SSE) toward **Salares**.

With the main growth of pine to our left, we descend 200 metres to a shallow neck in a spur where there's a patch of clearish path (Wp.30), which immediately splinters into more minor ways. Favouring the traces to the right and keeping the pine on our left, we cross a small rise then descend steeply on loose, rough ground to a lower stand of pine backed by a small reservoir and the silver line of an *acequia*. Crossing the *acequia* (Wp.31 255M), we skirt to the right of the reed-choked reservoir and descend onto a clear path (Wp.32) doubling back to the North for a little over 50 metres to a junction with a rough way (Wp.33) descending (W) to the **Herreriza** ruins. Bearing left, we follow the rough trail (WNW), passing between two solitary oak above an old threshing circle and crossing a tiny rivulet, after which we continue on narrow but obvious ways following a contour line and terracing to pass just below the ruin of **La Herreriza** (Wp.34 270M).

Bearing left, we follow an ancient goat path, passing to the right of a knee high cairn, after which the path veers left briefly before curving back to the west, bringing us a glimpse of **Puente Romano** in the crux of the valley. The goat path resolves itself into a broad but badly eroded trail zigzagging down alongside an oleander choked gully to **Puente Romano** (Wp.35 280M). We now simply follow the broad trail and subsequent track into **Sedella**, passing 'Casa la Resculadera' and entering the village via a concrete lane.

Bearing left, we come to the **Colegio Publico Rural** and, 50 metres further on, the **Ermita de la Esperanza**, which is signposted from the main road to the east of the village and is the place to leave a car if you're in a two-car party. For refreshment, turn right at the *colegio* and follow **Calle Libertad** through the village. Turn right in front of House N°16 on long concrete steps climbing to the central square and **Bar Plaza**. For accommodation or to rendez-vous with a lift, cross the plaza into **Calle Baja**, then turn left after **Casa Camanillo** to join the main road. 250 metres to the west you'll find the English owned **Hostal Casa Pinta** (T: 952 508955 www.lacasapinta.com lacasapinta@terra.es)

(c) Sierra Almijara: The Apretaderos Ridge path (Walk 16) and Chillar acequia (Walk 15) from Pinarillo (Walk 17)

If you don't fancy all the splashing about in the **Río Chillar**, nor the gruelling ups-and-downs of the **Limán Trail**, but would like to enjoy some fabulous views and spectacular paths, an interesting alternative take on our itineraries would be to poach the easiest bit from Walk 17 and some of the best bits from Walks 15 & 16. (See Walk 15 for the vertigo warning.)

Access: by car

To reach the start, follow the signs from the motorway for 'Cuevas de Nerja' then, just before the entrance to the *cuevas* car-park, turn left on a track signposted 'Área Recreativa El Pinarillo 5km'/'Fuente del Esparto', setting the odometer at zero. Park in the main *área recreativa* car-park at km4.7.

Starting from the car-park (Wp.1 0M), we follow a minor track descending (N) into **Barranco de Coladilla**. After crossing the *barranco*, we fork left at a Y-junction (Wp.2) and continue straight ahead when the main, right hand branch curls back to form a crossroads (Wp.3 5M). We then climb through a sharp bend before joining the main **Fuente del Esparto** track (Wp.4 10M). Bearing left, we follow the track up to **Collado de los Galgos** (aka **Apretaderos**) (Wp.5 15M), where we turn left (S) on a path along the **Apretaderos** crest.

There are actually two paths along the crest, one skirting a small summit, the

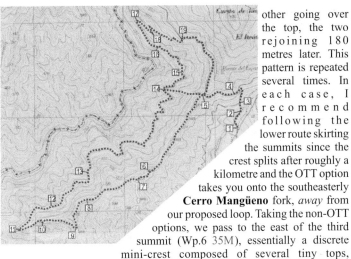

other going over the top, the two rejoining 180 metres later. This pattern is repeated several times. In each case, I recommend following the lower route skirting the summits since the crest splits after roughly a kilometre and the OTT option takes you onto the southeasterly **Cerro Mangüeno** fork, *away* from our proposed loop. Taking the non-OTT options, we pass to the east of the third summit (Wp.6 35M), essentially a discrete mini-crest composed of several tiny tops, identifiable by a path branching right onto the first of the tiny tops. This is a useful point of reference as the next OTT branch, forking left 75 metres later over the 603 metre top, the highest along the crest (Wp.7), is the one we really have to avoid, skirting its western flank in order to join the westerly branch of the ridge, where the path more or less levels out (Wp.8 50M).

300 metres later the path veers right (NW) between two small cairns (Wp.9 55M) to run along the southern flank of a westerly spur. The path crosses onto the northern flank, curving along the tapering spur from where we enjoy stunning views up the **Río Chíllar**. After bearing left onto a small promontory (Wp.10 65M) overlooking an *acequia*, we zigzag into a steeper descent, briefly interrupted by the tip of the spur before dropping down to the end of the *acequia* (Wp.11 70M).

We now simply follow the acequia to the north, passing a patch of uneven wall after 500 metres (Wp.12) and the first two stretches of protective fencing some 600 metres after that (Wp.13). There are two ways to leave the *acequia*, the first being the most direct, the second making the most of the views.

- Roughly 40 minutes from Wp.11 we pass a couple of red waymarks on the lip of the *acequia* wall, immediately after which new concrete slabs cover the *acequia,* and a narrow path on the right (Wp.14) climbs steadily to steeply (E) back to **Collado de los Galgos** (Wp.5).
- Alternatively, we can continue along the most vertiginous section of the *acequia*, passing a spectacular overhang (Wp.15) and a final fenced section (Wp.16) before reaching a crossroads with a clear wayposted path (Wp.17). Turning right, we climb steeply (ESE). After dipping down briefly, the path resumes climbing, doubling back to the left at a junction (Wp.18) above a roofless cabin. We then climb steeply to rejoin the **La Presa-Pinarillo** dirt track (Wp.19), which we follow to the right, back to **Collado de los Galgos** (Wp.5).

GPS Waypoints for the 30 walking routes included in **Walk! Axarquia** are quoted in Latitude/Longitude for the WGS84 Datum; the default datum for GPS receivers. Before loading waypoints into your gps please read 'Using GPS in Axarquia' on page 31.

Waypoints are quoted to four places of decimals, as recorded during Charles Davis' research. If your GPS will only accept three places of decimals then you should 'round off' the third decimal place; e.g. .0178 would 'round off' to .018, while .9224 would 'round off' to .922.

The edited GPS Track and Waypoint files for **Walk! Axarquia** can be downloaded from our **Personal Navigator Files (PNFs) CD** (version 2.01 onwards) via your PC into your GPS receiver, assuming you have a GPS-PC lead. For more information on our PNFs CD see our websites:-

www.walking.demon.co.uk   www.dwgwalking.co.uk

1.

CUEVA DE LA FAJARA FROM ALCAUCÍN

Wp	N	W
1	36 54.0960	4 06.8214
2	36 54.0672	4 06.8064
3	36 54.0810	4 06.7842
4	36 53.9604	4 06.7638
5	36 53.8530	4 06.7680
6	36 53.5386	4 06.9150
7	36 53.4864	4 06.6264
8	36 53.3304	4 06.6420
9	36 53.2074	4 06.4164
10	36 53.0352	4 06.4002
11	36 52.9464	4 06.5208
12	36 52.9350	4 06.2226
13	36 52.9050	4 06.1242
14	36 52.8846	4 05.9634
15	36 52.8966	4 05.9274
16	36 52.9986	4 06.0912
17	36 53.0556	4 06.0792
18	36 52.9638	4 05.9676
19	36 52.9884	4 05.9208
20	36 52.9974	4 05.8794
21	36 53.3436	4 06.1806
22	36 53.4396	4 06.2418
23	36 53.4792	4 06.2868
24	36 53.5644	4 06.3702
25	36 53.7258	4 06.5118
26	36 53.6904	4 06.6114
27	36 53.7204	4 06.6414
28	36 53.8122	4 06.7200

2.

LOS CASTILLONES FROM CORTIJO DE LA ALCAUCA

Wp	N	W
1	36 56.1000	4 04.4772
2	36 55.9752	4 04.5360
3	36 55.8804	4 04.5672
4	36 55.7952	4 04.6260
5	36 55.6236	4 04.6092
6	36 55.7808	4 05.2632
7	36 55.8696	4 05.6892

3.

LA MAROMA: EL ALCAZAR

Wp	N	W
1	36 55.0788	4 05.3406
2	36 55.0788	4 05.2596
3	36 55.1154	4 05.2086
6	36 55.0350	4 04.9362
7	36 55.1616	4 04.8006
8	36 55.1832	4 04.8162
9	36 55.2642	4 04.6968
10	36 55.3098	4 04.6260
11	36 55.3926	4 04.4568
12	36 55.4382	4 04.2432
13	36 55.1568	4 04.0398
14	36 55.0542	4 03.7929
15	36 55.1202	4 03.2340
16	36 55.0302	4 03.0192
17	36 54.8719	4 03.0137
18	36 54.6864	4 03.1254
19	36 54.5070	4 02.9100
20	36 54.2448	4 02.8068
21	36 54.1968	4 02.8014
22	36 54.1614	4 02.7348

4.

LA MAROMA: SENDERO EL ROBLEDAL

Wp	N	W
1	36 55.6266	3 59.6922
2	36 55.4784	3 59.9202
3	36 55.4730	4 00.1086
4	36 55.1268	4 00.4602
5	36 54.8058	4 00.7812
6	36 54.7776	4 00.8094
7	36 54.5790	4 01.0368
8	36 54.3918	4 01.1898
9	36 54.2742	4 01.4448
10	36 54.2172	4 01.5792
11	36 54.1578	4 01.5570
12	36 54.0853	4 01.6430
13	36 54.1104	4 01.9218
14	36 54.1392	4 02.2656
15	36 54.1602	4 02.7330
16	36 54.1308	4 02.7744

5.

EL ROBLEDAL

Wp	N	W
1	36 55.7550	3 59.7354
2	36 55.7358	4 00.0876
3	36 55.6842	4 00.2478
4	36 55.5192	4 00.3882
5	36 55.3380	4 00.5862
6	36 55.4082	4 00.5670
7	36 55.2965	4 00.4464
8	36 55.1184	4 00.4824
9	36 55.4688	4 00.1098

6.

LOMA DE LA FUENTE

Wp	N	W
1	36 51.6708	4 01.9008
2	36 51.8106	4 01.8270
3	36 52.0956	4 01.8066
4	36 52.1262	4 01.6758
5	36 52.1412	4 01.5708
6	36 52.1658	4 01.5834
7	36 52.2174	4 01.5222
8	36 52.2756	4 01.4946
9	36 52.3566	4 01.4766
10	36 52.4052	4 01.4040
11	36 52.4832	4 01.3518
12	36 52.7100	4 01.2702
13	36 52.7406	4 01.1982
14	36 52.9644	4 01.1676
15	36 52.9458	4 01.2570
16	36 53.1498	4 01.2246
17	36 53.0340	4 01.3206
18	36 53.0118	4 01.4040
19	36 53.0118	4 01.6590
20	36 52.9500	4 01.6860

Wp	N	W
21	36 52.9128	4 01.6836
22	36 52.9068	4 01.7730
23	36 52.9362	4 01.9848
24	36 52.9440	4 02.0712
25	36 52.8966	4 02.0760
26	36 52.2786	4 02.2532
27	36 52.1670	4 02.1510
28	36 51.9708	4 02.1060
29	36 51.8004	4 02.0586

7.
TWO SHORT WALKS FROM LA FÁBRICA DE LA LUZ
(a) Arroyo Turbilla

Wp	N	W
1	36 51.8280	3 58.2354
2	36 51.7386	3 58.2918
3	36 51.6624	3 58.4202
4	36 51.7470	3 58.5330
5	36 51.8214	3 58.4718
6	36 52.0740	3 58.5048
7	36 52.1448	3 58.4592
8	36 52.3938	3 58.4154
9	36 52.7322	3 58.0224
10	36 52.3698	3 57.8202
11	36 52.2168	3 57.8718
12	36 52.1892	3 57.9288
13	36 52.2186	3 57.9690
14	36 52.1016	3 58.2438

(b) Cerro de la Cueva del Agua

Wp	N	W
A1	36 51.8281	3 58.2355
A2	36 51.7386	3 58.2918
A3	36 51.6625	3 58.4203
A4	36 51.7470	3 58.5330
B1	36 51.4044	3 58.3026
B2	36 51.2214	3 58.9830
B3	36 51.4812	3 58.7160
B4	36 51.5328	3 58.6794
B5	36 51.6012	3 58.7694

8.
PUERTO BLANQUILLO FROM LA FÁBRICA DE LA LUZ via LOS PRADILLOS & ARROYO DEL CUEVA MELERO

Wp	N	W
1	36 51.8112	3 58.2192
2	36 51.8202	3 58.1316
3	36 51.6204	3 58.0416
4	36 51.6252	3 58.0314
5	36 51.1560	3 57.5022
6	36 51.0816	3 57.2202
7	36 51.0000	3 57.0558
8	36 51.5838	3 56.0844
9	36 51.6762	3 55.7538
10	36 51.9396	3 55.6914
11	36 52.1112	3 55.6416
12	36 52.1970	3 55.7634
13	36 52.3140	3 56.1798
14	36 52.3530	3 56.4036
15	36 52.3344	3 56.6394
16	36 52.3554	3 56.7726
17	36 52.2714	3 56.9958
18	36 52.2078	3 57.2214
19	36 52.0566	3 57.5280
20	36 52.0632	3 57.6036
21	36 51.8952	3 57.9534

9.
CAMINO DEL RÍO

Wp	N	W
1	36 50.8800	3 59.4385
2	36 51.0150	3 59.6017
3	36 51.2412	3 59.4943
4	36 51.3072	3 59.4751
5	36 51.4056	3 59.4510
6	36 51.4974	3 59.4672
7	36 51.5340	3 59.4762
8	36 51.6468	3 59.6706
9	36 51.6972	3 59.6916
10	36 51.7338	3 59.6988
11	36 51.6756	3 59.9244
12	36 51.4278	3 59.6262
13	36 51.0660	3 59.8266
14	36 50.9208	3 59.6574
15	36 50.8836	3 59.6136
16	36 50.8296	3 59.5824

10.
MALAS CAMAS via HAZA DEL AGUADERO

Wp	N	W
1	36 55.8534	3 56.4378
2	36 55.5546	3 57.0342
3	36 54.9216	3 56.7852
4	36 54.4686	3 56.9448
5	36 53.7126	3 57.1242
6	36 53.6700	3 57.2028
7	36 53.7888	3 57.9720
8	36 53.7517	3 58.2092
9	36 53.9328	3 58.3296
10	36 53.7300	3 58.1970
11	36 53.7120	3 58.1832
12	36 53.4984	3 58.0476
13	36 53.2548	3 57.4932
14	36 53.1624	3 56.7324
15	36 53.1798	3 56.6568

11.
PARAJE NATURAL DE LOS ACANTILLADOS DE MAR
Maro & Caleta

Wp	N	W
1	36 45.5778	3 50.7042
2	36 45.5436	3 50.7582
3	36 45.4548	3 50.8692
4	36 45.3396	3 50.9874
5	36 45.1188	3 51.0636
6	36 45.0654	3 51.0756
7	36 45.0834	3 51.0510
8	36 45.1140	3 50.9982
9	36 45.1218	3 50.9562
10	36 45.2088	3 50.8782
11	36 45.2508	3 50.8122
12	36 45.2232	3 50.7900
13	36 45.2112	3 50.7726
14	36 45.2664	3 50.6490
15	36 45.3234	3 50.5590
16	36 45.3408	3 50.5440
17	36 45.3894	3 50.5206

Torre de Maro

Wp	N	W
1	36 45.5400	3 50.5788
2	36 45.4086	3 50.5686
3	36 45.3942	3 50.5224
4	36 45.3450	3 50.0844
5	36 45.3498	3 49.9782
6	36 45.3498	3 49.9308
7	36 45.3576	3 49.7700
8	36 45.3192	3 49.6452
9	36 45.2796	3 49.7988
10	36 45.2502	3 49.8174
11	36 45.2148	3 49.7976
12	36 45.2166	3 49.7502
13	36 45.1830	3 49.7334
14	36 45.2070	3 49.8492
15	36 45.1692	3 49.6500
16	36 45.1632	3 49.5912
17	36 45.1056	3 49.5864
S1	36 45.4560	3 49.5870

Cerro Caleta

Wp	N	W
1	36 44.4666	3 46.6434
2	36 44.4114	3 46.6350
3	36 44.3742	3 46.7232
4	36 44.4240	3 46.7394
5	36 44.5212	3 46.8468
6	36 44.6652	3 46.8666
7	36 44.8296	3 46.9662
8	36 44.9118	3 46.9944
9	36 44.7270	3 47.3946
10	36 44.6124	3 47.2188
12	36 44.5782	3 47.2014
13	36 44.5296	3 47.0598

12.
PUERTO DE FRIGILIANA

Wp	N	W
1	36 48.8491	3 55.3609
2	36 49.4581	3 54.8935
3	36 49.5271	3 54.8635
4	36 49.5259	3 54.9949

5	36 49.7437	3 54.9979
6	36 49.8985	3 55.0735
7	36 50.0520	3 54.6948
8	36 50.2836	3 54.3582
9	36 50.5404	3 54.0816
10	36 51.2106	3 53.5968
11	36 51.4278	3 53.3934
12	36 51.3462	3 53.3682
13	36 51.3150	3 53.1714
14	36 51.2898	3 53.1390
15	36 51.3150	3 52.9890
16	36 51.3594	3 52.9782
17	36 51.5808	3 52.7580
18	36 50.8464	3 53.5098
19	36 50.8200	3 53.7750
20	36 50.0604	3 55.1184
21	36 49.9794	3 55.1610

13.

RÍO HIGUERON

Wp	N	W
1	36 47.4517	3 53.6808
2	36 47.4511	3 53.5860
3	36 47.7547	3 53.4510
4	36 48.1795	3 53.6148
5	36 49.3663	3 53.3460
6	36 49.6375	3 53.4474
7	36 49.9531	3 53.6881
8	36 50.1181	3 53.6137

14.

CUESTA DEL SORDO FROM FRIGILIANA

Wp	N	W
1	36 47.4517	3 53.6808
2	36 47.4511	3 53.5860
3	36 47.7547	3 53.4510
4	36 47.8230	3 53.2332
5	36 47.8296	3 53.1696
6	36 47.7852	3 53.1864
7	36 47.6952	3 53.2146
8	36 47.5620	3 53.2074
9	36 47.5236	3 53.2140
10	36 47.3940	3 53.2326
11	36 47.1462	3 53.2248
12	36 47.2698	3 53.3778
13	36 47.3712	3 53.5056
14	36 47.4601	3 53.5746
15	36 47.4835	3 53.5866
16	36 47.5878	3 53.5110

15.

RÍO CHILLAR

Wp	N	W
1	36 46.2990	3 52.7670
2	36 47.1090	3 52.9980
3	36 48.4014	3 51.7710
4	36 48.2604	3 51.5838

6	36 48.1314	3 51.4134
7	36 47.5416	3 52.1424
8	36 47.2332	3 52.6524
9	36 47.2008	3 52.8114

16.

THE LIMÁN TRAIL

Wp	N	W
1	36 46.2876	3 52.7568
2	36 46.2738	3 53.1198
3	36 46.2882	3 53.1414
4	36 46.4982	3 53.3352
5	36 46.5522	3 53.3346
6	36 47.0604	3 53.2506
7	36 47.0790	3 53.2428
8	36 47.1462	3 53.2248
9	36 47.2392	3 53.2446
10	36 47.3940	3 53.2326
11	36 47.5236	3 53.2140
12	36 47.5620	3 53.2074
13	36 47.7852	3 53.1864
14	36 47.8296	3 53.1696
15	36 48.0288	3 53.7088
16	36 48.2334	3 52.4472
17	36 48.2856	3 53.3260
18	36 48.3084	3 52.2882
19	36 48.3810	3 52.1478
20	36 48.5040	3 52.0350
21	36 48.5724	3 51.8754
22	36 48.5142	3 51.9138
23	36 48.4134	3 51.7674
24	36 48.0258	3 51.5568
25	36 47.9898	3 51.3018
26	36 47.5392	3 51.6774
27	36 47.5080	3 51.7428
28	36 47.3940	3 52.1214
29	36 47.2542	3 52.2216
30	36 47.2734	3 52.5060
31	36 47.2290	3 52.6578
32	36 47.2008	3 52.8114

17.

CORTIJO IMÁN FROM PINARILLO

Wp	N	W
1	36 47.8230	3 51.0252
2	36 47.9148	3 50.9976
3	36 47.9472	3 51.0078
4	36 47.9946	3 51.0420
5	36 47.9886	3 51.2880
6	36 48.3108	3 51.4368
7	36 48.5574	3 51.6816
8	36 48.8076	3 51.5244
9	36 49.5642	3 51.2562
10	36 49.6446	3 50.9934
11	36 49.8600	3 51.1146
12	36 48.4230	3 51.7776
13	36 48.3570	3 51.6636

18.

VENTA LOS PRADILLOS & CERRO GAVILÁN FROM CASA DE LA MINA

Wp	N	W
1	36 50.4732	3 56.8296
2	36 50.6958	3 56.8008
3	36 51.2370	3 56.0868
4	36 51.3259	3 55.9621
5	36 51.3036	3 55.9398
6	36 51.3510	3 55.9578
7	36 51.4296	3 55.9182
8	36 51.2094	3 55.7784
9	36 51.4488	3 55.7658
10	36 51.6570	3 55.7184
11	36 51.6762	3 55.7490
12	36 51.5886	3 56.0634
13	36 50.9946	3 57.0546
14	36 50.8332	3 57.1272
15	36 50.6772	3 57.0522
16	36 50.6586	3 57.1122
17	36 50.5380	3 57.2076
18	36 50.4588	3 56.9340

19.

LUCERO FROM RAMBLA DE LA MOTA

Wp	N	W
1	36 52.4940	3 54.8304
2	36 52.3824	3 54.3888
3	36 52.0860	3 53.9586
4	36 51.9912	3 53.6256
5	36 52.0506	3 53.4294

20.

NAVACHICA via BARRANCO DE LOS CAZADORES

Wp	N	W
1	36 48.1044	3 50.5188
2	36 48.2736	3 50.3664
3	36 49.3254	3 49.7622
4	36 49.9026	3 49.0620
5	36 50.1438	3 48.8118
6	36 50.1918	3 48.7536
7	36 50.2710	3 48.6714
8	36 50.3778	3 48.6546
9	36 50.5128	3 48.9168

21.

TAJO ALMENDRÓN & LA PUERTA

Wp	N	W
1	36 48.1044	3 50.5188
2	36 48.2736	3 50.3664
3	36 49.3254	3 49.7622
4	36 49.5462	3 50.0706
5	36 49.5894	3 50.1294
6	36 49.5366	3 50.2470

Wp	N	W
7	36 49.5234	3 50.2944
8	36 49.4622	3 50.3298
9	36 49.3650	3 50.3670
10	36 49.1934	3 50.5710
11	36 49.0674	3 50.7972
12	36 48.9366	3 50.7228
13	36 48.8340	3 50.9778
14	36 48.4590	3 50.8560
15	36 48.2874	3 50.7948
16	36 48.1878	3 50.4426
17	36 48.1464	3 50.6544

22.
TOUR OF TAJO DE LOS BUEYES

Wp	N	W
1	36 45.5892	3 50.4744
2	36 45.7620	3 50.4000
3	36 45.9276	3 50.4888
4	36 46.0848	3 50.5896
5	36 46.5144	3 50.1384
6	36 46.6524	3 50.1240
7	36 46.5480	3 50.0316
8	36 46.6788	3 49.7292
9	36 46.8942	3 49.9686
10	36 47.2362	3 50.1750
11	36 47.1660	3 50.2638
12	36 46.9680	3 50.9166
13	36 47.0166	3 51.0264
14	36 46.9620	3 51.0522
15	36 46.1646	3 51.2664
16	36 46.1484	3 51.2550
17	36 45.7332	3 51.1410

23.
ALTO DE CIELO FROM BARRANCO DE LA HIGUERA via CORTIJOS DE LA CIVILIA

Wp	N	W
1	36 48.1062	3 50.5158
2	36 48.1950	3 50.3664
3	36 48.1626	3 50.2182
4	36 48.2124	3 49.8138
5	36 48.2808	3 49.6068
6	36 48.3918	3 49.3044
7	36 48.4026	3 49.2690
8	36 48.3624	3 49.2402
9	36 48.3342	3 49.1298
10	36 48.3570	3 49.0668
11	36 48.2892	3 48.9036
12	36 48.2832	3 48.9924
13	36 48.0642	3 49.0164
14	36 47.8254	3 49.1178
15	36 47.5248	3 49.1748
16	36 47.4870	3 49.5312
17	36 47.1696	3 50.2650
18	36 47.5074	3 50.4084
19	36 47.7612	3 50.3220
20	36 47.9328	3 50.4324

24.
TWO SHORT WALKS OFF LOMA DE LAS CUADRILLAS

Wp	N	W
1	36 47.4774	3 46.0272
2	36 47.5500	3 46.0746
3	36 47.8842	3 46.1370
4	36 47.8500	3 46.2360
5	36 47.8705	3 46.2575
6	36 47.9227	3 46.2347
7	36 47.9599	3 46.1669
8	36 48.0757	3 45.9773
9	36 48.5881	3 46.4465

25.
PICO DE LOPERA via THE 'BACK DOOR'

Wp	N	W
1	36 52.6212	3 44.1840
2	36 52.6650	3 44.3604
3	36 52.7454	3 44.8830
4	36 52.9086	3 45.4212
5	36 52.9140	3 45.5700
6	36 53.0022	3 45.7740
7	36 53.1108	3 45.8772
8	36 53.1162	3 46.0830
9	36 52.9746	3 46.0584
10	36 52.4988	3 45.8748
11	36 52.3776	3 45.8718
12	36 52.5438	3 45.4002
13	36 52.5738	3 45.4710
14	36 52.6998	3 45.1422
15	36 52.6356	3 44.9808

26.
BARRANCO BACAL & CUERDA DE LOS MORROS

Wp	N	W
1	36 55.4712	3 48.7620
2	36 55.1064	3 48.6546
3	36 54.9798	3 48.6558
4	36 53.2056	3 47.6028
5	36 53.8314	3 47.9454
6	36 53.5242	3 47.9958
7	36 53.5416	3 48.3390
8	36 53.7450	3 48.7914
9	36 54.0186	3 48.8340
10	36 54.1446	3 48.9738
11	36 55.3688	3 49.4341

27.
RÍO CEBOLLON

Wp	N	W
1	36 55.7622	3 50.9484
2	36 55.0386	3 50.2836
3	36 54.9162	3 50.1402
4	36 52.6074	3 48.8394

28.
THE WATERFALL OF PETRIFIED WOOD

Wp	N	W
1	36 51.5874	3 43.3404
2	36 51.6384	3 43.4022
3	36 51.5832	3 43.4748
4	36 51.4320	3 44.2758
5	36 51.2982	3 44.3058
6	36 51.1638	3 44.5110
7	36 51.0966	3 44.7072
8	36 51.1980	3 44.8224
9	36 51.3918	3 45.1878
10	36 51.5712	3 44.8428
11	36 51.6252	3 44.4726
12	36 51.6846	3 44.1882
13	36 51.6984	3 43.9434
14	36 51.8178	3 43.4508

29.
RÍO VERDE

Wp	N	W
1	36 50.7990	3 43.0728
2	36 50.7948	3 43.6434
3	36 51.0234	3 44.1480
4	36 51.0426	3 44.3904
5	36 50.9760	3 44.5944
6	36 50.8944	3 44.6478
7	36 50.4222	3 44.7756
8	36 50.3868	3 44.6706
9	36 50.4348	3 44.5350
10	36 50.4630	3 44.4432
11	36 49.6752	3 43.2006
12	36 49.6296	3 43.0794
13	36 49.3050	3 42.7644
14	36 49.0626	3 42.1710
15	36 49.0788	3 42.0444
16	36 49.1688	3 41.9904
17	36 49.1846	3 41.9194
18	36 49.1570	3 41.9158
19	36 49.2278	3 41.8528
20	36 49.1984	3 41.8522
21	36 49.0370	3 41.7976

30.
ALTERNATIVE WALKS
(a) Traverse of the Sierra Tejeda to Canillas de Aceituna

Wp	N	W
1	36 55.0788	4 05.3406
2	36 55.0788	4 05.2596
3	36 55.1154	4 05.2086
6	36 55.0350	4 04.9362
7	36 55.1616	4 04.8006
8	36 55.1832	4 04.8162
9	36 55.2642	4 04.6968
10	36 55.3098	4 04.6260
11	36 55.3926	4 04.4568

Wp	N	W	Wp	N	W	Wp	N	W
12	36 55.4382	4 04.2432	2	36 55.4784	3 59.9202	30	36 52.2504	4 01.2114
13	36 55.1568	4 04.0398	3	36 55.4730	4 00.1086	31	36 52.0860	4 01.3650
14	36 55.0542	4 03.7929	4	36 55.1268	4 00.4602	32	36 52.0722	4 01.3818
15	36 55.1202	4 03.2340	5	36 54.8058	4 00.7812	33	36 52.1082	4 01.3878
16	36 55.0302	4 03.0192	6	36 54.7776	4 00.8094	34	36 52.1394	4 01.5576
17	36 54.8719	4 03.0137	7	36 54.5790	4 01.0368	35	36 52.1046	4 01.8006
18	36 54.6864	4 03.1254	8	36 54.3918	4 01.1898	**(c) Sierra de Almijara**		
19	36 54.5070	4 02.9100	9	36 54.2742	4 01.4448	Wp	N	W
20	36 54.2448	4 02.8068	10	36 54.2172	4 01.5792	1	36 47.8230	3 51.0252
21	36 54.1968	4 02.8014	11	36 54.1578	4 01.5570	2	36 47.9148	3 50.9976
22	36 54.1614	4 02.7348	12	36 54.0853	4 01.6430	3	36 47.9472	3 51.0078
23	36 54.2064	4 03.1662	13	36 54.1104	4 01.9218	4	36 47.9946	3 51.0420
24	36 54.1926	4 03.2634	14	36 54.1392	4 02.2656	5	36 47.9886	3 51.2880
25	36 54.1290	4 03.4836	15	36 54.1602	4 02.7330	6	36 47.5392	3 51.6774
26	36 53.9418	4 03.9792	16	36 54.1308	4 02.7744	7	36 47.5080	3 51.7428
27	36 53.7360	4 03.7176	17	36 54.0966	4 01.3920	8	36 47.3940	3 52.1214
28	36 53.6112	4 03.5640	18	36 54.1056	4 01.2924	9	36 47.2542	3 52.2216
29	36 53.2584	4 03.3870	19	36 53.9418	4 00.9666	10	36 47.2734	3 52.5060
30	36 52.8798	4 04.0056	20	36 53.9257	4 00.8126	11	36 47.2332	3 52.6524
31	36 52.6902	4 04.4670	21	36 53.8974	4 00.8166	12	36 47.3598	3 52.4046
32	36 52.5720	4 04.5954	22	36 53.8134	4 00.7566	13	36 47.5416	3 52.1424
33	36 52.4898	4 04.8258	23	36 53.7300	4 00.5886	14	36 48.0258	3 51.5568
34	36 52.4760	4 04.8966	24	36 53.6574	4 00.4998	15	36 48.1314	3 51.4134
35	36 52.4196	4 04.9380	25	36 53.4534	4 00.1422	16	36 48.2604	3 51.5838
(b) Traverse of the Sierra Tejeda to Sedella			26	36 53.0040	4 00.8118	17	36 48.4230	3 51.7776
Wp	N	W	27	36 52.6398	4 00.9192	18	36 48.3570	3 51.6636
1	36 55.6266	3 59.6922	28	36 52.4022	4 01.1628	19	36 48.3108	3 51.4368
			29	36 52.3530	4 01.2300			

GLOSSARY

This glossary contains Spanish words found in the text (shown in *italics*), plus other local words that you may encounter.

a

abandonado	abandoned
abierto	open
acantilado	cliff
aceite de oliva	olive oil
aceituna	olive
acequia	water canal
acueducto	aqueduct
adosados	terraced houses, lean-tos
agua	water
agua no potable	water (not drinkable)
agua potable	drinking water
ajo, ajillo	garlic
alcornoque	cork oak
aldea	hamlet, small village
aljibe	sunken water tank
alto	high
apaño	annual gathering of chestnuts
aparcamiento	parking
arroyo	stream
ayuntamiento	town hall

b

baetyl	magical or holy stone
bajo	low
barranco	ravine
bellota	acorn
betel	house or seat of the Gods
bocadillo	bread roll
bodegón	inn
bosque	wood

c

cabra montes	Spanish Ibex
café	coffee
cahorro	narrow chicane
calle	street
camino	trail, path, track
camino particular	private road
camino real	old donkey trail (lit. royal road)

carne	meat	hoya	depression (geological)
carretera	main road	huerta	smallholding,
carril	lane		vegetable/fruit plot
carta	menu	huevos	eggs
casa	house	**i**	
casa rural	country house	iglesia	church
	accommodation to let	información	information
caserío	hamlet, village	izquierda	left (direction)
castaña	chestnut	**j**	
castaño	chestnut tree	jamón	ham
castillo	castle	lavadero	public laundry area
cementerio	cemetery	**l**	
cerrado	closed	leche	milk
cerveza (caña,	beer (small, large,	librería	bookshop
jarra, presión,	draught, can)	llano	plain
lata)		lluvioso	rainy
chiringuito	beachside eating place	lomo	broad-backed ridge, or
chuleta de cerdo	pork chop		pork
clínica	clinic, hospital	**m**	
colmena	bee hive	malvasía	Malmsey grapes and wine
comida	food	mapa	map
cordillera	mountain range	menú del día	daily menu
correos	post office	mercado	market
cortijo	farmstead	miel	honey
coto privado de	private hunting area	mirador	lookout/viewing point
caza		molino	mill
Cruz Roja	Red Cross (medical aid)	montaña	mountain
cuenta	bill (in restaurant, bar etc.)	museo	museum
cuesta	slope	musulmán	Moslem
cueva	cave	**n**	
cumbre	summit	natillas	custard
d		norte	north
degollado	pass	nublado	cloudy
derecha	right (direction)	**o**	
desayuno	breakfast	oeste	west
desprendimiento	landslide	oficina de turismo	tourist office
e		olivo	olive tree
embutido	sausage	oveja	sheep
encina	holm oak	**p**	
ermita	chapel	panadería	bakery
este	east	parque natural	designated natural park
f		pastelería	cake shop
farmacia	chemist	pechuga de pollo	chicken breast
fiesta	holiday, celebration	peligro	danger
filete de pescado	fish fillet	pensión	guesthouse
finca	farm, country house	pescado	fish
flan	custard	pico	peak
frutas	fruit	pista	dirt road/track
g		pista (forestal)	forest road/track
ganado	cattle	playa	beach
gasolinera	petrol station	plaza	square
guagua	bus	poblado	village
Guardia Civil	police	pocilga	pigsty
guía	guide	policía	police
guiso	stew	postre	dessert
h		pozo	well
helados	ice cream	prohibido el paso	no entry
horno de calc	lime kiln	puente	bridge
hostal	hostel, accommodation	puerto	port, mountain pass

q			
quercus	oak	*tormentoso*	stormy
queso	cheese	*torre*	tower
r		*tostado*	thick toast and topping for breakfast
retema	broom (botanical)	*tubería*	water pipe
risco	cliff	**u**	
roble	oak	*umbria*	dark side of the mountain
roque	rock	*unto*	lard
ruta	route	**v**	
s		*vacuno(a)*	cow
salida	exit	*valle*	valley
santon	Muslim saint	*vega*	meadow
senda	path, track	*venta*	shop/inn, often in small villages and settlements
sendero	foot path		
sierra	mountain range	*ventoso*	windy
sin salida	no through road/route	*vereda*	path
solana	sunny side of the mountain	*vino (blanco, tinto, rosado)*	wine (white, red, rosé)
sur	south	**z**	
t		*zona de acampada*	camping area
tapas	bar snacks	*zona recreativa*	recreation area
té	tea		
tienda	shop		
tipico	traditional bar/eating place		

Please note:

Telephone numbers are shown in red, and fax numbers in blue. When dialling from outside Axarquía, prefix these numbers with 00 34. Websites and email addresses are shown in green.

A USEFUL INFORMATION

ACCOMMODATION
Hotel & Apartment Accommodation

www.alpha-beds.com/costa_del_solhotels.aspx
www.costavacations.com
www.holiday-apartments.co.uk/spain-costa-del-sol
www.hostelworld.com/findabed/costadelsolspain.php
www.hotels.com
www.hotelstogo.co.uk
nerja-costa-del-sol.godirect4holidays.co.uk
www.totalstay.com

Casas Rurales

www.allrural.com (English version)
www.antiquanatura.com (English version)
www.clubrural.com
www.holiday-rentals.com
www.masrural.com (English version)
www.proeco-rural.com
www.toprural.com (English version)
www.turismoruralyaventura.com

Casas Rurales in Canillas (see Walk 30(a) - there's no hotel)
www.antiquanatura.com and www.visitacostadelsol.com
Among phone numbers currently listed are:
952 518 004 / 952 518062 / 952 518 096 / 952 518102 /
952 518210 / 952 518284

Accommodation Recommendations

Camping

If money's tight there are six free camping zones in and around the *Parque Natural* at **La Fábrica de la Luz** above **Canillas de Albaida**, **La Rahiga** near **Canillas de Aceitunas**, **El Alcazar** above **Alcaucin**, **La Alcauca** east of **Zafarraya**, **El Robledal** behind **La Maroma**, and **El Bacal** south of **Jayena**. **Alcazar** and **Alcauca** enjoy the most dramatic location, **Bacal** the best facilities. Apart from **La Rahiga**, there are described itineraries from all of them. Camping is also tolerated though not as yet officially sanctioned at the **Pinarillo Área Recreativa** behind **Nerja**.

Hostals & Hotels

Jayena (see area introduction) is an interesting option for those who want to get right off the beaten track. It has all the services, including the *zona de acampada* mentioned above, a small, cheap (€30 per night for a double room, around €50 including half board), friendly *hostal* (**La Almijara Bar El Nota** 958 364157), and comes as a breath of fresh air after the colony-villages on the southern flanks of the sierras. Equally off the beaten track though somewhat more upmarket both in price (€50 per night for a double room) and pretensions is **Hotel Los Caños de la Alcaiceria** (958 350325, Fax: 958 360088) on the A335 behind **La Maroma**, where one can enjoy moderate luxury and a reasonable menu alongside some lively local colour, the bar being used (heavily) by local farmers and truck-drivers. If you're sticking with the coast, you'll have to go a long way to find better value for money than **Hostal Balcón de Maro** (952 529523 Fax: 952 522608), where double rooms with cupboard kitchenettes cost around €40 per night. Finally, for a peaceful retreat within sight of the sea, you can't go far wrong with **Hotel Casa la Mina** (687 564525) - see Walk 19 for access.

MISCELLANEOUS INFORMATION

Bus Information

www.alsinagraells.es

Background Information

www.almunecar.com/Visitors_Guide
www.andalucia.com
www.costasol.com
www.discover-costa-del-sol.co.uk
www.webmalaga.com
www.ultracosta.com

Official Websites

www.juntadeandalucia.es
www.ctd.junta-andalucia.es
www.tourspain.es
www.spain-info.com
www.visitacostadelsol.com

Phone Numbers

Medical emergencies	061
Guardia Civil	062
Police	091
Lost Credit Card	915 811 811
Victim Support	952 136 675
Málaga Airport	952 048 484

B CYCLE ROUTES

Dirt tracks suitable for mountain bikes

- **(A)** **Alcaucín** to **Canillas de Aceituno** (see Walk 1)
- **(B)** **Alcaucín** to **Llanos de Zafarraya** (see Walk 2)
- **(C)** **Venta de Zafarraya** to **Jatar via El Robledal** (see Walk 4)
- **(D)** **Puerto Blanquillo** from **Canillas de Albaída** (see Walk 8)
- **(E)** **Puerto de Frigiliana** (see Walk 12)
- **(F)** **Frigiliana** to **Cómpeta via Cortijo** de **Daire** (see Walks 12&18)
- **(G)** **Cómpeta** to **Canillas de Albaída** via **Puerto del Collado**, **Cerro Gavilán** and **Cruz de Canillas** (see Walks 8&18)
- **(H)** **La Resinera** to **El Lucero** (see Walk 19)
- **(I)** **La Resinera** to **Casa de la Monticana** (as per Walk 19 access but stay on the main **Río Cacin** track past the **Vivero La Resinera**)
- **(J)** **Cueva de Nerja** to **Fuente del Esparto** and/or **Cortijo de la Civila** (see Walks 20&22)
- **(K)** **Loma de las Cuadrillas** (see Walk 24)
- **(L)** **Pico de Lopera** (see Walk 25)
- **(M)** **La Resinera**, **Fornes** or **Jayena** to **Prados de Lopera** (see Walk 26&27) - various routes possible

C BIBLIOGRAPHY

Please note that some of these titles are only available in Spain (S), but most can be purchased second hand or new on
www.amazon.co.uk

SPANISH WALKING GUIDES (S)

Excursiones por el Sur de España (2 Volumes) (Desnivel) - Juan

Carlos García Gallego
The Bible of Andalusian walking.

🐚**Andar por la Axarquía: las Sierras de Tejeda & Almijara**
(Penthalon) - Francisco Jose Herrero Ruiz & Alicia Franco Alvarez
The book that first took me and many others into these sierras.

🐚**Disfrutar Caminando por el Parque Natural de las Sierras Almijara y Tejeda** (Arguval) - Jesús Cuartero Zueco & Cayetano Casado Bolívar
The latest Spanish publication. Occasionally as clumsy as its title, but earns its place on the shelves for some hitherto undescribed routes.

WALKING GUIDES IN ENGLISH

🐚**12 Walks Around Nerja 12 Walks Around Maro**
12 Walks Around Torrox   12 Walks Around Frigiliana
Elma & Denis Thompson. Pocket-sized booklets available in **Nerja** (S).
Coastal and mid-range mountain walks from the doyenne of Andalusian walking writers and her late husband.

🐚 **Sierra de Aracena - A Walk! Guidebook** (Discovery Walking Guides) - Ros & David Brawn pub 2004 **ISBN 1-899554-96-3**
The first serious guide in any language to one of Andalusia's least well-known sierras.

🐚**34 Alpujarras Walks** (Discovery Walking Guides) - Charles Davis pub 2003 **ISBN 1-899554-83-1**
Full range of itineraries in the mountains made famous by Chris Stewart's 'Driving Over Lemons'.

🐚**Walking on the Costa del Sol** (Santana) - Charles Davis pub 2004 **ISBN 8-489954-39-9**
Thirty-four itineraries between **Nerja** and **Manilva**.

LOCALLY PUBLISHED BOOKS IN ENGLISH

🐚**Wildflowers of Southern Spain** (Santana) - Betty Molesworth Allen
Excellent guide to selected flora

MAPS
Two Spanish organisations publish the closest equivalents to traditional Ordnance Survey style maps. They are:-

Centro Nacional de Información Geográfica
Oficina Central, Monte Esquinza, 41
28010 Madrid, Spain
Tel: 00 34 91 5979453   Fax: 00 34 91 5532913
www.cnig.es   consulta@cnig.es.

Servicio Geográfico del Ejército
Dario Gazapo, 8
28024 Madrid, Spain
Tel: 00 34 91 7115043   Fax: 00 34 91 7115033

	TEXT	MAP
A		
Acantilados de Maro	71	
Acebuchal	79, 80	*80*
Acequia de Lisar	84	
Alcaiceria	48, 51	
Alcauca	42, 43	
Alcaucín	3, 13, 17, 25,	*28, 39*
	36, 38, 40, 42,	
	44. 138	
Alcázar	3, 6, 36, 44,	*43*
	138	
Alhama de Granada	25, 26, 140	*54, 142*
Alhambra	26	
Almáchar	15, 25	
Almuñécar	18, 25, 134	*29*
Alto de Cielo	6, 11, 69, 109,	*117*
	116, 118	
Antequera	26	
Apretaderos	7, 91, 144	
Arenas del Rey	65, 103	
Arroyo -		
de Cantarriján	77	
de Juan Rojo	100, 101	*61, 101*
de la Alcauca	42	
de la Cueva		
del Melero	4, 60, 62	*61*
de la Fuente	53, 55	*54*
de la Minilla	64	
de Limán	110	
de los Pradillos	62, 100, 101	*101*
de los Presillejos	51, 52	
de los Tejos	47	*47, 48*
del Acebuchal	80	*80*
Turbilla	4, 58, 62	
Turillas	126	
B		
Barranco -		
Almendrón	98	
Bacal	6, 125	*126*
Cárcomo	39, 41	*39*
Culebra	130	
de Atajo	81	*81*
de Chortales	133	*131*
de Coladilla	96, 106, 113,	*107, 113,*
	115, 117, 144	*117*
de Contadero	96, 97	
de la Cueva d		
Don Pedro	139	
de la Cueva		
de Funes	132	
de la Higuera	6, 45, 70, 80,	*80, 81,*
	106, 107, 116,	*107, 117*
	117	
de la Hoya	40	*39*
de las Angustias	82	
de las Cabrerizas	131	*131*
de las Cabrerizas	133	*131*
de las Chorreras.	135, 136	*136*
de los		
Almanchares	140	
de los Caños		
del Rey	107	
de los		
Cazadores	5, 69, 70,	*107, 117*
	106-112, 117	
	119	
de los Gigantes	6, 120, 122	*121*
de los Pradillos	97	
de Malinfierno	65-67	*66*
de Maro	74	*73*
de Mina Rica	136	*136*
de Tajos Lisos.	139	
del Almirez	84	
del Arco	84	
del Bartolo	81	*81*
del Espino	46	
del Imán	98	*98*
del Lagarto	135	
del Marmól	80, 83, 84	*80, 84*
del Mojón	45, 46, 47	*47*
del Potril	65, 67	
del Rey	106-109	*107*
la Charca	106, 108	*107*
Orihuela	125	*126*
Sanguino	113	*113*
Selladero	52	
Boquete		
de Zafarraya	12, 16, 37	
C		
Cala Barranco		
de Maro	73, 74	*73*
Cala de los		
Cañuelos	77	*77*
Cala del Moral	10	
Camino de la Cas		
de las Nieves	6, 138	
Camino de		
Colmenares		*46*
Camino del Río	4, 63	
Campiñuelas	66	
Canillas de Aceituno	6, 25, 36, 38,	*28*
	44, 140	
Canillas de Albaida	13, 35, 36, 57,	*28, 64*
	63, 102	
Cantarriján	15, 71, 72, 77,	*77*
	120	
Cañuelos	77	
Carretera de		
la Cabra	135	*136*
Casa Cuascuadra	55, 142	*143*
Casa de la Junta	55	
Casa de la Mina	5, 100	

	TEXT	MAP		TEXT	MAP
Casa de la Nieve	139		de la Civila	6, 114, 116,	
Casa Montilla	100	*101*		118	
Casas de la			de la Cueva		
Monticana	109		del Umbria	132	
Castillones	43, 45		de la Herreriza	14, 53, 143,	*54, 142*
Central Eléctrica				144	
del Chíllar	88, 95		de la Junta		*54*
Cerro -			de la Lagunilla	62	
Albucaz	67, 68		de la Parra	57, 58, 62	*59*
Atalaya	60, 61, 102	*61, 101*	de la Parrilla	64	*64*
Caleta	77, 78	*77*	de las Bovedas	122	
de Cisne	61, 80, 85, 105		de los Llanos	58	
de la Chapa	57	*59*	de los Prados	123	
de la Cruz	133		de Roma	84	
de la Cueva			del Alcázar	42-44	*46*
del Agua	57, 59	*59*	del Daire	80, 104	
de la Mota	104	*104*	del Nevazo	22	
de las Monjas	124, 132		del Robledal Alto	51	
de los Gigantes	120, 122	*121*	Imán	5, 14, 96, 98	*98*
de Rajas Negras	57, 104	*59*	Melero	60, 62	*61*
del Aguila	46		Rafaeta	63, 64	*64*
del Luche	139		Cortijos de		
del Pinto	92		los Nacimientos	120, 121	*121*
El Cenacho	103		Cortijos Machiche	130	
Gavilán	5, 60, 102	*101*	Cortijos Masajate	130	
Gordo	4, 77		Cruz de Canillas	60, 61, 102	*61, 101*
Lucero		*104*	Cuerda de		
Mangüeno	95, 96, 145		los Morros	6, 127, 128	*126*
Martos	131	*131*	Cuerda		
Mojón	46		de Nevazo	68	*66*
Verde	80, 102	*101*	Cuesta -		
Chortales	135		Anamaria	121	
Coladero de			de la Luna	117	*117*
los Mosquitos	103, 104	*104*	de las Pulgas	123	*124*
Collada -			de los Galgos	11, 98	*98, 107,*
de la Orza	65	*66*			*110*
de Sablazo	65	*66*	del Espartal	109	
Blanquilla	79, 80	*80*	del Sordo	5, 86, 87	*87*
de Carneros	65, 67	*66*	Jiménez	94	*93*
de la Perdiz	104		Cueva -		
de los Charcones	140		Colica	69	
de los Galgos	91, 97, 144,		de la Fajara	3, 38, 40	*39*
	145		de la Rábita	140	
de Páez Blanca	79		de los Morros	125	*126*
Collado Nido			del Agua	4	
del Buitre	111		del Melero	58, 60	*59, 61*
Comares	25, 26		del Tesoro	10	
Competa	25, 36, 57, 60,	*28*	Cuevas de Nerja	12, 26, 115,	
	80, 100, 101			116	
Cordoba	26		**E**		
Corral del Pinto	87	*87*	El Alcázar	3, 6, 36, 44,	*43, 46*
Cortijo -				48	
Almáchar	14, 114	*114*	El Carrascal	79	
Chaparral	62		El Chorro	26	
de Cabañeros	69, 124		El Fuerte	84	
de Camacho	62		El Imán		*98, 110*
de Conca	14, 83, 84		El Pastical	130	
de Corzola	125, 127	*126*	El Robledal	4, 7, 11, 51	
de la Alcauca	3, 42	*43*	Embalse de		
de la Almijara	132		la Viñuela	36	

	TEXT	MAP		TEXT	MAP
Embase de la Cueva de Funes	132	*131, 136*	Llanos de Zafarraya	36	
Ermita de la Esperanza	53, 144	*54*	Loma - Contadero	48, 49	*49*
F			de Atalaya	109	*107*
Fornes	103		de Canillas	39	*39*
Frigiliana	5, 13, 18, 25, 70, 79, 83, 86, 87, 90	*29, 84, 87, 93*	de Cuascadra	50, 55, 142	*143*
			de Enmedio	70	
Fuensanta	46		de la Fuente	4, 53	*54*
Fuente - Agria	140		de la Garza	94	*84, 89*
de la Rábita	140		de las Cuadrillas	6, 120	*121*
de las Cabrerizas	132		de las Viboras	42, 43, 45	*46, 47*
del Esparto	97, 106, 112, 144	*107, 110, 145*	Lomas Llanas	109	
			Lomilla del Albarcón	140	
del Tío Pelegrán	44, 45		Lomilla del Huertezuelo	140	
Espino	46		Lopera	129	*124*
Tacita de Plata	140		Los Barracones	51, 52	
del Robledal	51	*143*	Los Cahorros	88	
H			Los Caracolillos	78	*77*
Haza del Aguadero	4, 11, 65, 67, 68	*66*	Los Castillones	3, 42	
			Los Charquillos	137	*136*
Hazuela de Puntas	130		Los Pradillos	4, 60, 61	
Higuerón	79		Lucerillo	84, 104	
Hoya de Gutiérrez	67		Lucero	9, 11, 14, 61	*104*
Hoya del Pico	142	*143*		68, 69, 80, 81	
Huerto Alegre	123			84, 92, 103, 105, 127	
I			**M**		
Iznate	25		Málaga	17, 26, 35, 103	*28*
J					
Jayena	71, 109, 125		Malas Camas	4, 65, 67	*66*
Junta de los Ríos	137	*136*	Marbella	35	
L			Maro	13, 18, 70, 73, 75, 76, 113, 115	*73, 75*
La Concha	35				
La Fábrica de la Luz	4, 35, 57-60, 62	*59*	Mina - de la Buena Fe	70	
			de la Cruz	70	*107, 110*
La Herradura	72		de la Furia	70, 106, 107	*107, 110*
La Maroma	3, 4, 6, 9, 10, 12, 17, 19, 35, 42, 44, 47-49, 52, 67, 138-140	*48, 142*	del Tajo	70, 107	*107*
			Mirador de la Cabra Montes	123, 131, 135	*136*
			Mirador de Masajate	129, 130	
			Moclinejo	25	
La Presa	90, 94-96, 98, 99, 145		Mojón de las Diferencías	124	
La Puerta	5, 108, 110, 111, 117	*98, 107, 110*	Molinero	116	
			Montes de Málaga	15, 25	
La Rabita	10. 138		Montosa	57	
La Resinera	14, 124, 128		Morterillas	133	
Las Cabrerizas	135		**N**		
Las Cañadas	65, 67	*66*	Nacimientos de Maro	114, 121	*121*
Las Chorreras	135, 136	*136*			
Las Nogueras	38		Navachica	5, 69, 106, 108-110	*107*
Lentegi	134				
Limán Trail	5, 83, 84, 90, 92, 93, 99, 144	*98*	Nerja	13, 18, 24, 69, 70, 73, 88, 91, 92, 96, 105, 115	*29*
Llanadas de Sedella	7, 11, 50, 67, 68, 142	*142, 143*			
Llano de los Cabanitos	135	*136*	**O** Otívar	25, 134	

	TEXT	MAP		TEXT	MAP
P				134	
Palacete de Cazulas	137		Ronda	26	
Paraje Natural de			**S**		
los Acantilados	4, 73		Salares	25, 55, 142, 143	
Pastizal	130		Salto de Caballo	50, 52	*49, 143*
Pedregal	79		Santa Ana	57, 59	
Peña Escrita	69, 122		Sedella	7, 25, 36, 37,	*54*
Peñon de los				53, 55, 56, 140,	
Castillejos	6, 18, 120, 122	*121*		142-144	
Peñon del Fraile	78	*77*	Sendero el Robledal	48	
Peñon Grande	140		Seville	26	
Periana	25		Sierra Almijara	61	*66*
Pico de Lopera	6, 123, 124,	*124*	Sierra de Alhama	37, 42	
	132		Sierra de Chaparral	124, 132	
Pinarillo	5, 94-96, 115,	*117*	Sierra de Játar	66	*66*
	116, 119, 145		Sierra del Enmedio	84, 86, 94	*93*
Pinarillo Espeso	84		Sierra Nevada	35	
Playa de la Caleta	73, 74	*73*	Sima de las Nieves	12, 35	
Playa de Maro	75	*73, 75*	**T**		
Playa Molino			Tacita de la Plata	7, 11	
del Papel	121		Tajo Almendrón	5, 11, 92, 96,	*93, 98*
Portichuelos	102			98, 107-110,	
Pozo Bátan	83, 85			117	
Pozo Romance	127		Tajo de los Bueyes	6, 113, 114	*113*
Prados de Lopera	17	*124*	Tajo del Águila	107, 108	*108*
Proa del Barco	139		Tajo del Sol	11, 49, 50, 52,	*49, 93*
Puente de Aguila	74			92, 96, 109,	
Puente de Piedra	42			111	
Puente Don Manuel	26		Tajo Perruchino	107	
Puente Romana	63, 64, 142,		Tajo Volaero	50	
	144		Tajos de Capellania.	140	
Puerto Blanquillo	4, 57, 60, 62,	*61*	Tajos del Púlpito	139	
	80		Torcal de Antequera	26	
Puerto de Competa	13-15, 62, 105	*61*	Torre Caleta	78	
Puerto de Frigiliana	5, 13, 69, 79,	*81, 98*	Torre de Maro	73, 76	*75*
	85, 98, 109		Torrecillas	35	
Puerto del Collada	100, 102		Torrox	18, 100	*28*
Puerto Lobera	49, 50, 52		**U**		
R			Umbria del Fuerte	79	
Rambla de la Mota	103		Umbría del Lobo	119	*117*
Rincón de la Victoria	25		**V**		
Río Alhama	65, 67		Velez Malaga		*28*
Río Bermuza	38, 39	*39*	Venta Camila	81	*81*
Río Cacín	104, 128		Venta Cándido	61, 101	
Río Cájula	63, 64	*64*	Venta Cebollera	79, 80	
Río Cebollon	6, 127-130	*129*	Venta de Cardenas	26	
Río Chillar	5, 7, 11, 18, 83,	*87, 93, 98*	Venta de Cazulas	134, 137	
	84, 86, 88-90		Venta Los Pradillos	5, 61, 100, 101	*101*
	92, 94-96, 111,		Venta Maria		
	144, 145		Guerrero	61, 100, 102	
Río Cueva			Venta Panaderos	79, 81	*104*
del Melero	57	*61*	Ventas de Zafarraya	25	*28*
Río de la Fuente	53, 55,	*54*	Vereda de Competa	60, 61	
Río de la Llanada	63		**W**		
Rio de la Miel	18, 120		Waterfall of		
Río Grande	125, 126	*126*	Petrified Wood	6, 131	
Río Higerón	5, 11, 18,	*87, 93*	**Z**		
	83-87, 93		Zafarraya	42, 52	
Río Nacimiento	132	*131*			
Río Verde	15, 19, 124,	*136, 137*			

DISCOVERY WALKING GUIDES LTD.TITLES LIST

GPS

GPS The Easy Way
Manual — **£4.99**

PERSONAL NAVIGATOR FILES
Version 2.01 Downloadable GPS records for all Walk!/Walks Guidebooks + GPS Utility Software
CD — **£7.99**

CANARY ISLANDS

Walk! Lanzarote
Guidebook — **£11.99**
Lanzarote Super-Durable
Tour & Trail Map — **£7.99**
Lanzarote Indestructible Map **£4.99**
Lanzarote Plant&Flower Guide **£2**

Walk! La Gomera (2nd edition)
Guidebook — **£11.99**
La Gomera Super-Durable
Tour &Trail Map — **£7.99**
Drive! La Gomera
Touring Map — **£2.50**

35 Tenerife Walks
Guidebook — **£9.99**
Walk! Tenerife South
Guidebook — **£5.99**
Tenerife Super-Durable
Walkers' Maps — **£4.99**
Tenerife Paper Edition
Walkers' Maps — **£2.99**
Tenerife Indestructible Map **£4.99**

Drive! Tenerife Touring Map **£2.50**
Tenerife Plant&Flower Guide **£2**

Gran Canaria Mountains
Tour & Trail Map — **£5**
Gran Canaria Plant&Flower Guide **£2**

Walk! La Palma
Guidebook — **£11.99**
La Palma Super-Durable
Tour & Trail Map — **£7.99**

SPANISH MAINLAND

Walk! Axarquía — **£11.99**
Guidebook

Sierra de Aracena - a Walk! Guidebook
Guidebook — **£11.99**
Sierra de Aracena
Tour & Trail Map — **£2.99**
34 Alpujarras Walks
Guidebook — **£9.99**
Alpujarras Super-Durable
Tour & Trail Map — **£7.99**

ANDORRA

Walk! Andorra
Guidebook — **£11.99**

BALEARIC ISLANDS

Walk! Mallorca (North & Mountains)
Guidebook — **£11.99**
Mallorca North & Mountains Super-Durable
Tour & Trail Map — **£7.99**
Walk! Mallorca West
Guidebook — **£11.99**

Walk! Menorca
Guidebook — **£11.99**
Menorca Super-Durable
Tour & Trail Map — **£7.99**

PORTUGAL, INCLUDING MADEIRA

Madeira Super-Durable
Tour & Trail Map — **£7.99**
35 Madeira Walks
Guidebook — **£9.99**
Madeira Bus & Touring Map **£2.50**

Algarve - Loule
Walking Guide — **£5**
Algarve - Silves
Walking Guide — **£5**

DWG Ltd.
10 Tennyson Close
Northampton NN5 7HJ
www.walking.demon.co.uk
www.dwgwalking.co.uk

Stanfords Bookshops
Tel 020 7759 7137
sales@stanfords.co.uk
www.stanfords.co.uk

The Map Shop
Upton Upon Severn
Tel 01684 593146
themapshop@btinternet.com
www.themapshop.co.uk
- or ask in bookshops